THE CHURCH AT PRAYER

Introduction to the Liturgy

THE CHURCH AT PRAYER

Introduction to the Liturgy

edited by
A G MARTIMORT

with the collaboration of

BERNARD BOTTE   I H DALMAIS
PIERRE JOUNEL   A M ROGUET
OLIVIER ROUSSEAU

editors of the English edition
AUSTIN FLANNERY OP   VINCENT RYAN OSB

Desclée Company
New York

Translated from *L'Église en prière*, 3rd edition, published by Desclée & Co., Tournai (Belgium).

Material from *The Jerusalem Bible* is © 1966 Darton, Longman & Todd Limited and Doubleday & Company, Inc. and is used by permission of the publishers.

Material from *The Mystery of Christian Worship* is © 1962 Darton, Longman & Todd Limited and Newman Press and is used by permission of the publishers.

We acknowledge with thanks permission of Geoffrey Chapman Limited to quote from their edition of *Documents of Vatican II*.

Nihil obstat: Thomas Corbett DD

Imprimatur: ✠Michael Harty DD
Ennis, 23 August 1968

Library of Congress Catalog Card Number: 68-56153

AUTHORS

BERNARD BOTTE OSB, Honorary Director of the Institut Supérieur de Liturgie, Paris; Honorary Lecturer in Liturgy, Faculty of Theology, Louvain.

IRÉNÉE-HENRI DALMAIS OP, Professor, Institut Supérieur de Liturgie, Paris.

PIERRE JOUNEL, Professor, Institut Supérieur de Liturgie, Paris.

AIMÉ-GEORGES MARTIMORT, Professor, Faculty of Theology, Toulouse; Professor, Institut Supérieur de Liturgie, Paris.

AIMON-MARIE ROGUET OP, Director of *La Maison-Dieu*.

OLIVIER ROUSSEAU OSB, Monk of the Monastery of Chevetogne.

NOTE TO THE ENGLISH EDITION

Thanks to the collaboration of a group of American and Irish liturgists, a translation of Part One of the great French manual *L'Église en prière* has at last appeared. Students of liturgy in the English-speaking world now have at their disposal a comprehensive and up-to-date handbook which will enable them to explore at depth every aspect of the Church's worship.

The translators have sought to produce a clear and faithful rendering of the original. This has proved an exacting task: the nuances of the French language are not always easily conveyed in good English idiom. The question of terminology has also posed problems: such frequently recurring terms as *"monition"* and *"pastorale liturgique"* have no really satisfactory equivalents in English and one can only aim at approximations. We hope that in spite of these limitations, inherent in any translation, students will be able to benefit to the full by the scholarship contained in these pages.

Wherever possible, the editors have included English-language editions of works referred to in the bibliographies. In some cases the original bibliographies have been expanded to include pertinent material available in English and not mentioned in the French edition.

Translators

Robert Fisher SVD
Anselm Hufstader OSB
John E. Rotelle OSA
Gerald Watt OSA
John Whelan

PREFACE TO THE ENGLISH EDITION

This is a translation of the first part of a work that first appeared in French in 1961, i.e. when preliminary commissions were busy preparing for the Second Vatican Council. In a motu proprio of July 25, 1960, Pope John XXIII had announced that he was entrusting to the Council the determination of the fundamental principles (*altiora principia*) for the complete renewal of the liturgy, a renewal towards which the Holy See had taken the first steps some years earlier. Several of the authors of these volumes were members of the liturgical commission whose work was favorably received by the fathers of the Council and which culminated in the Constitution promulgated on December 4, 1963. This Constitution was seen as the culmination of the great liturgical movement in which Pope Pius XII had seen "the passage of the Holy Spirit over the Church." After discussion, and even debates, it ended by winning over all Christian countries, stirring up interest in the missions, and contributing to the ecumenical dialogue.

In fact, the Constitution *De sacra liturgia* should be, above all, a point of departure. In 1964 Pope Paul VI appointed for its implementation a *consilium* composed of bishops and experts from all over the world. Again, several of the authors of the present work were included. They were to collaborate on a vast and profound reform, such as the history of the Church had not known before.

The different editions of *L'Église en prière*, in French and in other languages, bear testimony in their own way to the rapid evolution of rites and of liturgical discipline. The present English edition includes the revisions incorporated into the third French edition (1965), and adds further changes in the text, footnotes and bibliographies. The English edition will be brought out in several volumes so that its publication can follow more closely the work of the liturgical *consilium* and take into account all official documents as they appear.

Do we expect that the work of liturgical reform will reach its termination when these volumes are published? We think not, and for two reasons. While legislation is being recast and liturgical rites are being reformed, priests and people must continue to live day by day the liturgy of the Church as it is; they cannot defer initiation to a distant future. And to discern better the import of contemporary evolution it is necessary to know what is essential and what is accessory, what is changeable and what is unchangeable, what remains constant in the course of diverse manifestations. Hence the importance of keeping up the study of the history of the liturgy and the comparison of different liturgical traditions of East and West which characterize the present work. The liturgy of tomorrow could be as different from the Roman rite of today as that rite was from the Byzantine, and people could think that history would be of no help to understand it. But on the contrary, a knowledge of history is the best means of discerning the future and preparing oneself to live it; the Church is a tradition. The past may never repeat itself, but the study of it uncovers—beyond the diversity of contexts and usages—the demands of the deposit of faith which the Church has received from the Lord.

Finally, it seems worthwhile to recall the limitations of the present work as outlined in the first French edition. In the following pages, the reader will not find a complete course of rubrics. It would have been difficult, even harmful, to include this at a time when such monumental change is taking place before our very eyes.

We presume too that the reader has at hand the liturgical books in present use. Far from abandoning them, we urge him to read them again and again. The most essential study is that of the liturgical texts themselves. By meditating on those of the past and present, by participating in the liturgy of today with all the fervor of which we are capable, we will be ready to receive the new forms that the Church, in her perennial youth and assisted by the Holy Spirit, will offer us tomorrow.

Aimé-Georges Martimort

LIST OF ABBREVIATIONS

1. *Biblical references:*

Ac	Acts	Lk	Luke
Am	Amos	Lm	Lamentations
Ba	Baruch	Lv	Leviticus
1 Ch	1 Chronicles	1 M	1 Maccabees
2 Ch	2 Chronicles	2 M	2 Maccabees
1 Co	1 Corinthians	Mi	Micah
2 Co	2 Corinthians	Mk	Mark
Col	Colossians	Ml	Malachi
Dn	Daniel	Mt	Matthew
Dt	Deuteronomy	Na	Nahum
Ep	Ephesians	Nb	Numbers
Est	Esther	Ne	Nehemiah
Ex	Exodus	Ob	Obadiah
Ezk	Ezekiel	1 P	1 Peter
Ezr	Ezra	2 P	2 Peter
Ga	Galatians	Ph	Philippians
Gn	Genesis	Phm	Philemon
Hab	Habakkuk	Pr	Proverbs
Heb	Hebrews	Ps	Psalms
Hg	Haggai	Qo	Qoheleth (Ecclesiastes)
Ho	Hosea	Rm	Romans
Is	Isaiah	Rt	Ruth
Jb	Job	Rv	Revelation
Jdt	Judith		(Apocalypse)
Jg	Judges	1 S	1 Samuel
Jl	Joel	2 S	2 Samuel
Jm	James	Sg	Song of Songs
Jn	John	Si	Sirach (Ecclesiasticus)
1 Jn	1 John	Tb	Tobit
2 Jn	2 John	1 Th	1 Thessalonians
3 Jn	3 John	2 Th	2 Thessalonians
Jon	Jonah	1 Tm	1 Timothy
Jos	Joshua	2 Tm	2 Timothy
Jr	Jeremiah	Tt	Titus
Jude	Jude	Ws	Wisdom
1 K	1 Kings	Zc	Zechariah
2 K	2 Kings	Zp	Zephaniah

2. *Works frequently cited:*

AAS
: *Acta Apostolicae Sedis* (Rome, then Vatican City, 1909 ff).

Acta sanctorum
: *Acta sanctorum collecta. . . a Sociis Bollandianis*, 3rd ed. (Paris: Palmé, 1863 ff, then Brussels: Bollandistes).

ALW
: *Archiv für Liturgiewissenchaft* (Regensburg: F. Pustet, 1950 ff).

Andrieu OR
: M. Andrieu, *Les "Ordines Romani" du haut moyen âge* (Louvain: Spicilegium, 1931 ff). Five volumes have appeared; the sixth is in preparation (*Spicilegium sacrum Lovaniense* 11, 23, 24, 28, 29).

Andrieu PR
: M. Andrieu, *Le pontifical romain au moyen âge*, 4 vols. (Vatican City, 1938–41; *Studi e testi*, 86–88, 99).

ANF
: *Ante-Nicene Christian Library*, A. Roberts and J. Donalson ed. (Edinburgh: Clark, 1870 ff).

BR
: *Breviarium Romanum* . . . (unless otherwise noted, this refers to the edition of April 5, 1961).

Brightman
: F. E. Brightman, *Liturgies Eastern and Western*, vol. 1 (the only volume to have appeared), *Eastern Liturgies* (Oxford: Clarendon, 1896).

CC
: *Corpus christianorum collectum a monachis O.S.B. abbatiae S. Petri in Steenbrugge* (Tournhout: Brepols, 1954 ff).

Caer. ep.
: *Caeremoniale episcoporum* . . . (corresponds to the edition of Leo XIII, 1886).

CIC
: *Codex iuris canonici Pii X pontificis maximi iussu digestus. Benedicti papae XV auctoritate promulgatus* . . . (Typis polyglottis Vaticanis, 1917, with numerous re-editions).

CSCO
: *Corpus scriptorum christianorum orientalium editum consilio Universitatis catholicae Americae et Universitatis catholicae Lovaniensis* (Louvain, 1903 ff).

CSEL
: *Corpus scriptorum ecclesiasticorum Latinorum editum consilio et impensis Academiae litterarum . . . Vindobonensis* (Vienna: Tempsky, 1866 ff).

CSL
: *Sacrosanctum Concilium oecumenicum Vaticanum secundum, Constitutio de sacra liturgia*, AAS 56 (1964) 97–138.

DACL
: *Dictionnaire d'archéologie chrétienne et de liturgie*, published under the direction of F. Cabrol, H.

	Leclercq [and H. Marrou], 15 tomes in 30 vols. (Paris: Letouzey et Ané, 1907–53).
Denz	*Enchiridion symbolorum, definitionum et declaratio-num de rebus fidei et morum*, quod primum edidit H. Denzinger et quod funditus retractavit . . . A. Schönmetzer, 32nd ed. (Barcelona: Herder, 1963).
EL	*Ephemerides liturgicae* . . . (Rome: Edizioni liturgiche, 1887 ff). For years in which there are two series, all references, unless otherwise noted, will be to the series *Analecta ascetico-historica*.
EO	*Echos d'Orient*, 39 vols. (Constantinople and Paris: Bonne Presse, 1897–1942).
Fabre-Duchesne	P. Fabre and L. Duchesne, *Le Liber censuum de l'Église romaine publié avec une introduction et un commentaire* . . . 3 vols. (Paris: Ed. [Fontemoing] E. de Boccard, 1910–52).
GCS	*Die griechischen christlichen Schriftsteller der ersten Jahrhunderte*, hrsg. von der . . . deutschen Akademie der Wissenschaften zu Berlin (Berlin: Akademie Verlag, 1897 ff).
GeS	The old Gelasian sacramentary, Vatican Library MS Reginen. Lat. 316.—L. K. Mohlberg, P. Siffrin and L. Eizenhöfer ed., *Liber sacramentorum Romanae ecclesiae ordinis anni circuli* . . . (Rome: Herder, 1960; *Rerum ecclesiasticarum documenta* . . . , Series maior, Fontes, 4);—H. A. Wilson, *The Gelasian Sacramentary* (Oxford: Clarendon, 1894);—PL 74, col. 1049–1244 (=Muratori).
GrS	Gregorian sacramentary.
H	H. Lietzmann, *Das Sacramentarium Gregorianum nach dem Aachener Urexemplar* (Münster: Aschendorff, 1921; LQF 3).
HBS	*Henry Bradshaw Society for Editing Rare Liturgical Texts* (London, 1891 ff).
JLW	*Jahrbuch für Liturgiewissenschaft* . . ., O. Casel ed., 15 vols. (Münster: Aschendorff, 1921–41).
JTS	*Journal of Theological Studies* (London: Macmillan, then Oxford: Clarendon, 1900 ff).
LeS	The sacramentary formerly known as the Leonine; Verona, Biblioteca Capitolare, MS LXXXV [80].—L. K. Mohlberg, L. Eizenhöfer and P. Siffrin ed., *Sacramentarium Veronense* (Rome: Herder, 1955–56; *Rerum ecclesiasticarum documenta*, Series maior 1);—C. Feltoe, *Sacramentarium*

	Leonianum (Cambridge: University Press, 1896); —PL 55, col. 9-156 (=Ballerini).
LMD	*La Maison-Dieu, Revue de pastorale liturgique* (Paris: Ed. du Cerf, 1945 ff).
LP	L. Duchesne, *Le Liber pontificalis texte, introduction et commentaire*, 2nd edition by C. Vogel, 3 vols. (Paris: E. de Boccard, 1955–57)
LQF	*Liturgiegeschichtliche* (then *Liturgiewissenschaftliche*) *Quellen und Forschungen* (Münster: Aschendorff, 1919 ff).
LXX	The Greek Septuagint. A. Rahlfs ed., *Septuaginta id est Vetus Testamentum graece iuxta LXX interpretes*, 3rd ed., 2 vols. (Stuttgart: Württembergische Bibelanstalt 1935 [1949]).
Mansi	J. D. Mansi, *Sacrorum conciliorum nova et amplissima collectio*, 31 vols. (Florence-Venice edition, 1757–98); reprinted and continued, vols. 1-53 (Paris, Leipzig and Arnhem, 1901–27).
Martène	E. Martène, *De antiquis Ecclesiae ritibus*. References to this work will correspond to the three editions (Paris, 1700–06; Antwerp, 1736–38; Bassano-Venice, 1788), 4 vols. The edition of 1700 includes only 3 vols.; vol 4 is counted as the *Tractatus de antiqua ecclesiae disciplina in divinis celebrandis officiis* (Lyons, 1706); but to this must also be added the *De antiquis monachorum ritibus*, 2 vols. (Lyons, 1690), which is also included in the editions of Antwerp and Bassano.
MD	Pius XII, encyclical *Mediator Dei*, November 20, 1947. The numbers accompanying this abbreviation are those of the paragraphs in the English-language edition, published with an introduction and notes by G. Ellard (New York: The America Press, enlarged and revised edition, 1954).
MGH	*Monumenta Germaniae historica . . .* (Hanover, Hahn, Berlin: Weidmann, 1826 ff).
MR	*Missale Romanum . . .* (edition of June 23, 1962).
NPF	*Nicene and Post-Nicene Fathers* (2nd series), H. Wace and P. Schaff ed. (New York: The Christian Library Co.; Oxford: Parker, 1890 ff).
NRC	*Novus rubricarum breviarii ac missalis codex*, promulgated by the Congregation of Rites, July 26, 1960, in execution of the motu proprio,

	Rubricarum instructum, of John XXIII, dated the previous day, AAS 52 (1960) 593-734.
OC	*Oriens christianus, Halbjahrshefte für die Kunde des christlichen Orients* (Rome, then Leipzig: Harrasowitz, 1901 ff).
OCP	*Orientalia christiana periodica* (Rome: P. Institutum orientalium studiorum, 1935 ff).
OHS	*Ordo hebdomadae sanctae instauratus* (corresponds to the edition of November 30, 1955). The same abbreviation is used in transcribing the titles of various other liturgical books which deal with the restored Holy Week.
OR 23, 34 . . .	*Ordo Romanus* . . . Unless otherwise noted, the figure which accompanies this abbreviation corresponds to the numbering of Andrieu OR.
OR Mab	*Ordo Romanus*, following the numbering of J. Mabillon, *Musaei Italici*, vol. 2 (Paris, 1689; PL 78, col. 851-1372).
PG	J. P. Migne, *Patrologiae cursus completus, Series graeca*, 161 vols. (Paris-Montrouge, 1857-66).
PL	J. P. Migne, *Patrologiae cursus completus, Series latina*, 221 vols. (Paris-Montrouge, 1844-64).
PO	*Patrologia orientalis*, first edited by R. Graffin and F. Nau (Paris: Firmin-Didot, 1903 ff).
PR	*Pontificale Romanum*, following the edition of February 28, 1962 (parts 1 and 3) and, for the 2nd part, that of April, 13, 1961.
PRG	C. Vogel and R. Elze, *Le Pontifical romano-germanique du Xe siècle, Le texte*, 2 vols. (Vatican City, 1963; *Studi e testi*, 226-7); a 3rd volume of introduction and indexes is in preparation.
QLP	*Questions liturgiques et paroissiales* (Louvain: Abbaye du Mont César, 1910 ff).
RAC	*Reallexikon für Antike und Christentum* . . . T. Klauser ed. (Stuttgart: Hiersemann, 1950 ff).
RB	*Revue bénédictine* (Abbaye de Maredsous, 1884 ff).
RechSR	*Recherches de science religieuse* (Paris, 1910 ff).
Renaudot	E. Renaudot, *Liturgiarum orientalium collectio* (Paris, 1716);—Ed. 2ª correctior, 2 vols. (Frankfurt: J. Baer, 1847).

RevSR	*Revue des sciences religieuses* (Strasbourg: Palais Universitaire, 1921 ff).
RHE	*Revue d'histoire ecclésiastique* (Louvain, 1900 ff).
ROC	*Revue de l'Orient chrétien* (Paris: Leroux, then Picard, 1896).
RR	*Rituale Romanum*, following the edition of January 25, 1952.
RTAM	*Recherches de théologie ancienne et médiévale* (Louvain: Abbaye du Mont César, 1929 ff).
SC	*Sources chrétiennes*, under the direction of H. de Lubac and J. Daniélou [then C. Mondésert] (Paris: Ed. du Cerf, 1942 ff).
SE	*Sacris erudiri, Jaarboek voor Godsdienstwetenschappen* (Steenbrugge: Sint Pietersabdij, 1948 ff).
SL	*Cours et conférences des semaines liturgiques* (Abbaye de Maredsous, then Louvain: Abbaye du Mont César), vols. 1 (meeting of 1912, published 1913) to 14 (meeting of 1937, published 1938). The numbers following the abbreviation correspond to the volume (not to the order of meetings), then to the year of the meeting (not to the year of publication), thus conforming to the policy adopted by the editors in the original presentation of these volumes.
SRC	*Sacrorum rituum Congregatio.* When a number follows this abbreviation, it refers to the *Decreta authentica Congregationis sacrorum rituum* (Rome: Typographie de la Propagande, then Typographie Vaticane, 1898–1927), in 7 vols. (5 vols., plus 2 *Appendices*).
TA	*Texte und Arbeiten*, published by the Archabbey of Beuron (1917 ff). Unless otherwise noted, the number given refers to the 1. Abteilung, format in-8°.
TS	*Texts and Studies, Contributions to Biblical and Patristic Literature* (Cambridge: University Press, 1882 ff).
TU	*Texte und Untersuchungen zur Geschichte der altchristlichen Literatur* (Leipzig, then Berlin: Akademie Verlag, 1882 ff).
ZKT	*Zeitschrift für katholische Theologie* (Innsbruck: Theologische Fakultät, 1877 ff).

Contents

PART ONE

General Introduction

B

CHAPTER ONE

Preliminary Concepts

A. G. Martimort

1 Definitions

I THE TERM "LITURGY"

BIBLIOGRAPHY

P. Oppenheim, "Name und Inhalt der Liturgie bei den Alten" in *Theologische Quartalschrift* 113 (1932) 35-53.

P. Oppenheim, *Notiones liturgiae fundamentales* (Turin: Marietti, 1941; *Institutiones systematico-historicae in sacram liturgiam* 6) pp. 1-16.

E. Raitz von Frentz, "Der Weg des Wortes 'Liturgie' in der Geschichte" in EL 55 (1941) 74-80.

A. Romeo, "Il termine λειτουργία nella grecità biblica" in *Miscellanea liturgica in honorem L. Cuniberti Mohlberg* 2 (Rome: Edizioni liturgiche, 1949) pp. 467-519.

H. Schmidt, *Introductio in liturgiam occidentalem* (Rome: Herder, 1960) pp. 33-46.

H. Strathmann, "λειτουργέω," in G. Kittel, *Theologisches Wörterbuch des neuen Testaments* 4 (Stuttgart: Kohlhammer, 1942) pp. 231-8.

"Liturgy," a term which today is classic and rendered official by the solemn magisterium, is of fairly recent usage in the West. It is scarcely to be found in the official acts of the Church before the twentieth century.[1] It was popularized in the nineteenth century by numerous books and articles written for the general public, after having been introduced into the Latin language by scholars at the end of the sixteenth and in the seventeenth centuries,[2] probably under the influence of Byzantine texts.

[1] From 1832, SRC 2692, the expression *libri liturgici* is found and soon becomes classic; in 1897, SRC 3948, *liturgia ambrosiana* and in 1898, SRC 3999: "*de usu linguae slavicae in sacra liturgia.*" The Codex of 1917 gives distinct authority to *liturgia*, can. 447, §1, 4°; 1257, etc.—Cf. a definition in Pius XI, *Divini Cultus*, December 20, 1928, no. 1; A. Bugnini, *Documenta pontificia ad instaurationem liturgicam spectantia . . .* (Rome: Edizioni liturgiche, 1953) p. 60.

[2] The adjective *liturgicus* appears, perhaps for the first time, in G. Cassandre, *Liturgica de ritu et ordine dominicae coenae quam celebrationem Graeci liturgiam, Latini missam appellarunt* (1558); it is taken up again by Jacques de Joigny, known as Pamelius, *Liturgica latinorum*, 2 vols. (Cologne, 1571) and will be made famous by the work of Cardinal Bona, *Rerum liturgicarum libri duo* (Rome, 1671). The name *liturgia* is still a Greek one for Cassandre and for C. de Sainctes, *Liturgiae sive missae sanctorum patrum Jacobi*, etc. (Antwerp, 1562); it is defini-

In the Greek Church, however, the word λειτουργία, with its correspondents λειτουργός, λειτουργικός, has a more limited and exact meaning: it refers exclusively to the Mass and its various formularies.[3] It is true that the early ecclesiastical writers, above all in the New Testament and the Septuagint, already tended to use λειτουργία as meaning the service of God, worship, although they did not exclude less exact meanings such as spiritual sacrifice or charitable services.[4]

There are witnesses, at least late ones, to the use of the word in classical Greek, but the normal and technical meaning is that of public service: a function, whether it be in the political, technical or religious sphere, exercised in the interests of all the people.[5]

II DEFINITION OF THE LITURGY

BIBLIOGRAPHY

L. Beauduin, "La liturgie, définition, hiérarchie, tradition" in QLP 29 (1948) 123-44.

L. Bouyer, *Liturgical Piety* (University of Notre Dame Press, 1955) pp. 1, 29 and *passim.*

I. H. Dalmais, "La liturgie, acte de l'Église" in LMD 19 (1949) 7-25.

tively latinized in the seventeenth century, as is clear from the usage of J. Mabillon, *De liturgia gallicana libri tres* (Paris, 1685).—Until the sixteenth century Latin authors spoke of *De divinis officiis;* so Isidore of Seville, Alcuin, Rupert, etc., and still in 1568, M. Hittorp,—or *De ritibus ecclesiae, De sacris ritibus:* in 1588 Sixtus V founded the *Congregatio sacrorum rituum* which still keeps the same name, and in 1700 E. Martène could still give to his great collection the name *De antiquis ecclesiae ritibus.*

[3]From the first appearances of these words until Bona and Mabillon, *liturgica, res liturgicae* and *liturgia* still refer exclusively to the Mass. The extension to the present meaning, which includes all acts of worship and not just the Mass, evidently did not occur until the eighteenth century.—On the usage of the Greek church, see J. M. Hanssens, *Institutiones liturgicae de ritibus orientalibus* 2 (Rome: Gregorian Univ., 1930) pp. 21-41.

[4]For the meaning of λειτουργία (λειτουργός, λειτουργεῖν) among the ecclesiastical authors of antiquity, see J. M. Hanssens, *op. cit.*, p. 62; A. Romeo, *op. cit.*, pp. 513-17. — In the New Testmanent, meaning a service of Jewish worship: Lk 1:23; Heb 9-10, and the work of Christ which Jewish worship prefigured: Heb 8:2-6; — only once is the word used perhaps to mean Christian worship: Ac 13:2;—with the meanings of non-cultic service: Rm 13:6; 15:16, 27; 2 Cor 9:12; Ph 2:17, 25, 30, etc.— For the LXX, usually service of worship: Ex 28-39 (13 times); Nb 4:8, 18 and *passim;* 2 Ch 31:2; Ex 40-46 (16 times), etc.; more rarely in a non-cultic sense: Jos 1:1 (MSA.); 1 K 1:15, 19, 21; 2 Ch 22:8.—The Latins translated λειτουργία by *ministerium:* St Augustine, *Enarrationes in psalmos, In ps.* 135:3 (CC 40), p. 1959 (PL 37, col. 1757); or by *officium* (for example, the Vulgate at Lk 1:23); or finally by *munus:* O. Casel, "Leitourgia munus" in OC 3rd ser. 7 (1932), 289ff; H. Frank in JLW 13 (1933) 181-5.

[5]J. Oehler, "Leiturgie" in Pauly-Wissowa-Kroll, *Real Encyclopädie der klassischen Altertumswissenschaft* 12, 2 (Stuttgart: Metzler, 1925) col. 1871-9.

J. H. Miller, "The Nature and Definition of the Liturgy" in *Theological Studies* 18 (1957) 325-56.

H. Schmidt, *Introductio in liturgiam occidentalem* (Rome: Herder, 1960) pp. 47-87.

A. Stenzel, "Cultus publicus, ein Beitrag zur Begriff und ekklesiologischen Ort der Liturgie" in ZKT 75 (1953) 174-214.

C. Vagaggini, *Theological Dimensions of the Liturgy* 1, translated from the second Italian edition by L. Doyle (Collegeville, Minnesota: Liturgical Press, 1959) pp. 13-19.

1 First attempts at definition (1909-1947)

From the beginning of the liturgical movement (1909) to the present, most of the manualists have tried to give a definition of the liturgy which would sum up briefly its nature and essential characteristics. A difficult task, all the more so because the liturgy is a living reality, at once complex and unified. It can be understood only through participation, nor does it easily allow itself to be forced into concepts. This is why none of the proposed definitions has yet appeared to be satisfactory.

Some of them, it must be noted, were reprehensible, even though patronized by great names. Two such definitions were expressly rejected by Pius XII in his encyclical *Mediator Dei* of November 20, 1947:[6]

It is an entirely false notion to consider the sacred liturgy as only an external and outwardly perceptible part of divine worship, or as a decorative ceremony;[7] nor is it any less an error to consider it as a mere collection of laws and precepts by which the Church's hierarchy orders sacred rites to be carried out.[8]

Following this, the Congregation of Rites, in its instruction of September 3, 1958, made a very clear distinction between "liturgical actions" and *"pia exercitia,"* thus ending the confusion which had occurred when, at the opposite extreme, attempts were made to eliminate from the definition of the liturgy those conditions which the Church requires of it.[9]

[6]MD 25.

[7]*Utpote divini cultus partem . . . externam solummodo ac sensibus objectam, vel quasi decorum quemdam caerimoniarum apparatum:* this formula refers to the definition given by J. J. Navatel, "L'apostolat liturgique et la piété personnelle" in *Études* 137 (1913) 452, and which P. Oppenheim, *Notiones liturgiae fundamentales* (Turin: Marietti, 1941), p. 17, translated thus into Latin: *partem mere sensibilem, caerimonialem et decorativam cultus catholici.*

[8]This last definition, still extèrior to the liturgy itself, is more or less that of C. Callewaert, *De sacra liturgia universim* (1919; 4th ed., Bruges: Beyaert, 1944), p. 6: *cultus publicus ab Ecclesia quoad exercitium ordinatus, seu ordinatio ecclesiastica exercitii cultus publici.*—It was above all against this definition that J. M. Hanssens directed his "La définition de la liturgie" in *Gregorianum* 7 (1927) 204-28.

[9]Such was the attempt of J. A. Jungmann, "Was ist Liturgie" in ZKT 53 (1931)

Finally, the word "liturgy" has too often been used indiscriminately to refer both to the act of the Church at prayer, and to the science of the liturgy.

2 Definitions of the liturgy in the documents of the magisterium

(i) In his encyclical *Mediator Dei,* Pius XII did more than merely remove those definitions which made of the liturgy something external and accessory. Emphasizing the liturgy's supernatural reality, he suggested, as most pioneers of the liturgical movement already had, that we seek to understand this reality in the *priesthood of Christ* and in a true idea of *the Church as the mystical Body of Christ:*[10] "The Church continues the sacerdotal office of Jesus Christ primarily through the sacred liturgy."[11]

(ii) The Second Vatican Council opened its declaration of "general principles for the restoration and promotion of the sacred liturgy" with an instruction on "the nature of the sacred liturgy and its importance in the Church's life." Although this instruction purposely avoids textbook phrases in order to return to the language and categories of the Bible and the Fathers, it is nonetheless possible to extract from it the following as a definition of the liturgy:

> Rightly, then, the liturgy is considered as an exercise of the priestly office of Jesus Christ. In the liturgy the sanctification of man is manifested by signs perceptible to the senses, and is effected in a way which is proper to each of these signs; in the liturgy full public worship is performed in the mystical Body of Jesus Christ, that is, by the Head and his members.[12]

It is easy to notice here the echoes of *Mediator Dei,*[13] but the Council adds to these several important aspects:

(a) The liturgy, whose essence is formed by the sacraments, is in its entirety a sacred *sign,* as indeed is the Church itself.[14] The visible element is an efficacious sign of a supernatural reality. Although there is a difference between the efficacity of a sacramental

---

83-102; however cf. *id.,* "Liturgie und pia exercitia" in *Liturgisches Jahrbuch* 9 (1959) 79-86.—Without insisting on it, CSL 13 takes this distinction for granted; see below, footnote 23.

[10]V. Talhofer and L. Eisenhofer, *Handbuch der katholischen Liturgik* 1, 2nd ed. (Freiburg: Herder, 1912) pp. 6–15; L. Beauduin, "Essai de manuel fondamental de liturgie" in QLP 3 (1912) 58-62; 5 (1920) 85-90, 217-28; G. Lefebvre, *Liturgia, ses principes fondamentaux* (Lophem-lez-Bruges, 1920) pp. 2-10; T. Michels, "Die Liturgie im Lichte der katholischen Gemeinschaftsidee" in JLW 1 (1921) 109-16, etc.

[11]MD 3, cf. 22: "The liturgy is nothing other than the exercise of this priestly office [of Christ]."

[12]CSL 7. See also 26.

[13]MD 20.

[14]Cf. CSL 2, 5.

sign and that of other signs, the two remain analogous. The liturgy is therefore a *"sacramentum,"* a "mystery," in the sense in which the Fathers used these expressions.[15]

(b) The liturgy does more than cause the Church's prayer of adoration and supplication to rise towards God; it also causes the graces of the redemption to descend upon the members of the Church. This twofold motion, which is affirmed implicitly as soon as the liturgy is referred to the priesthood of Christ, was not sufficiently emphasized in certain older definitions of the liturgy.[16]

(iii) The precise place and nature of the liturgy can be clearly seen by situating it in the *plan of salvation.* The liturgy realizes in the mystery of signs what the Old Testament announced in figures, what Christ accomplished in passing from men to his Father, what will appear in the liturgy of heaven. This is why the Council insists at length on these perspectives in the first pages of the Constitution.[17]

(iv) At the same time it must be affirmed that the liturgy can only be carried out by the action of the Church's hierarchy, and that the *Christian people* are delegated, through baptism, to take an active part in this same liturgy.[18]

All that has been said explains in what sense and with what qualifications we may apply to the liturgy the categories of worship, external worship, public worship and others, accepted as standard by authors and the documents of the magisterium, notably by the Council. It is a fact that these concepts, established and distinguished from each other on a rational basis, are of themselves poorly qualified to express the supernatural richness of the Church's prayer, a prayer

---

[15]In addition to the text cited above, see, in the same sense, CSL 33, 59, 60.— Cf. J. H. Miller, *op. cit.,* pp. 344-50, 352; C. Vagaggini, *op. cit.* pp. 14, 17, 18f; one cannot accept the opinion of M. Righetti, *Manuale di storia liturgica* 1, 2nd ed. (Milan: Ancora, 1950) p. 6, that the sensible and material element is only *"integrante e accessorio."* The scholarly author has completely revised his study in the 3rd edition (1964).

[16]The Council returns to this point in several places: CSL 2, 5, 6, 10, 33, 59, 102. The two aspects were already emphasized in MD 20-22, 27, etc.:—see also L. Beauduin, *op. cit.,* p. 126; I. H. Dalmais, *op. cit.* p. 23f; J. H. Miller, *op. cit.,* pp. 338f; C. Vagaggini, *op. cit.,* pp. 15, 18. See below, ch. 8.

[17]CSL 5-8; L. Bouyer, *op. cit.,* p. 29; C. Vagaggini, *op. cit.,* p. 19; A. Bugnini, "La liturgia è l'esercizio del sacerdozio di Gesù Cristo per mezzo della Chiesa" in *Asprenas* 6 (1959) 4.—See below, ch. 9.

[18]"Mother Church earnestly desires that all the faithful be led to that full, conscious, and active participation in liturgical celebrations which is demanded by the very nature of the liturgy. Such participation by the Christian people as 'a chosen race, a royal priesthood, a holy nation, a purchased people' (1 P 2:9; cf. 2:4-5), is their right and duty by reason of their baptism" (CSL 14). See below, ch. 5.

which certainly satisfies the needs of men's hearts, but far exceeds their preconceptions.[19]

III LITURGICAL "ACTIONS"

Instead of words previously used, such as "rites," "ceremonies," or "functions," modern official documents speak rather of "liturgical actions,"[20] thus including every one of the gatherings of which the liturgy is composed: vespers, the dedication of a church, the celebration of a baptism, the blessing of crops, etc. This word "action," familiar to antiquity, had already been advocated by many liturgists.[21] It emphasizes the fact that the liturgy uses to the highest possible degree the activities of those who are present; that it has an effective and objective result, independent of edifying feelings which may be experienced; that it "does" something, that it has its own movement and rhythm, a dynamic unity, even though we may afterwards study separately the different actors, the various moments in succession, the words and gestures, the visible elements and the invisible realities. The liturgy only exists at the moment that it is put into action. That is why it remains unintelligible to one who does not take part, why it can only be grasped to the degree that one is engaged in it.

The Eucharist is the one *action* above all others: *Hoc facite in meam commemorationem.* It is a sacrifice, in other words the highest activity of human life.

IV "PIA POPULI CHRISTIANI EXERCITIA"

The term *pia populi christiani exercitia* is applied to all gatherings, celebrations or prayers in common which do not meet all the conditions required to constitute a liturgical action.[22] The term therefore encompasses a wide variety. It includes chiefly: ceremonies imposed by the Apostolic See itself, but which cannot be called liturgical;[23] "devotions proper to individual churches," celebrated upon the order of bishops according to custom or duly approved books—these

[19]See below, ch. 8.

[20]CSL 7, 26, 48, 112; SRC, instruction of September 3, 1958, n. 1 and 12. Already in Pius XI, *Divini cultus: quasi actio sacra praecellenter.*

[21]G. Dix, *The Shape of the Liturgy,* 2nd ed. (Westminster: Dacre Press, 1945) pp. 2, 12f; P. Bayart, *Les divins offices* (Paris: Bloud et Gay, 1948) p. 52; I. H. Dalmais, "La liturgie, acte de l'Église" in LMD 19 (1949) 8-11.

[22]SRC, instruction of September 3, 1958, n. 1, 12, 15, 19f; Martimort-Picard, *Liturgie et musique* (Paris: Ed. du Cerf 1959) pp. 24f, 41f, 62-5; J. H. Miller, *op. cit.,* pp. 355f.

[23]Cf. CSL 13: *praesertim cum de mandato Apostolicae sedis fiunt.*

last enjoy a special dignity recognized by the Vatican Council.[24]
We must also include among the *pia exercitia* traditional devotions
such as the stations of the cross, the rosary, holy hours, or finally
those more modern forms, among which the first place is held by
those "celebrations of the Word of God" which the council recommends,[25] and which have found a special place in ecumenical
gatherings.[26]

This last example shows how slender the division can sometimes
be between liturgical actions and *pia exercitia*. The structure and
value of some of these latter make it possible for the Church occasionally to raise them to the rank of liturgical actions for a diocese,
a religious order, or even for the universal Church.[27] All that is
needed for this is official recognition. On the other hand, to avoid
regrettable abuses, the Council asks that "these devotions . . . be so
drawn up that they harmonize with the liturgical seasons, accord
with the sacred liturgy, are in some fashion derived from it, and lead
the people to it, since the liturgy by its very nature far surpasses any
of them."[28]

These exercises must therefore be clearly distinguished from the
liturgy in the strict sense: they possess neither its grace nor its
authority.[29] Yet, if it is not permitted to mix *pia exercitia* and
liturgical actions, there is nothing to prevent their being set side by
side, the *pia exercitia* preceding or following immediately upon
liturgical actions.[30] When their nature permits, the *pia exercitia* may
be celebrated in places of worship, and even be presided over by the
hierarchy as in the liturgy.[31]

An important characteristic of *pia exercitia* is that most of them
do not depend on supreme authority, being subject only to the local
bishop, who must approve their content and prayer-formulas.[32] In
fact, these too conform eventually to local customs, and some are
even fixed in books. Nonetheless, their organization enjoys a liberty

---

[24]*Ibid.*

[25]CSL 35, 4⁰.

[26]*Directorium de re oecumenica*, n. 32-7.

[27]This was the case with the Corpus Christi procession in the fourteenth century
and the renewal of baptismal promises in 1951.

[28]CSL 13; cf. MD 179.

[29]J. H. Miller, *op. cit.*, pp. 339, 352ff; B. Capelle, "Liturgique et non liturgique"
in QLP 15 (1930) 3-15 (= *Travaux liturgiques* 1 [1955] 44-53).—SRC, instruction of
November 16, 1955, n. 23.

[30]SRC, instruction of September 3, 1958, n. 12.

[31]SRC, *op. cit.*, n. 1.

[32]CIC, can. 1259; SRC, *op. cit.*, n. 12.

which cannot be accorded to the liturgy itself. That is why they can
constitute a sort of path towards the liturgy for those who have
become too far removed from it, and can allow of a collective expression for groups or for forms of piety which could not be recognized by the liturgy.

Under these various conditions, the *pia exercitia* are not only
legitimate, but praiseworthy and sometimes necessary. Their pastoral
importance, recalled especially in our own day,[33] is made evident
by the popular traditions of Christian countries.

2 The science of the liturgy

BIBLIOGRAPHY

On the science of the liturgy in general:

L. Eisenhofer, *Handbuch der katholischen Liturgik* 1 (Freiburg: Herder, 1932)
pp. 53-7.

L. Eisenhofer and J. Lechner, *The Liturgy of the Roman Rite* (Edinburgh-
London: Nelson, 1961) based on the 6th ed. of *Liturgik des römischen Ritus*
(Freiburg: Herder) pp. 17-19.

R. Guardini, "Über die systematische Methode in der Liturgiewissenschaft"
in JLW 1 (1921) 97-108.

P. Oppenheim, *Introductio in scientiam liturgicam* (Turin: Marietti, 1940;
Institutiones systematico-historicae in sacram liturgiam 5).

On the history of liturgical science:

L. Eisenhofer, *op. cit.*, pp. 118-48; L. Eisenhofer – J. Lechner, *op. cit.*, pp. 19-43.

P. Oppenheim, *Introductio historica in litteras liturgicas,* 2nd ed. (Turin:
Marietti, 1945; *Institutiones . . .* 1).

M. Righetti, *Manuale di storia liturgica* 1, 3rd ed. (Milan: Ancora, 1964) pp.
75-99.

This science aims at acquiring a more profound and organic understanding of the liturgy.

Like all sacred sciences, this one presupposes *faith,* which alone
makes it possible to perceive the supernatural realities contained
under the signs, and more generally to understand the liturgy's
whole manner of speaking, based on revelation. Nor is faith alone
sufficient. Since the liturgy, as has been seen, is an action, it is
intelligible only to those who participate in it actively, intelligible
in the very proportion of this participation. Before being an object
of study it is life, to the point that a liturgical science which did not
base itself on this life would not attain its object. Of course it would
describe, more or less exactly, external features, but it could never
grasp their true meaning. To describe the night office of Byzantine
monks, even to read the texts, would still not permit us to enter

---

[33]MD 168-80; cf. CSL 13.

into that knowledge from within which active participation alone can provide.

On the other hand, an understanding of the liturgy, lived in faith, must be developed by the resources of scientific disciplines. The three most important of these must be possessed simultaneously: first that of the historian, then that of the theologian, and finally that of the rubricist.[34]

I THE IMPORTANCE OF LITURGICAL HISTORY

BIBLIOGRAPHY

A. Baumstark, *Vom geschichtlichen Werden der Liturgie* (Freiburg: Herder, 1923; *Ecclesia orans* 10).

F. Cabrol, *Les origines liturgiques* (Paris: Letouzey et Ané, 1906) pp. 23-44, 197-202.

F. Cabrol, *Introduction aux études liturgiques* (Paris: Bloud, 1907).

C. Callewaert, *De sacra liturgia universim* (1919; 4th ed., Bruges: Beyaert, 1944; *Liturgicae institutiones,* tract. 1) pp. 172-86.

A. Coelho, *Cours de liturgie romaine* 1 (1924), tr. by G. Lefebvre (Lophem-lez-Bruges: Abbaye de Saint–André, 1928) pp. 109-33.

K. Mohlberg, *Ziele und Aufgaben der liturgiegeschichtlichen Forschung* (Münster: Aschendorff, 1919; LQF 1).

K. Mohlberg, *Nochmals Ziele und Aufgaben für das Studium des christlichen Kultes . . .* (Rome: Herder, 1957).

P. de Puniet, "La méthode en matière de liturgie" in SL 2 (1913, published in 1914) 41-77.

Th. Vismans – L. Brinkhoff, *Critical Bibliography of Liturgical Literature* (Nijmegen: Bestelcentrale der V.S.K.B. Publ., 1961) pp. 22-9.

Current bibliographies in ALW, EL, QLP, *Yearbook of Liturgical Studies* (Notre Dame, Indiana, 1960 ff); *Studia Liturgica* (Nienwendam-Rotterdam, 1962 ff).

Both the encyclical *Mediator Dei* (1947)[35] and the decree restoring the paschal vigil (1951)[36] have attributed an important role in the liturgical renewal to the researches of historians. The Vatican Council also counted heavily on their contribution.[37] The historical science of the liturgy has in fact, since its creation in the seventeenth century, enabled the clergy and faithful to discover the value and richness of the liturgy, its importance in the Church's tradition, the exact meaning of rites and prayers, the distinction between the

---

[34]SRC, instruction of September 3, 1958, n. 98. Cf. CSL 16, 23.—It is no longer possible to describe liturgical science simply as "a branch of canon law," a phrase of A. Vigourel, *Manuel de liturgie . . .,* 3rd ed. (Paris: Roger-Chernoviz, 1921) p. 7. (This author did in fact recognize the importance of the historical and theological study of the liturgy.)

[35]MD 4f.

[36]*Decretum de solemni vigilia paschali instauranda* (February 9, 1951): *nostra autem aetate, succrescentibus de antiqua liturgia investigationibu*s . . .

[37]CSL, 23, 50, 62.

essential and accessory, the unity and diversity in its heritage of prayer.

The historical science of the liturgy has as its primary goal to show and explain *how the liturgy became what it is.* The origin of rites clarifies their authentic meaning, helps to determine their greater or lesser importance, enables us to appreciate either their transcendence of or their dependence on cultural contexts. As long as liturgical history was not scientific, it was thought enough to explain rites by external and arbitrary allegories, and to study them in the light of artificial categories which today, happily, have been rejected.[38]

Yet it is not enough to account for the exterior and material unfolding of rites. The historian must also try to discover the inward attitude with which, in every age, these rites have been practised and lived by clergy and faithful.

The diversity of liturgies in the Church affords an opportunity to use the *comparative method,* which has thrown great light on other fields, for example that of language. Traits which are common to several liturgies can sometimes be explained by the borrowing of one from the other, but sometimes also by a common source, and in this case it may be possible to establish the state of rites as they were before the known documents. The comparative method is moreover of considerable importance for appreciating the greater or lesser spread of the Church's practice, and thus for evaluating its importance from the theological point of view.[39]

Also to be noted is the important role of the historical science of language, or philology, in the study of liturgy. Prayers and rubrics are found in texts of very diverse dates: in the same language, Latin for example, words and expressions have a meaning which differs according to the usage of periods, regions and groups. When a text has been translated into another language, a knowledge of the original is then equally necessary in resolving that text's difficulties and in understanding all its implications.[40] More generally, liturgical texts must be subjected to literary analysis, such as universities practise with regard to literary and philosophical masterpieces. And finally, apart from written evidence (liturgical books, acts of the

[38]See especially M. Righetti, *Manuale di storia liturgica* 1, 3rd ed. (Milan: Ancora, 1964) pp. 57-66, 73-4.

[39]The fundamental work is, A. Baumstark, *Liturgie comparée*, 3rd. ed., revised by B. Botte (Chevetogne, 1953; coll. *Irénikon*). Engl. tr., *Comparative Liturgy* (Westminster, Maryland: Newman Press, 1958; London: Mowbray, 1958).

[40]It is especially the works of B. Botte and C. Mohrmann that have shown at what point scientific philology is necessary for the liturgist. Some of these works are indicated in various chapters of the present volume.

Church) and descriptive or didactic documents, the liturgical historian draws great profit from ancient objects and places of worship, brought to light by archeology and by the knowledge of figured documents: ancient representations of the liturgy on mosaics, frescoes and murals, sculptures, engravings, miniatures, etc. Archeological discoveries have often been at the origin of a renewal of interest in liturgical history. On the other hand, perhaps it was occasionally forgotten that archeology could be no more than an auxiliary science.[41]

II THEOLOGICAL REFLECTION ON THE LITURGY

BIBLIOGRAPHY

C. Vagaggini, *Theological Dimensions of the Liturgy* 1, translated from the second Italian edition by L. Doyle (Collegeville, Minnesota: Liturgical Press, 1959).

The results of liturgical historians' researches must then become the object of theological study.[42] Now that the practice of the Church has been observed, how can it be evaluated? In which cases are we confronted with an unimpeachable tradition, and in which cases a corrupt development? Does the evolution which has been observed constitute progress or regression? What, at the level of supernatural realities, is the value of the signs which have been analysed? These questions are of the greatest importance for the liturgist. Their solution requires an attentive submission to the teachings of the magisterium, a very advanced general knowledge of theology, and especially a sound notion of the *loci theologici,* the nature of the Church and the sacraments.[43] No less necessary, in order to maintain a balanced judgment in such delicate subjects, is a deep and authentic spiritual life and a sharp sense of pastoral responsibilities. Liturgy, after all, belongs directly to these two fields.

The theological task, while always obliging us to respect its own methods, also includes the examination of the liturgy in the light of contemporary problems or various human sciences: religious psychology, sociology, history of religions, depth psychology, etc.[44]

---

[41]In the absence of recent major works on the contribution of archeology and iconography, one may profitably consult certain monographs, especially L. de Bruyne, "L'initiation chrétienne et ses reflets dans l'art paléo-chrétien" in RevSR 36 (1962) 27-86.

[42]This point was perhaps left somewhat in the dark by scholars who had to work to give historical science its rightful place at the basis of liturgical science.

[43]See below, ch. 10.

[44]Cf. Pius XII, allocution to the Assisi Liturgical Conference in *The Assisi Papers* (Collegeville, Minnesota: Liturgical Press, 1957) p. 236: "The present-day

III THE SCIENCE OF RUBRICS

The knowledge of the rubricist is less a science than an art, whose object is the faithful carrying out of the liturgy in the manner desired by the Church. This is learned chiefly and traditionally by living usage (such was the great way of handing on liturgical rules in the past). It is, however, no less traditional that the liturgy become the object of a legislator's written decisions, and then be subject to official descriptions having force of law. A true juridical science has thus been formed to organize systematically our knowledge and interpretation of liturgical legislation. This science cannot however be used correctly without competence in history and theology. Its methods will be discussed further on.[45]

liturgy interests itself also in a number of particular problems concerning, for example, the relation of the liturgy with the religious ideas of the world today, contemporary culture, social questions and depth psychology.''

[45]See below, ch. 4.

CHAPTER TWO

Rites and Liturgical Groups

Dom B. Botte

BIBLIOGRAPHY

A. Baumstark, *Liturgie comparée*, 3rd ed. (Chevetogne, 1953; collection *Irénikon*). Engl. tr., *Comparative Liturgy* (London: Mowbray, 1958; West-minster, Maryland: Newman Press, 1958).

L. Duchesne, *Origines du culte chrétien*, 5th ed. (Paris: De Boccard, 1920) pp. 1-46. Engl. tr., *Christian Worship—Its Origin and Evolution* (London: SPCK, 1931).

M. Righetti, *Manuale di Storia Liturgica* 1, 3rd ed. (Milan: Ancora, 1964) pp. 101-85.

Christian liturgy has taken various forms in various churches. The principle of this diversity is to be found neither in the language nor in the dogmatic confession of those who practise it. Different liturgies are celebrated in the same language and, on the other hand, the same liturgy can be practised simultaneously by Catholics and separated Christians. The principle of distinction is, at least in its beginnings, a geographical one.

We must then begin with the two great divisions of the ancient Christian world: the East and the West.

1 Liturgies of the East

BIBLIOGRAPHY

A good introduction may be found in:

I. H. Dalmais, *Les liturgies d'Orient* (Paris: Librairie A. Fayard, 1959; *Je sais, je crois* III). Engl. tr., *The Eastern Liturgies* (New York: Hawthorn Books, 1960; *Twentieth Century Encyclopedia of Catholicism;* London: Burns and Oates, 1960; *Faith and Fact* 3).

A. King, *The Rites of Eastern Christendom*, 2 vols. (Rome: Catholic Book Agency, 1947–48).

S. Salaville, *An Introduction to the Study of Eastern Liturgies* (London: Sands, 1938).

A general survey and extensive bibliography in:

J. M. Hanssens, *Institutiones liturgicae de ritibus orientalibus* (Rome: Gregorian University, 1930-32). Only vols. 2 and 3 (with an appendix in fascicle) on the Mass have appeared.

A. Raes, *Introductio in liturgiam orientalem* (Rome: P. Istituto Orientale, 1947).

J. M. Sauget, *Bibliographie des liturgies orientales* 1900–1960 (Rome: P. Istituto Orientale, 1962).

Principal collections of texts, for the Mass:

F. Brightman, *Liturgies Eastern and Western* . . . 1, *Eastern Liturgies* (Oxford: Clarendon, 1896; photo-mechanically reproduced 1965). This is the only volume to have appeared.

A. Hamman and T. Halton, *The Mass. Ancient Liturgies and Patristic Texts* (Staten Island, New York: Alba House, 1967; *Alba Patristic Library* 1).

A. Hänggi and I. Pahl, *Prex Eucharistica* (Fribourg: Ed. Universitaires, 1968: *Spicilegium Friburgense* 12).

E. Renaudot, *Liturgiarum orientalium collectio* (Paris, 1716); ed. 2a correctior, 2 vols. (Frankfurt: J. Baer, 1847).

For the sacraments:

J. A. Assemani, *Codex liturgicus ecclesiae universae*, 13 vols. (Rome, 1749–66). Reproduced in facsimile by Welter, 1902.

H. Denzinger, *Ritus orientalium*, 2 vols. (Würzburg: Sumptibus Stahelıanis, 1863-64; photo-mechanically reproduced 1961).

A common characteristic of all Eastern rites is that, for the Mass, they use fixed *anaphoras* (formularies corresponding to the Latin canon), which never change, whatever the feast may be. Each rite, however, possesses a greater or lesser number of these anaphoras.

The Eastern rites must be divided into two groups, corresponding to the two most ancient patriarchates, Antioch and Alexandria. Their respective anaphoras may be distinguished by the position of the prayers of intercession and, secondarily, of the epiclesis. The anaphoras of the Antiochene group end with the prayers of intercession for the members of the Church living or dead. In the Egyptian group they come immediately after the initial thanksgiving and precede the *Sanctus*. The epiclesis is an invocation of the Holy Spirit, that he may come to consecrate the offerings. It follows the recital of institution and anamnesis in the Syrian Masses. The Egyptian group contains two epicleses, one before the recital of institution, the other after the anamnesis.

I THE ANTIOCHENE GROUP

The Antiochene group in its turn subdivides into two different types. The authority of the patriarch of Antioch did in fact reach into the territories of the Roman empire and the territories subject to the Persians. The Christian communities established in the valley of the Tigris and Euphrates spoke Syriac and lived under Persian rule. In this relative isolation their organization was, from the beginning of the fifth century, all but completely autonomous. It is therefore hardly surprising that they formed a different liturgy: this is the *East Syrian rite*. The other communities of the patriarchate of Antioch have liturgies of the *East Syrian* type, with very numerous variations.

1 *West Syrian type*

Of this West Syrian type are the Syrian rite of Antioch, the Maronite rites, the Byzantine rite, and the Armenian rite.

(a) The Syrian rite of Antioch (*Jacobites, uniate Syrians, Malankars*)

BIBLIOGRAPHY

H. W. Codrington, "Studies of the Syrian Liturgies" in *Eastern Churches Quarterly* (1936–37), reprinted as a pamphlet (London: Coldwell, 1952).

C. E. Hammond, *The Ancient Liturgy of Antioch and Other Liturgical Fragments* (Oxford: Clarendon, 1879).

L'Orient syrien (first volume, 1956) periodically publishes numerous texts and studies on the Syrian liturgy.

A. Raes, "L'étude de la liturgie syrienne" in *Miscellanea liturgica in honorem L. Cuniberti Mohlberg* 1 (Rome: Ed. liturgiche, 1948) pp. 333-46.

I. Ziadé, "Syrienne (église)" in *Dictionnaire de théologie catholique* 14 (Paris: Letouzey et Ané, 1941) col. 2024-28.

Antioch was, after Jerusalem, the first center for the spread of Christianity, and its influence extended very widely. As a Roman province in which the cultural language was Greek, West Syria constructed a liturgy in the Greek language, at least in the cities. Only the region of Edessa, the Osrhoene, which remained an independent kingdom until nearly AD 200, was a center of Syriac culture.[1]

The Greek liturgy of Antioch is known to us through the preaching of St John Chrysostom,[2] through that of Theodore of Mopsuestia,[3] and to a certain extent through the *Didascalia apostolorum* (third century)[4] and the *Apostolic Constitutions*.[5] The Greek anaphora of St James[6] has come down to us in a late text containing developments foreign to its primitive state.

[1] The liturgy of Edessa disappeared very quickly; there are perhaps some traces of it in rare documents: R. H. Connolly, "Sixth-century Fragments of an East Syrian Anaphora" in oc, neue Folge 12-14 (1925) 99-128; F. C. Burkitt, "The Early Syriac Lectionary System" in *Proceedings of the British Academy* 10 (1921-23) 301-38;—the works of St Ephrem also provide some information on this liturgy.

[2] To the texts concerning the Mass assembled by F. Brightman, *op. cit.*, pp. 470-81, should be added especially the baptismal catecheses edited by A. Wenger in 1957 (sc 50).

[3] The Catechetic Homilies (*Homélies catéchétiques*, ed. and tr. by R. Tonneau [Vatican City, 1949; *Studi e testi* 145]) might be earlier than his episcopate and thus describe the liturgy of Antioch, but this is not at all certain. There are notable divergences from the practices attested to by the catecheses of St John Chrysostom, which were certainly preached at Antioch.

[4] Ed. H. Connolly (Oxford: Clarendon, 1929);—French tr., F. Nau (Paris: Lethielleux, 1912).

[5] Ed. F. X. Funk, *Didascalia et Constitutiones apostolorum*, 2 vols. (Paderborn: Schöningh, 1905).

[6] Ed. and Latin tr. by B. Mercier (Paris: Didot, 1946; po 26, 2).

C

While the liturgy of Jerusalem and Palestine was very close to that of Antioch, the development of pilgrimages to the holy places gave to the former a very distinctive quality which in its turn influenced other liturgies, notably the Armenian and Georgian. It is attested to by an unrivaled set of documents: the catecheses of St Cyril (or of his successor John),[7] the diary of Egeria,[8] the ancient Armenian lectionary,[9] the Georgian calendar and Kanonarion,[10] and also by traces which remain in documents of the Melkite rite.[11]

The Council of Chalcedon (451) provoked a division in the church of Antioch. An orthodox patriarchate continued, of course, to exist, but in time its membership consisted mainly of subjects of the empire, whence the name which was given to them—*Melkites*. They ended by adopting almost completely the liturgy of Byzantium.[12]

The victory, therefore, remained with the Monophysites, and the Jacobite church of Antioch rallied around itself the Christian communities of both Greek and Syriac tongues. On the other hand, the Arab invasions separated Syria from the Roman empire, and Greek, which had been the language of the large cities, was abandoned first in favor of the national language, then of Arabic. The Antiochene rite was organized by means of some elements translated from Greek,[13] and others which were authentically Syriac. The

---

[7]PG 33; tr. by J. Bouvet (Namur: Ed. du soleil levant, 1962); see W. J. Swaans, "A propos des Catéchèses mystagogiques attribués à saint Cyrille de Jérusalem" in *Muséon* 55 (1942) 1-43. Cf. A. Renoux, "Les catéchèses mystagogiques dans l'organisation liturgique hiérosolymitaine du IVᵉ et du Vᵉ siècle" in *Muséon* 78 (1965) 355-9.

[8]Since the discovery of the *Peregrinatio* this woman has been called first Sylvia, then Etheria.—Ethérie, *Journal de voyage,* ed. and tr. by H. Pétré (Paris: Ed. du Cerf, 1948; SC 21).

[9]An edition has been prepared by C. Mercier for the *Patrologie orientale* published by Didot. Collation of a related manuscript by A. Renoux, "Un manuscrit du Lectionnaire arménien de Jérusalem (Cod. Jerus. arm. 121)" in *Muséon* 74 (1961) 361-85; 75 (1962) 385-98.

[10]G. Garitte, *Le Calendrier palestino-géorgien du Sinaïticus* 34ʳ(Xᵉ *siècle*) (Brussels: Bollandistes, 1958; *Subsidia hagiographica* 30); M. Tarchnišvili, *Le grand lectionnaire de l'Église de Jérusalem* (Vᵉ-VIIIᵉ *siècle*), 2 vols. (Louvain, 1959-60; CSCO 189, 205).

[11]M. Black, *Rituale melchitarum, a Christian Palestinian Euchologion* (Stuttgart: Kohlhammer, 1938; *Bonner orientalische Studien* 22); M. Black, *A Christian Palestinian Syriac Horologion* (Cambridge: University Press, 1954; *Texts and Studies* 2nd ser. 1).

[12]On the history of the Melkites and the stages of their assimilation of the Byzantine rite: C. Charon, "Le rite byzantin dans les patriarcats melkites" in Χρυσοστομικά (Rome: Pustet, 1908) pp. 485-718.

[13]James of Edessa (d. 708) is the author of some of these translations: I. Ortiz de Urbina, *Patrologia syriaca* (Rome: P. Istituto orientale, 1958) pp. 169f.

works of St Ephrem furnished an abundant hymnology. Antioch also fell heir to some of Jerusalem's traditions.

In the second half of the twelfth century, the Syrian rite of Antioch received its definitive features, mainly through the work of Denis bar Salibi (d. 1171). Apart from the ancient anaphora of St James,[14] it possesses seventy anaphoras, many of which are extremely late.[15] The office is characterized by the predominance of hymns, which have all but entirely replaced the psalmody. The pontifical rites were fixed, also in the twelfth century, by Michael the Syrian; one can find there some usages which are unknown to all other rites. Thus in ordinations, before the bishop lays his hands on the ordinand, he places them over the sacred species as though to draw from them divine grace.

Syriac remains the official language of the liturgy, although in Syria the readings and a good number of the prayers are said in Arabic.

In the seventeenth century, some of the Antiochene Syrians went over to Rome; they formed a Catholic patriarchate in which the Syrian rite is always practised.

In the same period, on the western coast of India, certain Malabars[16] who did not want union with Rome joined the Monophysite patriarchate of Antioch and adopted the East Syrian liturgy. Since 1930 several of their bishops have again joined Rome. They are called Malankars and keep their Syrian rite, which they celebrate in their national language, Malayalam.[17]

(b) The Maronite rite

BIBLIOGRAPHY

P. Dib, *Étude sur la liturgie maronite* (Paris: Lethielleux, 1919).

P. E. Gemayel, *Avant-messe maronite, histoire et structure* (Rome: P. Istituto Orientale, 1965; *Orientalia Christiana Analecta* 174).

M. Hayek, *Liturgie maronite, histoire et textes eucharistiques* (Tours: Mame, 1964).

[14]For the Greek text of the anaphora of St James, see the preceding note.—For the Syriac text: ed. by O. Heiming in A. Raes, *Anaphorae syriacae* 2 (Rome: Istituto orientale, 1953) pp. 105-79; French tr. and notes by G. Khouri-Sarkis in *l'Orient syrien* 4 (1959) 385-448; 5 (1960) 3-32, 129-58, 363-84. Engl. tr., A. Hamman, *Early Christian Prayers* (Chicago: Regnery; London: Longmans, 1962) pp. 215-21.

[15]They are listed in A. Raes, *Anaphorae syriacae* 1 (Rome: Istituto orientale, 1939) pp. xi-xiv. Sixteen of these are published in what has already appeared of this work, which is eventually to give a critical edition of them all.

[16]See below, 2, c.

[17]See E. Tisserant, "Syro-Malabares" in *Dictionnaire de théologie catholique* 14 (1941) col. 3049-3162; C. Korolevskij, *Liturgie en langue vivante* (Paris: Ed. du Cerf, 1955; *Lex orandi* 18) pp. 89-92, 160-87. Engl. tr., *Living Languages in Catholic Worship* (London, New York, Toronto: Longmans, 1957) pp. 57-9, 117-40.

This rite is a variant of the Syrian rite of Antioch. It is practised by communities of Lebanon which were constituted as an autonomous church, probably during the eighth to ninth centuries, around the monastery of St Maron. At the time of the crusades they rejoined Rome. Apart from what they have in common with Antioch, the Maronites also possess a tradition of their own.[18] Unfortunately they have undergone far too many Latin influences.

(c) The Byzantine rite

BIBLIOGRAPHY

A. Couturier, *Cours de liturgie grecque melkite*, 3 vols. (Par:is Gabalda, 1912–30).

J. Goar, *Εὐχολόγιον sive Rituale Graecorum*, 2nd ed. (Venice: B. Javarina, 1730).

P. de Meester, *Studi sui sacramenti amministrati secondo il rito bizantino* (Rome: Ed. liturgiche, 1947).

E. Mercenier and F. Paris, *La prière des églises de rite byzantin* (Chevetogne, 1937 ff). Vol. 1 was reprinted in 1948; vol. 2 is in two volumes; vol. 3 has not yet appeared.

E. Wellesz, *A History of Byzantine Music and Hymnography*, 2nd ed. (Oxford: University Press, 1961).

While the Byzantine rite is related through its origins to Antioch, and has close affinities with the Syrian rite of Antioch, it nevertheless took form in the imperial city. Just as the Roman liturgy is the liturgy of the city of Rome, the Byzantine liturgy is that of Constantinople, and it was inspired in part by the celebrations of the imperial court. Apart from elements coming from Antioch, there are some which stem from Cappadocia.

The anaphora of St Basil, which is said on certain days, is probably the work of the bishop of Caesarea.[19] The anaphora of St John Chrysostom, which is said more often, is later; it is the reworking of an ancient Antiochene anaphora, and is certainly later than the time of St John Chrysostom.[20] The prayers of intercession are placed after the epiclesis, as in all liturgies of the West Syrian type. The Byzantine

---

[18]In particular the anaphora of St Peter Sarar, very archaic and related to the Chaldean liturgy of Addai and Mari: H. Engberding, "Urgestalt, Eigenart und Entwicklung eines altantiochenischen eucharistischen Hochgebetes" in OC 3rd ser. 7 (1932) 32-48.

[19]Brightman, pp. 309-44 (ninth-century text), 400-411 (modern text); tr. in Mercenier-Paris, *op. cit.*, 1, 2nd ed., pp. 267-80; Engl. tr., A. Hamman, *op. cit.*, pp. 222-5. Study by B. Capelle in J. Doresse and E. Lanne, *Un témoin archaïque de la liturgie copte de saint Basile* (Louvain, 1960; *Bibliothèque du Muséon* 47).

[20]Brightman, pp. 309-44 (ninth-century text), 352-99 (modern text); Mercenier-Paris, *op. cit.*, pp. 250-66; see Χρυσοστομικά (Rome: Pustet, 1908) pp. 245-471, 731-969; A. Raes, "L'authenticité de la liturgie byzantine de saint Jean Chrysostome" in OCP 24 (1958) 5-16. Engl. tr., A. Hamman, *op. cit.*, pp. 225-8.

rite possesses no other anaphora. For days on which Mass is not celebrated, there is a liturgy of the presanctified.[21]

The Byzantine rite has extensively developed its hymnology. Originally composed to fill out the psalms and biblical canticles, these poetic pieces soon took precedence over the biblical chants.[22]

Another trait of the Byzantine rite is the importance accorded to the cult of images. The chancel which closes the sanctuary became an iconostasis, adorned with icons according to fixed rules. The emphasis on the cult of images was a reaction against iconoclasm (eighth century).

The prayers of the Byzantine rite possess a tremendous theological wealth. One senses in them, far more clearly than in the Roman rite, a desire to express the great conciliar dogmas of Nicaea, Ephesus and Chalcedon.

To be classed with the Byzantine rite are the *Ruthenian* rite, practised by those Byzantine churches of the Ukraine which have been united with Rome since the seventeenth century, and the *Melkite* rite. The name Melkite (or "imperial") is given to the communities of Syria and Egypt which remained faithful to Chalcedon. At first they continued to practise their own rite, but progressively adopted the Byzantine.[23]

The Byzantine rite is practised both by the Orthodox and by Catholics (Ruthenians and Greeks). In the same way there are Orthodox Melkites and Catholic Melkites.

The original language of the Byzantine rite is Greek; liturgical books, however, were translated into Slavonic at the time of the Slavs' conversion. The Melkites celebrated at first in Syriac, but then adopted Arabic. Other languages are used according to country: Rumanian, Georgian, etc.[24]

(d) The Armenian rite

BIBLIOGRAPHY

G. Amadouni, *La divine liturgie du rite arménien* (Venice: Imprimerie Saint-Lazare, 1957).

F. C. Conybeare, *Rituale Armenorum* (Oxford: Clarendon, 1905).

P. Ferhat, A. Baumstark, A. Rücker, "Denkmäler altarmenischer Liturgie" in oc 2nd ser. 1 (1911) 204-14; 3 (1913) 16-31; 7-8 (1918) 1-82; 3rd ser. 1 (1927) 149-57; 5 (1930) 56-79.

A. Renoux, "Le rite arménien" in *Bulletin du comité des études* (Compagnie de Saint-Sulpice) 7 (1963) 245-78.

[21]Brightman, pp. 345-52 (ninth-century text); Mercenier-Paris, *op. cit.*, pp. 285-98.
[22]See below, ch. 6.
[23]See above, a, and below, II, 1.
[24]C. Korolevskij, *Liturgie en langue vivante*, pp. 23-6, 30-5, 42-87; *Living Languages in Catholic Worship*, pp. 9-12, 14-18, 23-57.

It was the Catholicos Sahak who, at the end of the fourth century, created the Armenian liturgy, as well as Armenian Christian literature. For the calendar and lectionary, he drew his inspiration chiefly from Jerusalem,[25] but it is difficult to say which elements are the most primitive since the Armenian liturgy has, in several periods, undergone the influence of Byzantium and Rome. It is one of the most latinized rites, even as it is practised by the non-Catholics. It must, however, be noted that the use of unleavened bread in the Mass is not due to a Latin influence; it goes back to a time when the question had not yet been raised. The liturgical language is classical Armenian, which differs notably from the spoken language of today.

2 *East Syrian type*

As we have said, the communities established in Mesopotamia under Persian domination escaped the Antiochene influence for geographical and political reasons. Dogmatic separation soon became another factor in this isolation. The East Syrians did not accept the decisions of Ephesus, and became Nestorians. It is thus that the East Syrian liturgy became mixed for several centuries with the Nestorian liturgy.

(a) *The Nestorian rite*

BIBLIOGRAPHY

R. H. Connolly, *The Liturgical Homilies of Narsaī* (Cambridge: University Press, 1909; *Texts and Studies* 8, 1).

R. H. Connolly, *Anonymi auctoris Expositio officiorum ecclesiae Georgio Arbelensi vulgo adscripta* . . . , 4 vols. (Louvain, 1911-15, 1953-54; CSCO 64 and 72 for the text, 71 and 76 for the translation).

A. J. Maclean, *East Syrian Daily Offices* (London: Rivington Percival and Co., 1894).

E. Tisserant, "Nestorienne (église)" in *Dictionnaire de théologie catholique* 11 (1931) col. 157-323.

In the form in which we know it, the East Syrian rite was organized in the seventh century by the patriarch Isho-'Yab III.

For the Mass, it includes these anaphoras: those of the Apostles Addai and Mari, of Theodore of Mopsuestia and of Nestorius. As will be seen later on, the anaphora of the Apostles raises a special problem: in the form in which it has come down to us in the manuscripts, it contains no recital of institution. Moreover, the epiclesis is placed after the prayers of intercession, and not before, as in the other Syrian rites.

The language is for the most part Syriac.

[25]See above, a.

(b) The Chaldean rite

In the fifteenth century, some of the Nestorians of Cyprus, and in the sixteenth century, of Chaldea, rejoined Rome and formed the Chaldean church. They have retained, with a few corrections, the liturgy practised by the Nestorians.[26] Although the names of Theodore of Mopsuestia and Nestorius were removed from the titles of the anaphoras, the anaphoras themselves remained in use.

(c) The Malabar rite

BIBLIOGRAPHY

L. W. Brown, *The Indian Christians of Saint Thomas* (Cambridge: University Press, 1956).

The Nestorians were great missionaries, bringing the gospel to the East.[27] Most of the communities founded by them have disappeared, except for the church of Malabar. In the sixteenth century, the Portuguese who occupied the region wished to lead this church back to Catholicism. They did this in a tactless way, attempting to impose the Roman liturgy, or at least to correct the Syrian liturgy then in use. It is today the most latinized rite, having kept only a small part of its traditions. Only the liturgy of the Apostles is in use; those of Theodore of Mopsuestia and of Nestorius have been suppressed. Unleavened bread and the Latin Mass were also imposed. Ordinations, since there was no bishop of the Syrian rite, were conducted in Latin. Later on, the resumption of ancient customs was prevented by the lack of a pontifical. At present, the Sacred Oriental Congregation has ordered the preparation of a pontifical for the East Syrian rite.[28]

Those communities which did not unite with Rome joined the Monophysite patriarchate of Antioch and formed the Malankar church, which practises the Syrian rite of Antioch.[29] In 1960 there appeared a new edition of the missal of Alwaye which contains the anaphora of the Apostles, revised according to the sources.

II THE ALEXANDRIAN GROUP

We have few very ancient documents concerning the origin of the

[26]C. Mousses, *Histoire du missel chaldéen* (Jerusalem: Ed. Proche-Orient chrétien, 1953); D. Dahane, *Liturgie de la sainte messe selon le rite chaldéen* (Paris: Enault, 1937).

[27]J. Dauvillier, "Les provinces chaldéennes de l'extérieur au moyen âge" in *Mélanges F. Cavallera* (Toulouse: Institut Catholique, 1948) pp. 260-316.

[28]Cf. C. Korolevskij, *op. cit.*, pp. 89-91. Engl. tr., pp. 57-9.

[29]See above, a.

liturgy of Egypt.[30] The euchology of Serapion (fourth century) is such an unusual document that it is no longer possible to draw from it any general conclusions.[31] What has been called the "Egyptian church order" is really nothing but the *Apostolic Tradition* of St Hippolytus, enclosed by other documents in a canonical collection.[32] It is impossible to find here a source for the primitive Egyptian liturgy.

Such as it appears over the course of the Middle Ages, the liturgy of the Alexandrian patriarchate may be seen under two forms: the Coptic rite and the Ethiopian rite.

1 The Coptic rite

BIBLIOGRAPHY

O. Burmester, "Rites and Ceremonies of the Coptic Church" in *Eastern Churches Quarterly* 9 (1951–52) 1-27, 245-60, 306-19; 10 (1953–55) 9-27, 217-29.

The liturgy was celebrated in Greek at Alexandria and in lower Egypt. It was probably celebrated in various Coptic dialects in upper Egypt; we still have some fragments of ancient manuscripts in Sahidic. In the ninth century, the Bohairic dialect became, and has remained, the official language of the liturgy of Alexandria, although Greek has still been occasionally employed. At present, a great deal is done in Arabic, which is the language of the country.

We have preserved a Greek version of the anaphora of St Mark.[33] It already existed in the fourth century in a shorter form.[34] The Copts use the anaphora of St Cyril, which is a translation and

[30]Evidence drawn from patristic works, above all St Athanasius, in Brightman, pp. 504-9.

[31]Greek text in F. X. Funk, *Didascalia et Constitutiones apostolicae* 2 (Paderborn: Schöningh, 1905) pp. 158-95; French tr. in A. Hamman, *Prière des premiers chrétiens* (Paris: Fayard, 1951) pp. 179-200.—On this collection, see B. Capelle, "L'anaphore de Sérapion" in *Muséon* 59 (1946) 124-42, 424-43; Engl. tr. by J. Wordsworth, *Bishop Serapion's Prayer-book*, 2nd ed. (London: SPCK, 1923). Also, A. Hamman, *Early Christian Prayers* (Chicago: Regnery; London: Longmans, 1961) pp. 117-31.

[32]R. H. Connolly, *The So-Called Egyptian Church Order and Derived Documents* (Cambridge: University Press, 1916; *Texts and Studies* 8, 4); B. Botte, *La Tradition apostolique de saint Hippolyte* (Münster: Aschendorff, 1963; LQF 39); cf. *id.*, "Les plus anciennes collections canoniques" in *Orient syrien* 5 (1960) 331-49.

[33]Brightman, pp. 113-43; a better edition may be found in C. A. Swainson, *The Greek Liturgies* (Cambridge: University Press, 1884) pp. 1-73.

[34]M. Andrieu and P. Collomp, "Fragments sur papyrus de l'anaphore de saint Marc" in RevSR 8 (1928) 489-515. See also an important fragment of the sixth century in C. H. Roberts, *Catalogue of the Greek and Latin Papyri in the J. Rylands Library* 3 (1938) 132 (n. 465).—The papyrus of Dêr Balizeh contains

adaptation of the Greek anaphora of St Mark.[35] These differ from the Syrian anaphoras in that the prayers of intercession are placed in the first part of the thanksgiving, before the *Sanctus*. Moreover, there is a short epiclesis which precedes the recital of institution, whereas a long epiclesis analogous to that of the Syrians, is found after the anamnesis. The question is whether this second epiclesis was part of the earliest Egyptian rite. Given the present state of the documentation, it is impossible to say.

Two other anaphoras are in use, apart from that of Mark-Cyril: one bears the name of St Basil and is an older form of that used by the Byzantines.[36] The other anaphora is that of St Gregory.[37] These two anaphoras are not of the Alexandrian, but of the Syrian type.

There are also to be found many influences of the anaphora of St James on that of St Mark. So too in the sacramental rites we find prayers which are of Syrian origin. The Syrian influence in Egypt has thus been considerable.

In Egypt, as in Syria, the national church rejected the Council of Chalcedon and professed Monophysitism. There has also remained a group of Melkites, faithful to orthodoxy, whose liturgy has taken on a Byzantine form.[38] Finally, there are Copts in union with the Roman Church.

2 The Ethiopian rite

BIBLIOGRAPHY

E. Hammerschmidt, *Studies in the Ethiopic Anaphoras* (Berlin: Akademie-Verlag, 1961; *Berliner byzantinische Arbeiten* 25).

Although Ethiopia already had a bishop in the time of St Athanasius, the country was not really evangelized until much later, for the most part by monks who came from Syria in the sixth century, and were therefore Monophysites. The first translation of the Bible into Ge'ez dates back to this period.

a fragment of an anaphora of the sixth to seventh century, and not of the fourth, as was previously held. The best edition is that of C. H. Roberts and B. Capelle, *An Early Euchologium* (Louvain, 1949; *Bibliothèque du Muséon* 23).

[35]Brightman, pp. 144-88; Swainson, *ibid.*—Cf. H. Engberding, "Das Verhältnis der syrischen Timotheusanaphora zur koptischen Cyrillusliturgie" in oc 42, (1958) 55-67.

[36]Latin tr. in E. Renaudot, *op. cit.* 1, pp. 1-25; French tr. by S. de Beaurecueil in *Cahiers coptes* 6 (1954) 6-12.—See J. Doresse and E. Lanne, *Un témoin archaïque de la liturgie copte de saint Basile* (Louvain, 1960; *Bibliothèque du Muséon* 47).

[37]Latin tr. in E. Renaudot, *op. cit.,* pp. 25-37; French tr. by S. de Beaurecueil in *Cahiers coptes* 7-8 (1954) 6-10.—See E. Hammerschmidt, *Die koptische Gregoriosanaphora* (Berlin: Akademie Verlag, 1957).

[38]C. Charon, "Le rite byzantin dans les patriarcats melkites," *op. cit.,* pp. 477-84.

The Ethiopian liturgy is known to us only through late manuscripts. All in all, it may be said that this is a liturgy translated from
Coptic.

It possesses, however, original poetry; the marian hymns in
particular are quite remarkable.[39]

Moreover, this liturgy contains a collection of seventeen or
eighteen anaphoras, most of which are not Alexandrian. The liturgy
of the Apostles, for example, is none other than the anaphora of
Hippolytus. Another one, called the anaphora of our Lord, is
drawn from an Ethiopian reworking of the *Testament of Our Lord,*
which is itself a reworking of the *Apostolic Tradition.* These two
anaphoras, drawn from literary writings, do not represent a very
old liturgical usage. That of the Apostles could not be used before
an Ethiopian translation was made from the Coptic canonical
collection which contained the *Tradition,* in other words probably
in the thirteenth century.

The liturgical language of the Ethiopians has remained Ge'ez,
which is today a dead language.

2 Liturgies of the West

BIBLIOGRAPHY

K. Gamber, *Codices liturgici Latini antiquiores* (Fribourg: Universitätsverlag,
1963; *Spicilegii Friburgensis subsidia* 1).
C. Vogel, *Introduction aux sources de l'histoire du culte chrétien au moyen âge*
(Spoleto: Centro italiano di studi sull'alto medioevo, 1966; *Biblioteca degli
Studi medievali* 1).

I THE ROMAN RITE

1 *The gradual extension of the Roman rite*

Although the Roman rite is practised today by nearly all of Latin
Christianity, it is in its origins the liturgy of the city of Rome, as it
was organized by the popes.

At a very early date the Roman liturgy was adopted, probably
with great freedom, by other churches of Italy. At the end of the fourth
century St Ambrose declares that he follows the Roman tradition,
but also reserves the right to keep or adopt customs which are
foreign to Rome.[40] In any case the Roman liturgy, with local
variants, won acceptance very rapidly throughout almost all of
Italy.[41]

---

[39]See the bibliography given in A. Baumstark, *Liturgie comparée*, 3rd ed. (Chevetogne, 1953), pp. 255f.
[40]*De sacramentis* III.1.5, ed. B. Botte (sc 25 bis) p. 94.
[41]The liturgy best known to us through the liturgical books which have been

It also spread beyond the Alps, at first spontaneously: the most ancient witnesses to the Roman canon are books of Gallican or Irish origin.[42] Then Charlemagne imposed the Roman liturgy within his empire, with the result that it almost entirely replaced the ancient local liturgies in Gaul and Germany.

Its penetration into Spain was slower and later, but it was imposed in the eleventh century by St Gregory VII to such an extent that the ancient Spanish liturgy remained in only a few churches.[43]

2 Sources and characteristics of the old Roman liturgy

The oldest liturgical collections which we possess—setting aside the *Apostolic Tradition* attributed to St Hippolytus,[44] which is of a very special nature and cannot be considered an official book—are the *sacramentaries*. These books contained only those prayers which the bishop was to say during various celebrations. The sacramentary which we call the Leonine (or the sacramentary of Verona),[45] preserved for us in only one copy and unhappily damaged in the first section, is not yet a well-organized sacramentary. It is a collection of texts of unequal length and gathered, though only approximately, in the order of the liturgical year. In certain pieces it has been possible to discern the hands of St Leo, Pope Gelasius I and Pope Vigilius.

The "old Gelasian" sacramentary has also come down to us in one copy (*Vat. Reginen. Lat.* 316).[46] This is a well-organized sacramentary, divided into three parts, the cycle of seasons being separated from the cycle of saints. Although written in Gaul and marked by Gallican influences, its origin is substantially Roman. Its idiosyncra-

preserved either in full or in part is that of Benevento (R. J. Hesbert, "L'antiphonale missarum de l'ancien rite bénéventain" in EL 52 [1938] 28-66, 141-58; 53 [1939] 168-90; 59 [1945] 69-95; 60 [1946] 103-41; 61 [1947] 153-210), and to some extent that of Naples (G. Morin, "La liturgie de Naples au temps de saint Grégoire" in RB 8 [1891] 480-93, 529-37; *Anecdota Maredsolana* 1 [Maredsous, 1893] 426-35), Capua (*ibid.*, 436-44), and Aquilea.—Cf. A. King, *Liturgies of the Past* (London: Longmans, 1959).

[42]*The Bobbio Missal*, E. A. Lowe ed. (London, 1920; HBS 58);—*Missale Francorum*, L. C. Mohlberg ed. (Rome: Herder, 1957; *Rerum ecclesiasticarum documenta*, Series major, *Fontes* 2);—*The Stowe Missal*, G. F. Warner ed. (London, 1915; HBS 32).

[43]J. F. Rivera, "Gregorio VII y la liturgia mozárabe" in *Revista española de teología* (1942) 3-33.

[44]*Tradition apostolique*, B. Botte ed. (Münster: Aschendorff, 1963; LQF 39).

[45]*Sacramentarium Veronense*, L. C. Mohlberg ed. (Rome: Herder, 1956; *Rerum ecclesiasticarum documenta*, Series major, *Fontes* 1); PL 55, col. 22-156.

[46]*Liber sacramentorum Romanae ecclesiae ordinis anni circuli*, L. C. Mohlberg ed. (*ibid.*, 1960; same collection IV); PL 74, col. 1055-1244.

sies are best explained by the hypothesis which considers it to be the sacramentary of a titular church in Rome towards the middle of the seventh century. It does not, therefore, represent the papal liturgy; in the city of Rome itself the liturgy was far from uniform.[47]

The Gregorian sacramentary is the work of Pope St Gregory. We do not know it in its original state, however; nearly all the copies which have come down to us derive from one which Pope Adrian sent to Charlemagne at the end of the eighth century.[48] This was a sacramentary for the pope's use, in which the cycle of saints was mixed in with that of the seasons, and which lacked many elements necessary for current usage. Alcuin, or more probably St Benedict of Aniane, therefore revised it and added a supplement.[49]

We also possess, in their original condition, other books of the liturgy as it was practised in Rome before the Carolingian period, notably the lectionaries for the Mass.[50] In addition, the *Liber Pontificalis,* the formulas of the *Liber Diurnus,* and above all the letters of the popes furnish us with valuable information on the details of this liturgy and on the changes which the Roman pontiffs introduced.

The canon of the Mass is characteristic of the Roman rite. The liturgies of Gaul and Spain have no fixed formula, the sacerdotal prayer being made up of changeable sections grouped around the recital of institution, while the Oriental rites have a greater or lesser number of anaphoras. Rome has a single formula, but one which admits of a certain latitude. Some sections have variations for certain solemnities: the preface (which was part of the canon), the *Communicantes,* the *Hanc igitur.*

Also characteristic is the style of the Roman prayers. They use a carefully balanced language, modelled after the *cursus.*[51] Their concision stands in contrast with the fulsomeness of the Gallican and Visigothic formulas.

The Roman rite also showed great reserve towards poetic composi-

[47]A. Chavasse, *Le sacramentaire gélasien* (Tournai: Desclée, 1958) pp. 77-86.

[48]H. Lietzmann, *Das Sacramentarium Gregorianum nach dem Aachener Urexemplar* (Münster: Aschendorff, 1921; LQF 3).

[49]H. A. Wilson, *The Gregorian Sacramentary under Charles the Great* (London: 1915; HBS 49); H. Lietzmann, "Handschriftliches zu Alkuins Ausgabe und Sacramentarium" in JLW 5 (1925) 68-79;—J. Deshusses, "Le supplément au sacramentaire grégorien: Alcuin ou saint Benoît d'Aniane?" in ALW 9 (1965) 48-71.

[50]A. Chavasse, "Les plus anciens types du lectionnaire et de l'antiphonaire romains de la messe" in RB 62 (1952) 3-94; T. Klauser, *Das römische Capitulare evangeliorum* (Münster: Aschendorff, 1935; LQF 28).

[51]See below, ch. 6.

tions. These were introduced only at a later period and in a secondary place. Almost all chant compositions have biblical texts.[52]

The language of the Roman liturgy was at first Greek, then Latin from at least the third quarter of the fourth century.[53] The only noticeable exception to this is the missal in Slavonic, known as the *Glagolithic,* granted to the churches of Bohemia and always used in the region of Dalmatia.[54]

In the seventh century, the presence in Rome of a large Byzantine colony and of Eastern monks required that certain parts of the liturgy, especially the readings, be bilingual. In addition, oriental customs were introduced, notably marian feasts, the adoration of the cross, and the chant at the fraction.

3 *The evolution of the Roman liturgy after its diffusion outside Italy*

In the course of its diffusion through Gaul and Germany, the Roman liturgy gathered foreign elements, either because old local customs remained or because new rites were created.

Thus, from the time of Pepin the Short's reign, sacramentaries known as "Gelasians of the eighth century" began to appear.[55] These were essentially a mixture of the Gelasian with the Gregorian, but there can also be found, in varying proportions, compositions of Gallican origin. In the same way, the Carolingian revision of the Gregorian sacramentary, the epistolary, etc., admitted certain local elements.

It is in Gaul and Germany that the *Ordines Romani,* small books containing descriptions of one or several ceremonies, were compiled. Beginning with the ancient Roman sources, their editors mixed in many elements of diverse origin.[56]

Of special importance, finally, is a collection known as the Romano-Germanic pontifical, composed at Mainz in the middle of the tenth century.[57] When brought to Rome by the bishops who

[52]See below, ch. 6.

[53]See below, ch. 6.

[54]A bibliography on this subject is to be found in LMD 53 (1958) 37f.

[55]See A. Chavasse, "Le sacramentaire gélasien du VIIIe siècle" in EL 73 (1959) 249-98.

[56]M. Andrieu, *Les Ordines Romani du haut moyen âge,* 5 vols. (Louvain, 1931-61; *Spicilegium sacrum Lovaniense* 11, 23, 24, 28, 29). A sixth and last volume, containing indices, is in preparation.

[57]C. Vogel and R. Elze, *Le Pontifical romano-germanique du Xe siècle. Le texte,* 2 vols. (Vatican City, 1963; *Studi e testi* 226-7); a third volume, containing an introduction and tables, is in preparation; cf. C. Vogel, "Précisions sur la date et l'ordonnance primitive du Pontifical romano-germanique" in EL 74 (1960) 145-62.

accompanied the emperor Otto I in the beginning of the eleventh century, the collection had a profound influence on the Roman liturgy; it has since served as the basis for the Roman pontifical.[58]

4 *Roman usage during the Middle Ages*

Thus, each of the churches in the old Carolingian empire used the liturgy which came from Rome while incorporating into it some local customs and subjecting it to an autonomous evolution, to the point that books and ceremonials varied from city to city and even from church to church. In Rome as well, each basilica had its own liturgy, different from that of the papal court.

The discovery of printing, and then the liturgical reform which issued from the Council of Trent, considerably reduced these variations. Certain churches, however, notably Braga and Lyons, have fortunately kept their venerable local customs, above all their *ordo missae;*[59] so have certain religious orders: the Dominicans, Premonstratensians, Carthusians.[60] Then too, local rituals for the administration of sacraments were not suppressed by the 1614 edition of the *Rituale Romanum.*[61]

II THE AMBROSIAN RITE

BIBLIOGRAPHY

P. Borella, E. Cattaneo, E. Villa, *Questioni e bibliografia ambrosiane* (Milan: Ambrosius, 1950; *Archivio ambrosiano* 2).

P. Borella, *Cenni storici sulla liturgia ambrosiana, sacramenti e sacramentali* (Milan: Ancora, 1953). This is an extract from M. Righetti, *op. cit.*, vol. 4; it is revised in the second edition of the latter work (1959) pp. 555-620.

P. Borella, "Il canon missae ambrosiano" in *Ambrosius* 30 (1954) 225-57.

P. Borella, "La messa ambrosiana" in M. Righetti, *Manuale di storia liturgica* 3, 2nd ed. (Milan: Ancora, 1956) pp. 551-614.

P. Borella, *Il rito ambrosiano* (Brescia: Morcelliana, 1964).

E. Cattaneo, *Il breviario ambrosiano* (Milan: Ambrosius, 1943).

A. King, *Liturgies of the Primatial Sees* (London: Longmans, 1957) pp. 286-453.

A. Paredi, "Messali antichi ambrosiani" in *Ambrosius* 35 (1959, *supplemento*) 1-25.

Problemi di liturgia ambrosiana (Milan: Ambrosius, 1949; *Archivio ambrosiano* 1).

[58] M. Andrieu, *Le Pontifical romain au moyen âge*, 4 vols. (Vatican City, 1938-41; *Studi e testi* 86-88, 99).

[59] A. King, *Liturgies of the Primatial Sees* (London: Longmans, 1957).

[60] A. King, *Liturgies of the Religious Orders* (London: Longmans, 1955); P. Lefèvre, *La liturgie de Prémontré* (Louvain: Warny, 1957).

[61] See below, ch. 3 and 4.

St Ambrose, as we have seen, claimed to follow the Roman tradition, but with a certain freedom[62]; we can still discern the same tendency in the rite practised in Milan today. The liturgy is of the Roman type, occasionally preserving ancient Roman customs which Rome subsequently abandoned, but also containing many of its own customs, for the Mass as well as for the office. One can also notice similarities to the rite of Gaul, notably in the choice of readings. We lack ancient documents, however, to show us this liturgy as it was before being altered in many places by the Carolingian reforms. The canon of the Mass differs slightly in form from the Roman canon. The prayers and prefaces are of the same type, and many may be found in the sacramentaries.[63] In no way, then, is the Milanese liturgy of Oriental origin, as Msgr Duchesne believed. It has benefited from excellent efforts of restoration, first in the sixteenth century, under the influence of St Charles Borromeo, and then at the end of the nineteenth century and at the beginning of the twentieth, thanks to a group of Milanese scholars, among whom was A. Ratti, the future Pope Pius XI.

III THE MOZARABIC OR VISIGOTHIC RITE

BIBLIOGRAPHY

Estudios sobre la liturgia mozárabe . . . (Toledo: Disputación provincial, 1965; *Publicaciónes del Instituto provincial de investigaciónes y estudios toledanos,* ser. 3, *estudios, introducciónes, repertorios,* 1).

A. King, *Liturgies of the Primatial Sees* (London: Longmans, 1957) pp. 457-631.

J. Pinell, "El oficio hispano-visigótico" in *Hispania sacra* 10 (1957) 385-427.

G. Prado, *Historia del rito mozárabe y toledano* (Santo Domingo de Silos, 1928).

The general name "Mozarabic" is given to the liturgy found in the missal and breviary printed by order of Cardinal Ximénès de Cisneros,[64] and which is still practised in several churches of the diocese of Toledo and in a chapel of the cathedral, and elsewhere on certain exceptional occasions. But the present usage and the two books mentioned can give no idea of the richness of the old Spanish liturgy, replaced by the Roman on the order of St Gregory VII at the end of the eleventh century. We possess some ancient manuscripts, primarily from the tenth and eleventh centuries, a

[62]See above, I, 1.

[63]A. Paredi, *I Prefazi ambrosiani* (Milan: Vita e pensiero, 1937).

[64]PL 85-6.

number of which have been published.[65] The liturgy which they contain was not created during the Arab occupation, but had been organized and extensively unified, as various councils indicate, in the Visigothic period.

While this liturgy was subject to strong Oriental influences in the seventh century which succeeded in giving it a set of characteristic features, it had in fact from the beginning been fundamentally different from the Roman liturgy. The Mass has no fixed canon; it is made up of movable sections grouped around the recital of institution: *Illatio* (corresponding to the Preface), *Vere Sanctus,* which makes a bridge between the *Sanctus* and the recital of institution, *Post pridie,* which follows the consecration and takes the place of the anamnesis, sometimes too of the epiclesis.

The prayers of the liturgy of Spain are written in a rich and sometimes diffuse style. The sacerdotal prayers addressed to Christ are numerous, contrary to the Roman usage, where they are rare and relatively late.

One can find sections drawn from Roman sacramentaries, in their original or an adapted form. In its turn, the Visigothic liturgy exercised a considerable influence on the liturgy of Gaul (southwest Gaul was part of the Visigothic kingdom, and kept its liturgy until the adoption of the Roman rite). It was through Gaul that some of its prayers came into the medieval Roman liturgy.

IV THE LITURGY OF GAUL

BIBLIOGRAPHY

H. Beck, *The Pastoral Care of Souls in South-East France during the Sixth Century* (Rome: Gregorian University, 1950; *Analecta Gregoriana* 51).
E. Griffe, "Aux origines de la liturgie gallicane" in *Bulletin de littérature ecclésiastique* 52 (1951) 17-43.
A. King, *Liturgies of the Past* (London: Longmans, 1957) pp. 186-275.
W. Porter, *The Gallican Rite* (London: Mowbray, 1958).
J. Quasten, "Oriental Influence in the Gallican Liturgy" in *Traditio* 1 (1943) 55-78.
P. Salmon, *Le lectionnaire de Luxeuil,* 2 vols. (Rome: Abbaye de St-Jérôme, 1944–53; *Collectanea biblica* 7 and 9).
A. Wilmart, "Germain de Paris (Lettres attribuées à saint)" in DACL 6 (1924) col. 1049-1102.

---

[65]*Liber ordinum,* M. Férotin ed. (Paris: Didot, 1904; *Monumenta ecclesiae liturgica* 5); *Liber mozarabicus sacramentorum,* M. Férotin ed. (*ibid.,* 1912; *Monumenta ecclesiae liturgica* 6); *Oracional visigótico,* J. Vives ed. (Barcelona, 1946; *Monumenta Hispaniae sacra, Serie liturgica* 1); *Liber commicus,* J. Pérez de Urbel and A. Gonzalez ed., 2 vols. (Madrid, 1950-55: same collection 2 and 3); "El commicus palimpsest Paris Lat. 2269," ed. A. Mundó in *Liturgica* 1 (Montserrat, 1956) 151-275; *Antifonario de la catedral de León,* L. Brou and J.

The liturgy practised in Gaul is less well known to us because it did not survive the reform of Charlemagne, at which time its organization was probably still rudimentary.

We can draw some idea of it from clues in the sermons of St Caesarius of Arles, the writings of Gregory of Tours (sixth century) and the Merovingian councils. An *Expositio missae gallicanae,* falsely attributed to St Germain of Paris,[66] describes a late form of this liturgy (eighth or, at the earliest, the end of the seventh century). We possess several lectionaries, but all of them very incomplete. As for the books intended for the celebrant, those which remain have already been more or less influenced by the Roman liturgy.[67]

From the structural point of view, the Gallican liturgy was closely similar to that of Spain. As in the Visigothic Mass, the great sacerdotal prayer is made up of variable sections. In the form in which we know it through documents of the seventh to eighth centuries, the Gallican liturgy is also influenced by Oriental practices, especially by Syrian rites. It must be added that nearly all the documents come to us from Burgundy, and give us no idea of the diversity which probably existed in other regions.[68]

Vives ed., 2 vols. (Barcelona-Madrid, 1953-59; *Monumenta Hispaniae sacra, Serie liturgica* 5).

[66]PL 72, col. 89-98; see the study of A. Wilmart noted above in the bibliography.

[67]*Missale Gallicanum vetus,* L. C. Mohlberg ed. (Rome: Herder, 1958; *Rerum ecclesiasticarum documenta,* Series major, *Fontes* 3); *ibid.,* pp. 74-91, an edition of the "Masses of Mone," following the important corrections of A. Wilmart;— *Missale Gothicum,* H. M. Bannister ed. (London, 1917-19; HBS 52 and 54); L. C. Mohlberg ed. (Rome: Herder, 1961; *Rerum ecclesiasticarum documenta,* Series major, *Fontes* 5).—For the *Missale Francorum* and the *Bobbio Missal,* see above, footnote 42.

[68]We are very poorly informed on the liturgy of the Celtic churches. The few documents which remain seem to be a very eclectic compilation of continental practices.—See L. Gougaud, *Les chrétientés celtiques,* 2nd ed. (Paris: Gabalda, 1911) pp. 295-313. Engl. tr., *Christianity in Celtic Lands* (London: Sheed and Ward, 1932).

D

CHAPTER THREE

A Brief History of the Liturgy

BIBLIOGRAPHY

C. Callewaert, *De sacra liturgia universim*, 4th ed. (Bruges: Beyaert, 1944; *Liturgicae institutiones* 1) pp. 57-122.

J. D. Crichton, "An Historical Sketch of the Roman Liturgy" in *True Worship*, L. Sheppard ed. (Baltimore: Helicon, 1963) pp. 45-82.

I. H. Dalmais, *Initiation à la liturgie* (Desclée de Brouwer, 1958) pp. 167-92. Engl. tr., *Introduction to the Liturgy* (Baltimore: Helicon, 1961; London: Chapman, 1961) pp. 148-73.

J. A. Jungmann, *The Early Liturgy to the Time of Gregory the Great* (Notre Dame University Press, 1959; London: Darton, Longman and Todd: 1960).

T. Klauser, *A Brief History of the Liturgy* (Collegeville, Minnesota: Liturgical Press, 1963).

J. H. Srawley, *The Early History of the Liturgy*, 2nd ed. (Cambridge: University Press; New York: Macmillan, 1947).

B. Steuart, *The Development of Christian Worship* (London, New York and Toronto: Longmans, 1953).

The history of the liturgy may be divided into two distinct periods, the Council of Trent (1545-63) being the boundary between them. Before Trent, there was a parallel evolution of the liturgy in the East and West. The Latin liturgy, submitted directly to the authority of the Apostolic See since Trent, is subject to reforms made both possible and necessary by its unification and centralization. The Eastern liturgies are better able to retain the purity and integrity of their ancient traditions.

1 From the beginnings to the Council of Trent (*Dom B. Botte*)

I STAGES IN THE DEVELOPMENT OF THE LITURGY

The development of the liturgy from its origins to the end of the Middle Ages falls into four periods, more or less identical in the various rites.

1 *Liturgical improvisation (to the fourth century)*

In the beginning there was no other liturgical book than the Bible. The Church inherited from Jewish tradition the practice of reading the Old Testament in the assemblies; to this she added the New Testament. The psalms and biblical canticles made up the community's book of chant. Some writers have claimed to find in apostolic writings the traces of other canticles used by the churches,[1] but we must be cautious here and avoid taking as historical reality what is only a debatable hypothesis.

As for the celebrant's prayers and liturgical formulas, texts were not fixed in a uniform manner. The comparative study of different rites does not take us back to a unique archetype, even for elements which we would think essential.

For the eucharistic consecration, for example, there is no uniformity to be found—neither in the various liturgies, nor even in the four accounts preserved in the New Testament.[2]

For baptism, the rites of the Syrian type use the formula, "N. is baptized . . ."[3] The Alexandrian rite uses the active form, "I baptize you . . ." As for the Roman rite, its most ancient witnesses contain no other formula than the three interrogations on trinitarian faith: "Do you believe in God, the Father almighty . . .?"[4]

It is therefore pointless to search for a single "apostolic liturgy" which would then have been diversified in the course of time.[5] There doubtless were, in each church, oral traditions for the essential points, but they were not uniformly established. This freedom produced a very great diversity in disciplinary and liturgical customs, one which the ancient historians and Fathers noted with pleasure: it only emphasized more the Church's unanimity in keeping the deposit of faith.[6]

The prayer was improvised; St Justin explains that the celebrant "gives thanks, as he is able."[7] The principle of improvisation is clearly affirmed by the *Apostolic Tradition,* a work which modern scholarship has attributed to St Hippolytus of Rome (*circa* 200). The author gives prayer texts for the Eucharist and for ordinations, but notes that these are models and not obligatory formulas.[8]

---

[1] See below, ch. 6, 2.

[2] See the comparative tables arranged by P. Cagin, *Eucharistia* . . . (Tournai: Desclée, 1912), especially pp. 307-20.

[3] A. Wenger, *Huit catéchèses baptismales inédites de saint Jean Chrysostome* (Paris: Ed. du Cerf, 1957; SC 50), pp. 96-8.

[4] To be treated in a subsequent volume.

[5] This was the mistake of some of the older scholars, notably P. Cagin, *L'anaphore apostolique et ses témoins* (Paris: Lethielleux, 1919).

[6] For example Eusebius of Caesarea, *H.E.* 5, 24.11-13, citing St Irenaeus; Socrates, *H. Eccl.* 5, 22; St Augustine, *Epist.* 55 *ad Januarium,* etc.

[7] St Justin, *First Apology* 67, 5, L. Pautigny ed. (Paris: Picard, 1904; *Textes et documents* 1) pp. 142f. A. Roberts and F. Donaldson ed. (Edinburgh: 1870; ANF 2) pp. 65-6.

[8] Hippolytus of Rome, *Apostolic Tradition,* n. 9, B. Botte ed. (Münster: Aschendorff, 1963; LQF 39) p. 29.—Even if this work still raises certain questions for

These written compositions nevertheless enjoyed great success; we find them again taken up and reworked in various collections of the fourth and fifth centuries.[9]

The year of the Edict of Milan, 313, is a decisive date in the liturgical life of the Church. Henceforth worship could take place freely and in handsome buildings; pilgrimages were organized regularly to the holy places of Palestine or to the tombs of the martyrs; imperial legislation favored the liturgical assemblies. It would, however, be a mistake to think that before 313 Christians had no buildings for worship, or that they had to take refuge in cemeteries, or that the liturgy was still rudimentary. The *Tradition* of Hippolytus, the Syrian *Didascalia,* the works of Tertullian and St Cyprian, the sermons of Origen, the letters of St Denis of Alexandria and archeological finds all allow us to form a more exact idea of this early liturgy.[10]

2 *The creation of fixed texts (fourth to seventh century)*

The use of written compositions gradually became more widespread. At the end of the fourth century, St Augustine complains that certain bishops use prayers composed by incompetent authors, i.e. by heretics.[11] The necessity for a stricter discipline was felt; some African councils forbade the use of formulas which had not been approved by a synod.[12]

historians, it nevertheless offers information on the liturgy of third-century Rome which was unavailable to liturgists before 1914. Ed. and English tr., G. Dix, *The Treatise on the Apostolic Tradition of St Hippolytus of Rome* 1 (New York: Macmillan; London: SPCK, 1937).

[9]Notably the *Epitome* and the *Apostolic Constitutions,* F. X. Funk ed., *Didascalia et Constitutiones apostolicae* (Paderborn: Schöningh, 1905);—the *Testamentum Domini,* I. Rahmani ed. (Mainz, 1899); tr. F. Nau, "La version syriaque de l'Octateuque de Clément" in *Le canoniste contemporain* 30 (1907) 669-77; 31 (1908) 78-83, 139-44, 301-8, 463-71, 587-94; 32 (1909) 203-9, 532-41;—the *Canons of Hippolytus,* R. Coquin ed. (Paris: Didot, 1966; PO 31, 2);—the Canons of the Egyptian church (preserved in Coptic, Arabic and Ethiopian), ed. and Engl. tr., G. Horner, *The Statutes of the Apostles* (London: Williams and Norgate, 1904).

[10]For the *Didascalia,* besides the edition of F. X. Funk cited in the preceding note, see *Didascalia Apostolorum,* H. Connolly ed. (Oxford: Clarendon, 1929); tr. F. Nau, *La Didascalie des douze apôtres,* 2nd ed. (Paris: Lethielleux, 1912);— on Tertullian, see E. Dekkers, *Tertulianus en de geschiedenis der liturgie* (Brussels: De Kinkhoren, 1947).

[11]St Augustine, *De baptismo contra Donatistas* 6, 25, Petschenig ed. (CSEL 51) p. 323 (PL 43, col. 213f);—cf. *De catechizandis rudibus* 9, 13.

[12]Council of Carthage III (397), can. 23, H. Bruns, *Canones apostolorum et conciliorum . . .* 1 (Berlin: sumpt. Reimeri, 1839) p. 126;—Carthage (407), can. 9 (*Codex canonum ecclesiae Africanae,* can. 103), H. Bruns, *op. cit.,* p. 186; there is a more developed text under the name of the Council of Milevus, can. 12, in *Collectio Hispana* (PL 84, col. 232).

From now on, the intervention of local councils[13] and the influence of the great churches of Rome, Antioch and Alexandria were to create the different liturgical types analysed in the preceding chapter.[14] A certain unity would exist, but only within the confines of specific regions.

The great creative period extended from the middle of the fourth century to the middle or end of the seventh century. These three centuries saw an immense creativity, of which the documents extant today can give us only an imperfect idea.

As early as about 390, St Ambrose cites fragments of a canon of the Mass which is the ancestor of the Roman.[15] The dominant features of the Roman liturgy are finally established by St Gregory the Great (590–604) and his immediate successors.[16] Between these two dates falls the important activity of St Leo, Gelasius I[17] and Vigilius.

It seems that the Spanish liturgy too, unable to develop during the Arab occupation, was fully crystallized in the seventh century.

Similar observations may be made of liturgical development in the Orient. The allusions and descriptions to be found in the Fathers of the fourth century—St Basil,[18] St John Chrysostom,[19] Theodore

---

[13]Apart from the councils of Carthage in 397 and 407, particular mention must be made of some others which are more important from a liturgical point of view: the Nestorian synod of Seleucia-Ctesiphon under the Catholicos Mar Isaac (410), in J. B. Chabot, *Synodicon orientale* (Paris: Imprimerie Nationale, 1902) pp. 265-8; the French councils of Vannes (465) and Agde (506), in C. Munier, *Concilia Galliae . . .* (Turnhout: Brepols, 1963; cc 148) pp. 150-7, 189-228; Orleans (511 and 541), Epaône (517), Vaison (529), Tours (567), Auxerre (*circa* 578) and Mâcon (583 and *circa* 613-28) in C. de Clercq, *Concilia Galliae . . .* (1963: cc 148a), *passim*: the Spanish councils of Gerona (517), Braga (563), Toledo III (589) and IV (633) in H. Bruns, *op. cit.,* 2, pp. 18-20, 33-7; 1, pp. 210-45.—The so-called canons of the council of Laodicea are an apocryphal collection of canonical documents of the fourth to fifth centuries.

[14]See ch. 2, 1, above.

[15]*De sacramentis* 5-6, 21-7, B. Botte ed. (sc 25 bis) pp. 114-16.

[16]Today the liturgical reform of St Gregory the Great is better known in its historical reality, and evaluated with more reserve: E. Bourque, *Études sur les sacramentaires romains* 1 (Vatican City, 1949; *Studi di antichità cristiana* 20) pp. 387-91; A. Chavasse, "Temps de préparation à la Pâque d'après quelques livres liturgiques romains" in RechSR 37 (1950) 125-45; "Les plus anciens types du lectionnaire et de l'antiphonaire romains de la messe" in RB 62 (1952) 3-94; "Peut-on dater le Sacramentaire grégorien?" in EL 67 (1953) 108-11.

[17]The role of Pope Gelasius (492-496) has been fully elucidated by B. Capelle, "L'oeuvre liturgique de saint Gélase" in JTS 52, n. ser. 2 (1951) 129-44.

[18]Brightman, pp. 521-6.

[19]*ibid.,* pp. 470-81, 530-4; St John Chrysostom, *Huit catéchèses baptismales inédites . . .* , A. Wenger ed. (Paris: Ed. du Cerf, 1957; sc 50).

of Mopsuestia,[20] St Cyril of Jerusalem[21]—allow us to reconstruct
the Eucharist and baptism at this period in the patriarchate of
Antioch. The details of these rites are set down in an eighth-century
manuscript of the Vatican library (*Barberini Gr* 336).[22]

The ancient collections written in Syriac take us back to James of
Edessa (684–88) for the West Syrians,[23] and to Isho-'Yab III (*circa*
650–58) for the East Syrians,[24] i.e. to the seventh century.

3 *Collections of texts* (*eighth to twelfth century*)

Creative activity did not entirely stop after the seventh century—
it will never stop altogether, since even today new prayers are being
composed—but it declined. Henceforth it was found preferable to
rework and compile old formulas rather than compose new ones.

The sacramentaries known as "eighth-century Gelasian" appeared
in Gaul in the latter half of that century; they contain prayers and
rites of Gallican origin as well as the formulas of older Roman
sacramentaries (Gelasian and Gregorian). The Roman rite spread
in Gaul and Germany, and while it was made official in these
countries by Charlemagne, it nonetheless gathered foreign elements.
In the eleventh century it was to return to Rome in this revised form
and become the Roman liturgy of today. Although the sacramentaries and pontificals all varied from church to church, the formulas
which they added to the old Roman base were repeated in a great
number of copies, thus allowing us to classify them by types, families,
regions and influences.

The same was true in the East, where we see anaphoras pass from
Antioch to Alexandria—the Alexandrian anaphora of St Basil, the
anaphora of St Gregory[25]—or Byzantine anaphoras translated into
Armenian.[26] It would be a mistake to think of the churches, even

---

[20]*Homélies catéchétiques,* R. Tonneau ed. (Vatican City, 1949; *Studi e testi* 145).

[21]*Catecheses,* PG 33; French tr. by J. Bouvet (Namur: Ed. du Soleil levant, 1962).
English tr., *Catechetical Lectures* (NPNF 8).

[22]Previous classification, *Barber.* III, 55; this is a *euchologion,* which was published
in part by J. Goar, *Euchologion sive Rituale Graecorum,* 2nd ed. (Venice, 1730);
cf. Brightman, pp. 309-52.—A. Strittmatter, "The 'Barberinum S. Marci' of
Jacques Goar" in EL 47 (1933) 329-67.

[23]On James of Edessa, see E. Tisserant, *Dictionnaire de théologie catholique* 8
(1924) col. 286-91; A. Baumstark, *Geschichte der syrischen Literatur* . . . (Bonn,
1922) pp. 248-56.

[24]On Ishô-'Yab III, see A. Baumstark, *op. cit.,* pp. 197f, and esp. p. 126.

[25]See above, ch. 2, "The Coptic rite."

[26]The anaphora of St Basil exists in three different states: see I. Catergian and
I. Dashian, *Les formulaires de la messe arménienne* (Vienna, 1897) pp. 120-59,

those separated by confessions of faith, as completely isolated from each other. The work of translators was particularly important in the East.

The liturgical development of this period is thus one of adaptation and appropriation rather than of original creation. Creative activity can scarcely be noticed, at least in the West, except at the periphery of liturgical action: private prayers to be said by the faithful or even by the celebrant,[27] *prosae* or sequences, devotional offices, etc.[28]

It is also at this time that liturgical treatises began to multiply. In contrast to patristic catechesis—sermons for the people—these were didactic works, based far more on written sources than on living usage and too often substituting allegorical interpretations for the true meaning of liturgical rites.

4 *Establishment of the liturgies (thirteenth to fourteenth century)*

It can be said that the work of original creation, then of adaptation and compilation, was over by the thirteenth century, and that the liturgies had by then taken the form that they have kept up to the present.

It is true that, in the West Syrian rite, further anaphoras were composed well after this date, but this does not mean that the basic liturgical structure—the liturgical year, the ritual for sacraments, the system of readings, the liturgical chant—was not fixed. It was possible for the Oriental Congregation to draw recent editions of texts for Catholics of the Syrian or Chaldean rite from manuscripts of the twelfth to thirteenth centuries without bringing about any notable changes.

How the formulas and rites of liturgies in the West came to be fixed is equally clear to us. Almost everywhere ordinals were composed, describing to the last detail the ceremony for the offices of the whole year. The great religious orders established their customaries and standardized their books. The Roman curia benefited from the reforming work of Innocent III (1198-1216),[29] whose pontifical would spread far and wide before being replaced by the pontifical of

---

180-216, 414-29. On the anaphora of St John Chrysostom, see G. Aucher, "La versione armena della liturgia di san Giovanni Crisostomo" in Χρυσοστομικά (Rome: Pustet, 1908) 371-98.

[27]Characteristic of this literary genre are the *Book of Cerne*, A. Kuypers ed. (Cambridge: University Press, 1902); *L'ordinaire de la messe du sacramentaire d'Amiens* (Paris, Bibl. Nat. MS Lat. 9432, IXᵉ s.), V. Leroquais ed., EL 41 (1927) 435-45, and the "Missa Illyrica" in PL 138, col. 1305-36.

[28]See A. Wilmart, *Auteurs spirituels et textes dévots du moyen âge latin* (Paris: Bloud et Gay, 1932).

[29]Andrieu PR 2, p. 310.

William Durandus, bishop of Mende, composed about 1294.[30] In turn, masters of ceremonies, setting down in instruction-books or ordos[31] the rite of the papal chapel and its smallest variations, began a work of codification which would emerge at the beginning of the sixteenth century in the ceremonial of the Roman church, and then later in the *Caeremoniale Episcoporum*. The role played by the Friars Minor was also very important in the establishment and diffusion of the missal, breviary and Roman ritual in their modern form. But while clerics and religious attached more and more importance to liturgical offices which vied with each other in length and complexity, the people were drifting farther and farther away from them. Despite the periodic reminders of councils, they preferred devotions, some of which were of very dubious value.

II FACTORS IN THE DEVELOPMENT OF LITURGIES

The various rites thus passed through different stages, and only achieved their definitive form after many centuries. What are the factors which contributed to this development?

1 The law of the Church's growth

Just as the Church has had progressively to clarify its dogma and perfect its juridical organization, it has also attempted to express more clearly the essential contents of the mysteries of faith in the liturgy. Thus the economy of salvation, originally celebrated by the Sunday and Easter liturgy, has been unfolded in the liturgical year. The essential rite of baptism has been enriched by the preparatory rites of the catechumenate. Ordination has seen accessory rites added to the laying on of hands, such as investiture and anointing in the West, while at Antioch hands were laid on after having touched the holy species on the altar.

Liturgical formulas also followed doctrinal development, and translated into prayers the dogmas of Nicaea and Chalcedon.

The monastic life played a very important role in developing the divine office, hymnology and chant.

2 Mutual influences

As we have already seen, rites do not develop independently of each other; many reciprocal influences may be found. The feast of

[30]Andrieu PR 3.
[31]Some have been published by Fabre-Duchesne, vol. 2, pp. 128-33 (Card. Albinus), 290-316 (=OR Mab 12, Cencio de' Savelli), others by Mabillon, OR 13 (ceremonial of Gregory X), 14 (Card. Gaetano Stefaneschi), 15 (Pierre Ameilhe), while some are still unedited: Bibl. Nat. MS Lat. 4162a; Toulouse, Bibl. Municipale, MS 67, etc.

Christmas spread from Rome to all the Western and Eastern churches; yet the feast of February 2 in Rome is certainly of Eastern origin. The Alexandrian liturgy was profoundly influenced by the rite of Antioch. The liturgical year of both Nestorian and Monophysite Syrians includes a preparation for Christmas (Sundays of the Annunciation) which is certainly later than the doctrinal separation which occurred after the Council of Ephesus.

Rome had a preponderant influence in the West, where Roman books finally supplanted the Gallican or Mozarabic ones. In the East, Byzantium exercised an analogous influence on the liturgies of Alexandria and Antioch, still practised after Chalcedon by the communities which had rallied to the Council (Melkites). And the liturgy of Rome experienced in its turn the influence of liturgical books adapted in German territories in the tenth century.[32]

3 External influences

Here two principal sources of influence may be distinguished: Judaism and the pagan cults.

(a) Influence of Judaism

The Christian liturgy was born in a Jewish milieu, and it is clear that its inspiration came from Jewish traditions, especially from the synagogue worship. But since the Jewish liturgy of that era is known to us only from sources which are several centuries later and which require critical analysis, we must avoid hasty conclusions. Then too, contact with Judaism had already been broken at the time when the various Christian rites were formed. Christianity nonetheless shared a common source with Judaism, the Old Testament, which inspired Christian prayer to a very great extent.

Sometimes the Old Testament has influenced Christian rites in an unexpected way. Thus for the rites of ordination, the anointing and investiture of the high priest had been given a symbolic sense in the ordination prayers, and then the symbolic sense led to the reintroduction of the ceremony: in the ninth century, both anointing and investiture were added to the rite of episcopal consecration. It is no less certain that the rite for the dedication of churches, such as we find it in the pontifical, draws many points of inspiration from the dedications described in the Old Testament, especially Ex 29:12–18.

(b) Influence of pagan cults

Christian worship matured in the world of Hellenism and had to adapt itself to the language and usages of that milieu. To what extent did it make use of pagan cults? Here we must distinguish between periods and modes of influence.

---

[32]See above, ch. 2, **2**.

In all that they tell us, the first Christian writers appear careful to avoid any compromise with paganism; even in their language they insist rather on what distinguishes and separates Christianity from paganism. It would therefore be false to suppose that the primitive Church made an effort to christianize pagan customs. Nevertheless, to the extent that the menace of paganism waned and the liturgy developed, the latter gradually admitted rites used by all religions: lustral water, blessed salt, lights, incense. It must be noted that some of these customs may also derive from the Old Testament.

Secondly, we must distinguish the kinds of influence that paganism exercised. To react is not to borrow. The feast of the Nativity was assigned to December 25, probably to compete with the *Natalis Invicti*, linked as it was with the sun worship which formed the hard core of paganism. While the Church did intend to oppose a Christian to a pagan feast, the object of the former was entirely different. To say that the Church christianized the *Natalis Invicti* is an inaccurate way of speaking. For the *Natalis Invicti*, she substituted the feast of Christ, the sun of justice.

There were also some customs, profane rather than pagan, which the Church tolerated, such as the *refrigerium* (commemorative meals taken at tombs), and which she very soon suppressed.

Pagan influences are not to be denied, but often they bear only on peripheral elements of worship. The Church used those modes of expression which were at hand in the Hellenistic milieu and which could be adapted to the symbolism of Christian worship without compromising its originality.

* * *

The history of the liturgy is thus very complex. Its study must take into account all its constitutive elements. In particular, a knowledge of Oriental rites is indispensable for an overall understanding of liturgy, as well as for the discernment of what is essential and what secondary. Although liturgies differ in various ways, they all bear witness to the same essential truths and to the same mysteries of salvation. This variety shows the richness of the Christian faith which is not exhausted by the diversity of expression which it has found in the course of history. Even for the history of a single rite, the comparative study of other rites is necessary, because of recip-rocal influences. And if the history of other rites is useful for the understanding of a particular rite, the history of that rite in its different phases is indispensable for an understanding of today's usages. The present texts, whether of the Mass, of baptism, of ordinations or of the liturgical year, are fully intelligible only after a study of their sources. We are not dealing with rites which were all composed at the same time. They were elaborated gradually, in the course of centuries, and bear signs of the stages through which they have passed.

2 From the Council of Trent to Vatican II (*P. Jounel*)

For the study of the evolution of the Latin liturgy, the four centuries from the Council of Trent to the Second Vatican Council may be divided into three periods: at the beginning and end there is a half-century of intense renewal (1562–1614 and 1903–62), separated by three centuries of immobility when liturgical questions faded into the background of the Church's life. With the promulgation of the constitution *De sacra liturgia* by the Second Vatican Council (December 4, 1963), a new period in the history of the liturgy has begun.

I THE LITURGICAL REFORM OF THE COUNCIL OF TRENT

The extreme liturgical decadence at the end of the Middle Ages was not unrelated to the birth of Protestantism. On the eve of the Council of Trent, numerous diocesan synods and provincial councils took stock of this abuse and called for a reform of liturgical books. Before books could be revised, however, some truths had to be recalled to Christian minds and discipline re-established. Such was the providential work of the Council.

1 *The liturgical work of the Council* (1562–63)

The dogmatic and disciplinary decrees of session 22 of the Council (September 17, 1562)[33] constitute the point of departure for all liturgical reform. The sacrificial value of the Mass is solemnly defined, together with the legitimacy of the rites which celebrate it and the dignity of the Roman canon, and the Council restored to their rightful place the two parts of the eucharistic assembly: that of the word of God, *ne oves Christi esuriant* (ch. 8), and that of the Lord's Supper, urging that *in singulis missis fideles adstantes non solum spirituali affectu sed sacramentali etiam eucharistiae perceptione communicarent* (ch. 6).[34] The disciplinary decree entitled *De observandis et evitandis in celebratione missae* allows us to see how grave were the abuses which had intruded into the celebration.[35]

---

[33]On the debates in the session itself and on the preparatory work, see J. Rivière, "Messe durant la période de la Réforme et du Concile de Trente" in *Dict. de théol. cath.* 10 (Paris: Letouzey, 1928), col. 1112-42.

[34]Denz. 1738-59.

[35]*Canones et decreta . . . Concilii Tridentini* (Rome: Colleg. de Propaganda fide, 1834) pp. 121f; J. Rivière, *op. cit.*, col. 1139-41; it is thus that bishops are obliged to prohibit all sorts of music, *ubi sive organo sive cantu lascivum aut impurum aliquid misceatur.*

The Council should then have taken up the revision of the breviary and missal, a task which had been in preparation by a special commission for several years, but many bishops were becoming impatient to return to their dioceses. The Fathers accordingly decided, in the twenty-fifth and last session, to hand the dossier over to the pope, entrusting to him the task of promulgating the reformed breviary and missal, as well as the Catechism and the Index of prohibited books (December 4, 1563).[36]

2 The Tridentine liturgical books (1568–70)

It was not long before the Council's decrees were being carried out: in 1568 appeared the *Breviarium romanum ex decreto sacrosancti concilii Tridentini restitutum, Pii V Pont. Max. iussu editum,* followed in 1570 by the *Missale romanum.* To learn the goal which St Pius V had set himself and even the method of work followed by the preparatory commission, one has only to read the two bulls of promulgation which for four centuries were printed at the beginning of each edition of the Roman breviary and missal.[37]

The pope, as a faithful custodian of the Council's intentions, had no thought of composing new liturgical books. He wanted rather to restore the Church's prayer *ad pristinam orandi regulam,* to revise the missal *ad pristinam sanctorum Patrum normam,* and to establish unity in the celebration of rites, *cum unum in Ecclesia Dei psallendi modum, unum missae celebrandae ritum esse maxime deceat.*

The desire for a return to tradition required first of all that nothing be changed of what was traditional: the *ordo missae* and *ordo psallendi,* as well as the ancient formularies to whose antiquity the liturgical manuscripts of the Vatican library bore witness.[38] The same desire was shown by the reduction of the additional offices (offices of our Lady and of the dead, gradual and penitential psalms); the suppression of certain votive Masses which were tainted with superstition; the simplification of the calendar, which would now contain only 182 feast days (of which 70 would be simple feasts and 30 semi-doubles). Also, a first effort was made to restore the celebration of Sunday and the ferial office; henceforth a Sunday would replace a double in Lent and a semi-double during the rest of the year, while ferial psalms would be recited on lesser feasts. With

[36]A. Michel, "Les décrets du Concile de Trente" in Hefele-Leclercq, *Histoire des conciles* 10 (Paris: Letouzey, 1938) p. 630.

[37]The bull *Quod a nobis* gives valuable details on the work preparatory to the reform of the breviary by Paul IV and Pius V.

[38]The two bulls give emphasis to this comparison of the printed editions *cum vetustis nostrae Vaticanae Bibliothecae codicibus.*

regard to texts, the commission turned to revising the legends of the office in order to suppress the most offensive ones, and eliminated from the missal a good number of sequences and compositions of later date.

Uniformity of celebration required the codification of rules. These were printed for the first time, at the beginning of each of the two books: either the *rubricae generales Breviarii*, or the *rubricae generales Missalis* and the *ritus servandus in celebratione missae*. The rubrics were drawn from the *Directorium divinorum officiorum* of L. Ciconiolano[39] and the *Rubricarium* of M. A. Frisco,[40] as well as the *ritus servandus* from the *Ordo Missae* of J. Burckard.[41] Modern *Ordines romani*, the rubrics of St Pius V were to exercise a considerable influence on the spread of the Roman liturgy throughout the world. This diffusion, coming into effect at the same time as improvements in printing, was just what the pope intended: the bulls *Quod a nobis* and *Quo primum tempore* made the adoption of the Council of Trent's breviary and missal obligatory for all churches which could not claim a local liturgical usage at least two centuries old.

3 The post-Tridentine liturgical books (1584–1614)

The immediate success of the reformed breviary and missal encouraged the popes to enlarge the enterprise. Thus, when Sixtus V instituted the Roman congregations in 1587, he included among the tasks of the new *Congregatio pro sacris ritibus et caeremoniis* that of correcting the liturgical books, *in primis Pontificale, Rituale, Caeremoniale, prout opus fuerit.*[42] The martyrology is not mentioned only because it had just been promulgated under the authority of Gregory XIII, the pope of the calendar reform (1584).

This work of revision and correction was carried out according to the spirit and method of St Pius V. In each case, books already in use were taken as a starting point. The pontifical of Patrizi (1485), a direct descendant of that of William Durandus, served to establish the text of the new Roman pontifical. Patrizi's Roman ceremonial (1488) and the work of Paride Grassi, *De caeremoniis cardinalium et episcoporum in eorum dioecesibus* (1587), provided the substance for

[39]*Directorium divinorum officiorum juxta Romane Curie ritum per Ludovicum Ciconiolanum regularis observantie provincie Campanie editum. Et per dominum Paulum Tertium Pontificem maximum approbatum* (Rome, 1539). The part of the *Directorium* which treats of the Mass has been edited by J. W. Legg, *Tracts on the Mass* (London, 1904; HBS 27) pp. 195-215.

[40]*Rubricarium pro divinis officiis ac missis rite celebrandis secundum ordinem Romane Curie* (Bologna, 1523), 112 pages (anonymous).

[41]On Burckard and his *Ordo missae,* more in a subsequent volume.

[42]Bull *Immensa,* January 22, 1588, in *Bullarium magnum Taurinense* 8, p. 989.

the ceremonial of bishops.[43] As for the ritual, it is dependent above all, as Paul V says, on the ritual which Santori, cardinal of San Severino, had prepared *longo studio, multaque industria et labore* (1584 ff).[44] These documents were subjected to a careful analysis and compared to the available manuscript sources, with a view to a better presentation of the rubrics. In the ritual itself, an attempt was made to simplify the rites as much as possible and to give pastoral directives.

The *Pontificale romanum* and the *Caeremoniale episcoporum* were published by Clement VIII in 1595 and 1600, the *Rituale romanum* by Paul V in 1614; but whereas Clement VIII "suppresses and abolishes" all other existing pontificals and makes observation of the new ceremonial forever obligatory, Paul V is content to invite all the bishops to accept the ritual of the Roman church, *omnium matris et magistrae.*

II THREE CENTURIES OF LITURGICAL IMMOBILITY

1 *The "era of rubricists"*

It is thus that the German liturgist Theodor Klauser characterizes the three centuries between the creation of the Congregation of Rites and the accession of St Pius X. The result of this "static period" he says, was "that spiritual life broke away from its liturgical sources and expression."[45] The Roman liturgy in this period, examined historically from within, is especially notable for the development of liturgical legalism and for the excessive growth of the cult of saints, which tended to submerge the seasonal cycle of the essential mysteries of redemption.

From the seventeenth to the twentieth centuries liturgical legalism and casuistry took an ever greater place in the practice and teaching of liturgy. These tendencies found ample nourishment both in the decrees and responses of the Congregation of Rites and in commentaries on the rubrics, all of which multiplied during this period. It was not long before private collections of the decrees and responses of the Congregation were being published; they were replaced in

---

[43]See P. Borella, *San Carlo e il Ceremoniale dei vescovi* (Varese: Tipografia Varese, 1937);—cf. EL 51 (1937) 64-80.

[44]On this ritual and the preparation of the ritual of Paul V, see B. Löwenberg, *Das Rituale des Kardinals Julius Antonius Sanctorius, Ein Beitrag zur Entstehungsgeschichte des Rituale Romanum* (Munich, 1937);—cf. ZKT 66 (1942) 141-7.

[45]T. Klauser, *A Brief History of the Liturgy* (Collegeville, Minnesota: Liturgical Press, 1963), p. 27. A similarly severe judgment is given by C. Callewaert, *De sacra liturgia universim*, 4th ed. (Bruges: Beyaert, 1944, *Liturgicae institutiones* I) pp. 103, 120.

1898 by Leo XIII's collection of the *Decreta authentica Congrega-tionis sacrorum rituum*.[46] As for commentaries on the rubrics, none had as much influence as B. Gavanti's *Thesaurus sacrorum rituum* (Milan, 1628); its re-edition by G. Merati (Rome, 1738) remains a classic.

As for the increase in the number of feasts, the figures speak for themselves. In the calendar of 1914, already simplified by the reforms of Pius X, 117 feasts were later than the calendar of St Pius V, and nearly all these feasts were doubles.[47] Since then the increase has continued, with 23 feasts added between 1920 and 1960. Doctors of the Church were the most numerous: there were 4 of them in the middle of the sixteenth century, 9 in 1568, 14 in 1751, 23 in 1899; since 1959 there have been 30. The development of the cult of saints is partly explained by the continual flowering of Christian sanctity. But its principal cause, until the end of the nineteenth century, was without any doubt the express desire to substitute festive for ferial offices, because the former were shorter. Thus we come to the decree of July 5, 1883, which authorizes the celebration of a votive Mass and office on every day of the week, *loco missarum et officiorum ferialium occurentium quocumque anni tempore: exceptis feria IV Cinerum, feriis totius temporis Passionis ac sacri Adventus a die 17 ad 24 Decembris inclusive*.[48] "The era of rubricists" thus ended in a profound liturgical decadence.

2 *Attempts at reform*

There were some who found the reforms of Pius V too cautious and held that the revision of liturgical books and the restoration of the Sunday cycle should be carried farther, especially since historical scholarship was making available the treasures of ancient prayer previously unpublished. But the most important of these attempts at reform was accomplished without the approval of the Holy See, others were included in doctrinal condemnations,[49] while the reform prepared by Pope Benedict XIV was never put into effect.

[46]See below, ch. 4, **2.**

[47]P. Jounel, "Les développements du Sanctoral romain de Grégoire XIII à Jean XXIII" in LMD 63 bis (1960) 74-81.

[48]*Missale Romanum* (1885); this is by and large the text of the decree SRC 3581. It is also possible, even in cathedral chapters, to say the office of the angels on Monday, that of the apostles on Tuesday, of St Joseph on Wednesday, of the Blessed Sacrament on Thursday, of the Passion on Friday, and of the Immaculate Conception on Saturday. According to the *Ordo divini officii* of the Lateran Basilica for 1909, only two Sundays were celebrated in green vestments that year.

[49]This was the case of the synod of Pistoia, condemned by Pius VI in 1794. Denz., 2628, 2631-3, 2651, 2655, 2662-7, 2669-74.

The local liturgies of French dioceses, which spread in an extremely disorganized manner during the eighteenth century, deserve neither all the reproaches which were directed at them around 1850 nor all the interest which some have shown in them today. To consider only the most widely diffused French books, the *Missale* and the *Breviarium Parisiense* promulgated by the archbishop of Paris, Charles de Vintimille (1736), it is clear that the author had no scruples about tradition in what concerned the gradual and antiphonary. In the general ordering of the offices, he often succumbed to an insipid, moralizing catechesis. On the other hand, the distribution of the psalter over all the offices of the week, with nine psalms in the Sunday and ferial as well as festal matins, has been the rule of the Roman breviary since 1911; the restoration of Sundays and lenten weekdays to their primal importance, the revision of the so-called historical lessons and the choice of epistles and gospels for Wednesdays and Saturdays of every week in the year, are all measures consonant with the present liturgical reform. The most basic criticism which can be made of these diocesan liturgies is that they were promulgated without the approval of the Holy See, although the latter accorded them its tacit recognition during negotiations on the Concordat of 1802.[50]

The history of the liturgical reform planned by Benedict XIV is that of an undertaking without issue, since the pope refused to ratify the work of the preparatory commission which he had set up (1741–47). The project was at once too radical in the revision of the calendar, eliminating as a matter of principle nearly all modern feasts, and too cautious in its refusal to make any changes in the *ordo psallendi*. Thus, it maintained the eighteen psalms of Sunday matins and the daily recitation of Psalm 118 during the little hours. It therefore had no effect, although the publication of some of the commission's work at the end of the nineteenth century helped to sustain the desire for a more thorough reform of the divine office faithful to tradition.[51]

---

[50]On these liturgies, see H. Leclercq, "Liturgies néo-gallicanes" in DACL 9 (1930), col. 1634-1730.—The Holy See upheld Dom Guéranger in his effort to restore the Roman liturgy in France as soon as it heard that the initiative of the abbot of Solesmes had won acceptance from numerous bishops and in wide circles of Catholic opinion; in the beginning, however, it remained in prudent expectation, as is clear from the brief of Gregory XVI to Archbishop Gousset of Rheims, August 6, 1842.

[51]A bibliography and résumé are given in S. Bäumer, *Histoire du bréviaire* 2, translated from the German by R. Biron (Paris: Letouzey, 1905) pp. 372-401. The original acts may be found in Rome at the Biblioteca Corsini, MS 361-3.

III FROM THE REFORM OF PIUS X TO VATICAN II (1903–62)

The half-century of liturgical renewal preceding the Second Vatican Council developed in a direction quite the opposite of that following the Council of Trent. In the sixteenth century liturgical reformers began by revising their books, in order to instil a new liturgical life into the clergy and Christian people. In the twentieth century, the first step was a pastoral effort which would result in a revision of rubrics and liturgical books. The influence of Popes Pius X and Pius XII, essentially pastoral popes, was certainly not without effect on this orientation.

A reawakening of the true Christian spirit through "active participation" of all the faithful in liturgical celebration—such was the objective which Pius X set at the opening of his pontificate in the motu proprio *Tra le sollecitudini*, in which he firmly recalled the rules of chant and sacred music (1903).[52] Pius XII was to give precise rules for this "active and enlightened" participation in the instruction *De musica sacra et sacra liturgia*, which marked the end of his own pontificate (September 3, 1958).

The two popes went to the heart of the people's participation in the holy mysteries by grouping the faithful around the eucharistic table. There is a striking continuity between the decrees of Pius X on frequent communion (1905) and communion of children (1910) and Pius XII's legislation on the eucharistic fast and evening Masses (1953 and 1957). A half-century of liturgical life had widened the perspectives: since the table of the word is also set for Mass, Pius XII made it more accessible by authorizing bilingual lectionaries; since the celebration of Easter, like the Mass, is also the "primary source of the true Christian spirit," Pius XII restored the Easter vigil (1951), then Holy Week (1955), and at the same time facilitated the participation of the faithful in sacramental rites by increasing the number of bilingual rituals.

It is in this context of a liturgical apostolate that the first significant reforms since the Council of Trent find all their importance: the promulgation of the *Graduale Romanum* (1907) and of the *Antiphonale sacrosanctae Romanae ecclesiae pro diurnis horis* (1912),

---

[52]The three principal reforming acts of St Pius X are the motu proprio *Tra le sollecitudini* (1903), published in Italian and Latin in SRC 4121; the apostolic constitution *Divino afflatu* of 1911 (SRC 4279), which is reprinted in breviaries; and the motu proprio *Abhinc duos annos* of 1913 (SRC 4307). These reforms were codified in *Additiones et Variationes in Rubricis Breviarii (Missalis) ad normam bullae "Divino afflatu" et subsequentium S.R.C. decretorum* (1914); until 1960 these were inserted in breviaries and missals after the *rubricae generales* of St Pius V.

E

the reform of the *ordo psallendi* (1911), the restoration of Sunday
and lenten weekdays (1913), the simplification (1955) and then the
new codification of the rubrics (1960),[53] the revision of Book II
of the Roman pontifical (1961)[54] and the re-establishment of stages
in the catechumenate for adults (1962).[55]

These last three documents were promulgated by Pope John
XXIII. It remained for him to crown the work of Pius X and Pius
XII by submitting to the Fathers whom he had called together in
the ecumenical Council the guiding principles of a general liturgical
reform (motu proprio *Rubricarum instructum* of July 25, 1960).

IV   THE LITURGICAL CONSTITUTION OF VATICAN II

The Second Vatican Council began its work with a discussion of
the schema for the liturgical constitution. This had been elaborated
by a pontifical commission composed of bishops and experts
chosen from all over the world. From October 22 to November 13,
1962, the conciliar Fathers devoted no less than fifteen general
sessions to a discussion of liturgical reform.[56] The many changes
which they introduced into the original text could not be incorporated before the end of the first session, and it was only at the end of
the second session that the constitution *De sacra liturgia,* approved
by a vote of 2,147 to 4, was promulgated by Pope Paul VI *una cum
Patribus Concilii* (December 4, 1963).

Promulgated exactly four centuries after the day on which the
Fathers of Trent had entrusted the revision of the missal and Roman
breviary to the pope, the liturgical constitution of the Second
Vatican Council[57] reveals a very different spirit from that which had

[53]Nearly all the documents concerning the liturgical reform carried out between
1903 and 1959 may be found in the two volumes of A. Bugnini, *Documenta
pontificia ad instaurationem liturgicam spectantia* (Rome: Ed. liturgiche, 1953-
1959) [*I. ab anno* 1903 *ad annum* 1952; *II. ab anno* 1953 *ad annum* 1959]. To
this must be added the "Codex rubricarum" in AAS 52 (1960) 593-740, and the
"Instructio de calendariis particularibus" in AAS 53 (1961) 168-80. R. Seasoltz
ed., *The New Liturgy: a Documentation,* 1903-65 (New York: Herder and Herder,
1966).

[54]AAS 54 (1962) 52.

[55]AAS 54 (1962) 310-15.

[56]On the preparation of the liturgical constitution and the conciliar debates,
see P. M. Gy, "Esquisse historique" in LMD 76 (1963) 7-17. Engl. tr., "The Constitution in the Making" in *Vatican II—The Liturgy Constitution,* 6th ed., A.
Flannery ed. (Dublin: Scepter, 1966) pp. 11-20. On the first session of the Council,
see A. Bugnini, "De sacra liturgia in prima periodo Concilii oecumenici
Vaticani III" in EL 77 (1963) 3-18.

[57]AAS 56 (1964) 97-138.

presided over the Tridentine reform; perhaps the novelty can best be appreciated by considering the differences.

A theology of the liturgy. Although the dogmatic decrees of the Council of Trent, in particular those concerning the sacraments, are of great importance for the theology of Catholic worship, the Fathers of Trent never intended to set out a formal theology of the liturgy. It is precisely on this point that the constitution of Vatican II is most striking. It presents the paschal mystery of Christ, to which "the wonders wrought by God among the people of the Old Testament were but a prelude," as the source and center of that worship which the mystical Body of Jesus Christ renders to God. Born from the death and resurrection of the Lord, the Church must first and last announce to men that they have been saved in the blood of Christ, join them through baptism to the paschal mystery of Christ and renew the sacrificial meal of the Lord "until he comes," thus anticipating in the liturgical assembly on earth the regathering of men in the new Jerusalem (art. 5–8).

A general reform of the liturgy. The Fathers of Trent had in mind nothing more than a correction of the missal and breviary used by the Roman church from the twelfth to thirteenth centuries; thus in the missal and breviary of St Pius V we have substantially the missal of Innocent III and the Franciscan breviary of 1223. While the constitution of Vatican II requires "that sound tradition . . . be retained" (art. 23) in the restoration of the liturgy, it also desires that "the way be open for legitimate progress" (*ibid.*), in order that "the rites . . . be within the people's powers of comprehension" (art. 34), adapted to "different groups, regions, and peoples" (art. 38), and "so that richer fare may be provided for the faithful at the table of God's word" (art. 51). The reform concerns not only the missal and breviary, but all liturgical books (art. 25), sacred chant (art. 112), the disposition of places for worship (art. 112), and above all the way in which the faithful should participate in the liturgy, "that full, conscious, and active participation in liturgical celebrations" which is the essential aim of liturgical renewal (art. 14).

Collegial action of pope and bishops. At the Council of Trent, the bishops had abandoned the project of effecting a liturgical reform by themselves. From that moment, all authority in matters of worship passed into the hands of the Apostolic See, represented from 1587 by the Congregation of Rites. The motu proprio *Pastorale munus* (November 30, 1963),[58] with its list of powers given to the bishops by Paul VI, throws a sharp light on the dependence in which the bishops had been held, as much for the organization of liturgical

[58]AAS 56 (1964) 5-12.

life in their churches as for the rest of their pastoral activity. Even before the promulgation of the dogmatic constitution on the Church, the Second Vatican Council in its liturgical legislation affirmed itself the council of episcopal collegiality. Thus it gives important powers in liturgical matters "to various kinds of competent territorial bodies of bishops legitimately established" (art. 22), above all in what concerns necessary adaptations, "especially in the case of the administration of the sacraments, sacramentals, processions, liturgical language, sacred music, and the arts" (art. 39).

Diversity within unity. The Tridentine ideal in liturgical matters consisted principally in bringing about a uniformity of rites. The missal and breviary of Pius V were imposed on all churches and religious orders which could not claim a liturgy at least two hundred years old. No one can deny the benefits of this effort at unification, an effort to which the spread of printed books gave considerable strength. Yet a certain diversity, such as we find in the Eastern rites, also constitutes a richness in the Church's tradition. This is why the Second Vatican Council wished to declare solemnly that "holy Mother Church holds all lawfully acknowledged rites to be of equal authority and dignity; that she wishes to preserve them in the future and to foster them in every way" (art 4). Even within the Roman rite, a place will be given to local usages "within the limits set by the typical editions of the liturgical books" (art. 39). It is left to competent ecclesiastical authority, in particular, to prepare individual rituals "following the pattern of the new edition of the Roman ritual" (art. 63), and wherever a deeper adaptation to the traditions and mentality of a people is required, the bishops will lay concrete proposals before the Holy See (art. 40).

A door opened wide to the use of living languages. The Council of Trent had flatly refused the request of those reformers who, for doctrinal reasons, had asked the Church to abandon the use of Latin in public worship (sess. 22, ch. 8). In the Second Vatican Council the pastoral necessity for the introduction of living languages into the liturgy became evident during the discussions among the Fathers. The constitution therefore gave them generous acceptance. While declaring that "particular law remaining in force, the use of the Latin language is to be preserved in the Latin rites," it affirms that "the use of the mother tongue . . . may frequently be of great advantage to the people" (art. 36). The faculty granted to bishops' conferences of introducing the vernacular into worship[59] immediately appeared as the most novel element of the constitution *De sacra liturgia.*

[59]See below, ch. 6.

3 The liturgical movement from Dom Guéranger to Pius XII
(*Dom O. Rousseau*)

BIBLIOGRAPHY

L. Alting von Geusau ed., *Liturgy in Development* (London and Melbourne: Sheed and Ward, 1965).

W. Barden, "Phases of the Liturgical Movement" in *Studies in Pastoral Liturgy* 2, P. Murray ed. (Maynooth: The Furrow Trust, 1961).

L. Beauduin, *La piété de l'Église* (Louvain: Mont César, 1914). Engl tr., *Liturgy the Life of the Church*, 2nd ed. (Collegeville, Minnesota: The Liturgical Press, 1929).

T. Bolger *et al.*, *Liturgische Erneuerung in aller Welt, ein Sammelbericht* (Maria Laach: Ars Liturgica, 1950).

L. Bouyer, *Liturgical Piety* (Notre Dame, Indiana, 1950); *Liturgy and Life* (London: Sheed and Ward, 1958).

L. Bouyer, *Dom Lambert Beauduin, un homme d'Église* (Tournai: Casterman, 1964).

J. Hofinger ed., *Liturgy and the Missions—the Nijmegen Papers* (New York: Kenedy; London: Burns and Oates, 1960).

E. Koenker, *The Liturgical Renaissance in the Roman Catholic Church* (Chicago University Press, 1954).

W. O'Shea, "Liturgy in the United States, 1889–1964" in *American Ecclesiastical Review* 150 (1964) 176-96.

Priests of St Séverin and St Joseph, *What is the Liturgical Movement?* (London: Burns and Oates, 1964; *Faith and Fact* 110); L. Sheppard, *The People Worship: a History of the Liturgical Movement* (New York: Hawthorn Books, 1967).

O. Rousseau, *Histoire du mouvement liturgique, Esquisse historique depuis le début du XIXᵉ siècle jusqu'au pontificat de Pie X* (Paris: Ed. du Cerf, 1945; *Lex Orandi* 3). Engl. tr., *The Progress of the Liturgy: an Historical Sketch from the Beginning of the Nineteenth Century to the Pontificate of Pius X* (Westminster, Maryland: Newman Press, 1951).

H. Schmidt, *Introductio in liturgiam occidentalem* (Rome: Herder, 1960) pp. 164-208: "Hodierna renascentia liturgiae" (with important bibliography).

I THE BEGINNINGS: DOM PROSPER GUÉRANGER (1837-75)

In the first period of its history the "liturgical movement," that is, the renewal of fervor among clergy and faithful for the liturgy, derives from Dom Guéranger (1805–75). Restoring the Benedictine Order in France at the Abbey of Solesmes (1837), Guéranger created a community whose spiritual life was above all centered in experienced contact with the prayer of the Church. Moreover, through various publications, notably *Année liturgique*, a historical and mystical commentary on the temporal and sanctoral cycles (15 volumes, from 1841), he caused this spirituality which was then new—because so neglected for centuries—to spread among centers of educated Christians.

Dom Guéranger's personality, and the various battles he joined, led him perhaps to see an element of counter-revolution in the liturgical movement and in the traditional values which the latter had restored. It remains nonetheless true that his move for a return to the sources awoke a current of renewal which was never to be stopped. He has been criticized for a certain extremist radicalism in his rejection of neo-Gallican liturgies in favor of the Roman liturgy, a decision which he had considered, perhaps excessively at least in the beginning of his literary career, as indispensable. A sworn enemy of anything which smacked of Jansenism—this position would in its turn exclude him from suspicion—Guéranger was a reactionary ultramontane who, through an unflinching logic, occasionally went beyond the bounds of sober reason. The Roman liturgy was for him the form *par excellence* of prayer.[60]

His renewal found a hearing in Germany, thanks to the Benedictine foundation of Beuron (1863). This was the work of two German priests, the Wolter brothers, who had earlier become Dom Guéranger's disciples. The country had moreover been prepared to receive the new seed by the studies and influence of renowned theologians, notably the great ecclesiologist, J. A. Moehler (d.1838). Less than a century later, Germany would be in the vanguard of the true liturgical renewal in the Church.

II DOM BEAUDUIN, DOM CASEL, PIUS PARSCH

The foundations made by Beuron in Belgium, at Maredsous in 1872, then from there at Mont César in 1899, were to be the springboard for a new development. It was from Mont César in 1909 that another Benedictine of genius, Dom Lambert Beauduin (1873–1960), launched the true liturgical renewal which spread rapidly in most Catholic regions before the First World War. Its characteristics were: (1) to aim at reaching the masses—in his first years as a diocesan priest Fr Beauduin had been, at the appeal of Leo XIII, a "workers' chaplain"—and (2) no longer to try, as Dom Guéranger had, to return to a past which would be dominated by the traditionalism of the time, but to look frankly towards the future while holding the richness of ancient institutions in the greatest respect. Dom Beauduin was able to put into practice—and he did so, extensively—Pius X's ideas of renewal concerning popular Gregorian chant and active participation in the mysteries of worship, "first and

---

[60]Although he had a very great veneration for the Oriental liturgies, Dom Guéranger was of the opinion that "any reunion of the two churches, in order to be lasting, should include in its program a modification of the Eastern liturgy which would put it more or less in relation with developments of Catholic forms in the West:" *Institutions liturgiques* 2 (Le Mans: Fleuriot, 1841) p. 724; 2nd ed. (Paris: Palmé, 1885) pp. 657f.

indispensable source of the true Christian spirit." The principal organ of Dom Beauduin's movement was, at first, a small people's missal published in fascicules, then a review entitled *Les Questions liturgiques,* which was soon changed to *Les Questions liturgiques et paroissiales*

The German liturgical movement known as that of Maria Laach, which spread immediately after the First World War, was not without relation to Dom Lambert Beauduin's movement; it was, however, of a less immediately pastoral and of a more theological character. The work of Dom Odo Casel (1886–1948) and his emphasis on the Christian mystery[61] are well known.

The work of the Rhineland abbey was completed in the same period by the Canons Regular of Klosterneuberg in Austria. Canon Pius Parsch (1884–1954)[62] gave to the movement a popular form particularly well adapted to German-speaking regions.

III FROM THE SECOND WORLD WAR TO VATICAN II (1940–62)

It was in Germany during the Second World War, where religion under pressure from National Socialism had to take refuge in the churches and limit itself to worship, that the two tendencies of Maria Laach and Klosterneuberg joined to bring the liturgical movement to its third stage, the one which we know today, characterized by effort at community participation almost entirely without the help of books, and speaking to the Christian assembly as such.

This stage has had its great theologians, among whom Father Josef Jungmann SJ, deserves mention. After the war, the movement spread in France, chiefly from Alsace.

In Paris at the same time, in 1943, the Centre de pastorale liturgique was created, its principal publication being *La Maison-Dieu.* Its goal was to channel the rush of initiatives which were then springing up in France, to give them foundation and form, and to prevent, thanks to the influence of some clearsighted men—in the first place Dom Lambert Beauduin, then living near Paris—those initiatives from straying off in misguided directions.

Faced with these new energies which had to be approved and restrained at the same time, Pope Pius XII, in several important acts of his magisterium, praised the liturgy and gave directives which thenceforth constituted the movement's official charter: the letter of Cardinal Maglione, secretary of state, to Cardinal Bertram, Decem-

[61]See below, ch. 9, **3,** II.
[62]See the notice by C. Rauch, "Un promoteur du mouvement liturgique" in LMD 40 bis (1954) 150-56.

ber 24, 1943;[63] the encyclicals *Mediator Dei* of November 2, 1947 and *Musicae sacrae* of November 25, 1955, and the speech to the congress of Assisi, September 22, 1956. At the same time, the pope was making reformatory decisions of exceptional importance for promoting the "active and enlightened" participation of the people in the liturgy.[64]

After that, the liturgical movement began to make progress in all countries. The bishops became its promoters and guides in publishing diocesan or national directories and in forming official structures to promote the liturgical apostolate: diocesan commissions, sometimes national commissions, etc. Missionaries took an interest in liturgical life and became aware of the problems that it raises for converts from paganism and in non-Western cultures. Lectures, seminars and congresses spread ever more widely the directives of the Church, the research of scholars and the experience of pastors.[65]

It is still too early to describe the efforts accomplished in most countries of the world by the bishops and their liturgical commissions in applying the decisions of Vatican II, in spreading its teaching and in putting into effect the various reforms which the executive council is rapidly elaborating.

[63]The text is given in H. Schmidt, *op. cit.*, pp. 174-6.
[64]See above, **2**, III.
[65]See H. Schmidt, *op. cit.*, pp. 722-85.

PART TWO

Fundamentals of the Liturgy

GENERAL BIBLIOGRAPHY

R. Aigrain, *Liturgia, Encyclopédie populaire des connaissances liturgiques* (Paris: Bloud et Gay, 1935).

P. Bayart, *Les divins offices*, 1: *Introduction générale* (Paris: Bloud et Gay, 1948).

L. Beauduin, *La piété de l'Église* (Louvain: Mont César, 1914). Engl. tr., *Liturgy the Life of the Church*, 2nd ed. (Collegeville, Minnesota: Liturgical Press, 1929).

L. Beauduin, *Mélanges liturgiques recueillis parmi les oeuvres de dom Lambert Beauduin* OSB *à l'occasion de ses quatre-vingts ans* (Louvain: Abbaye du Mont César, 1954).

L. Bouyer, *Liturgical Piety* (Notre Dame University Press, 1950); published in England as *Liturgy and Life* (London: Sheed and Ward, 1958).

F. Cabrol, *Le Livre de la priere antique* (Librarie H. Oudin, 1900). Engl. tr., *Liturgical Prayer—Its History and Spirit* (Westminster, Maryland: Newman Press, 1950).

F. Cabrol, *Les origines liturgiques* . . . (Paris: Letouzey et Ané, 1906).

C. Callewaert, *Liturgicae institutiones*, 1: *De sacra liturgia universim*, 4th ed. (Bruges: Beyaert, 1944; 1st ed., 1919).

B. Capelle, *Travaux liturgiques de doctrine et d'histoire*, 1: *Doctrine* (Louvain: Abbaye du Mont César, 1955).

O. Casel, *The Mystery of Christian Worship and Other Writings*, edited by B. Neunheuser (Westminster, Maryland: Newman Press, 1962; London: Darton, Longman and Todd, 1962).

H. Chirat, *L'assemblée chrétienne à l'âge apostolique* (Paris: Ed. du Cerf, 1949; *Lex Orandi* 10).

A. Coelho, *Cours de liturgie romaine*, tr. by Dom Gaspar Lefebvre, 1: *Liturgie fondamentale* (Bruges: Abbaye de Saint-André, 1928).

I. H. Dalmais, *Initiation à la liturgie* (Desclée de Brouwer, 1958; *Cahiers de La Pierre-qui-vire* 11). Engl. tr., *Introduction to the Liturgy* (Baltimore: Helicon ; London: Chapman, 1961).

G. Dix, *The Shape of the Liturgy*, 2nd ed. (Westminster: Dacre Press, 1945; reprinted in 1952).

L. Duchesne, *Origines du culte chrétien, Études sur la liturgie latine avant Charlemagne*, 5th ed. (De Boccard, 1920). Engl. tr., *Christian Worship—Its Origin and Evolution*, 3rd ed. (London: SPCK, 1949).

L. Eisenhofer–J. Lechner, *The Liturgy of the Roman Rite* (New York: Herder and Herder; Edinburgh-London: Nelson, 1961; this edition prepared with English bibliography by H. Winstone was made from the 6th ed. of *Liturgik des römischen Ritus*).

M. Festugière, *Qu'est-ce que la liturgie, sa définition, ses fins, sa mission; Un chapitre de théologie et de sociologie surnaturelle* (Abbaye de Maredsous, 1914).

T. Filthaut, *Learning to Worship* (London: Burns and Oates, 1965).

A. Gréa, *La sainte liturgie* (Paris: Bonne Presse, 1909).

R. Guardini, *The Spirit of the Liturgy* (London: Sheed and Ward, 1930; republished in 1940 with another work of the author, *The Church and the Catholic*).

P. Guéranger, *Institutions liturgiques*, 3 vols. (Le Mans: Fleuriot, 1840-1851).

J. Jungmann, *Pastoral Liturgy* (London: Challoner, 1962).

J. Miller, *Fundamentals of the Liturgy* (Notre Dame, Indiana: Fides, 1959).

P. Oppenheim, *Institutiones systematico-historicae in sacram liturgiam*, vol. 1: *Introductio historica in literas liturgicas*, 2nd ed. (Turin: Marietti, 1945); vol. 2-4: *Tractatus de iure liturgico* (1939-1940); vol. 5: *Introductio in scientiam liturgicam* (1940); vol. 6: *Notiones liturgiae fundamentales* (1941); vol. 9: *Principia theologiae liturgicae* (1947).

R. Paquier, *Traité de liturgique* (Neuchâtel: Delachaux et Niestlé, 1954).

P. Radó, *Enchiridion liturgicum* (Rome: Herder, 1961), 2 vols.

H. Reinhold, *The Dynamics of Liturgy* (New York: Macmillan, 1961).

M. Righetti, *Manuale di storia liturgica*, 1: *Introduzione generale*, 3rd ed. (Milan: Ancora, 1964).

L. Sheppard ed., *True Worship* (Baltimore: Helicon, 1963).

C. Vagaggini, *Il senso teologico della liturgia, Saggio di liturgia teologica generale* (Rome: Edizioni Paoline, 1957). Engl. tr., *Theological Dimensions of the Liturgy*, vol. 1 (Collegeville, Minnesota: Liturgical Press, 1959; only the first volume has been published).

A. Verheul, *Inleiding tot de liturgie haar theologische achtergrond*, 2nd ed. (Antwerp: Patmos, 1964). Engl. tr., *Introduction to the Liturgy* (London : Burns and Oates, 1968).

"La vrai visage de la liturgie", SL 14 (1937).

As the Church is both an institutional reality and a mystery, so also the liturgy, as one of the essential activities of the Church, is an ensemble of institutions—which can be described, studied, compared to institutions by lawyers, sociologists, historians—and at the same time a "mystery," in the sense that God is present, giving himself. This means that the liturgy is a supernatural reality which can only be perceived by faith, and on which one can only reflect with a theological method. We must say of the liturgy what Pope Pius XII, following Leo XIII, affirmed of the Church:[1] "We think how grievously they err who arbitrarily claim that the Church is something hidden and invisible, as they also do who look upon her as a mere human institution possessing a certain disciplinary code

[1] Pius XII, encyclical *Mystici Corporis* (Engl. tr., NCWC, 1943, n. 64); cf. CSL 2. See B. Capelle, "Théologie pastorale des encycliques *Mystici Corporis* et *Mediator Dei*" in LMD 47-8 (1956) 67-80; C. Vagaggini, *Initiation théologique à la liturgie* 1 (Bruges: Abbaye de Saint-André, 1959) pp. 205-9, "La liturgie et la loi de l'incarnation"; Engl. tr., *The Theological Dimensions of the Liturgy* (Collegeville, Minnesota: Liturgical Press, 1963) pp. 166-9, "The Liturgy and the Law of Incarnation."

and external ritual, but lacking power to communicate supernatural life. On the contrary, as Christ, head and exemplar of the Church, is not complete if only his visible human nature is considered . . ., or if only his divine invisible nature . . ., but he is one through the union of both and one in both . . . so is it with his mystical Body."

For this reason, in a general study of the liturgy we must place ourselves successively on these two planes. In the first section, we will analyse the structure and laws of liturgical celebration. We will examine first of all the legislation that governs it, then the assembly and the various functions which are performed there, the dialogue between God and his people, and liturgical symbolism. In the second section we will attempt to elaborate a theology of celebration, and for this reason to analyse the double movement which the liturgy implies: a movement of God towards men and of men towards God. We shall also try to determine the efficacy of the liturgy, what divine riches it brings, how it is a mystery of salvation. Finally we will try to point out the liturgy's value as a *locus theologicus*, the expression and teaching of the faith of the Church, and to examine in this wide range of perspectives the place and nature of pastoral liturgy.

The Structure and Laws of Liturgical Celebration

A. G. Martimort

CHAPTER FOUR

Liturgical Law

1 The special character of liturgical law

Since the Second Vatican Council, liturgical law has become the object of a thorough reform, as has church law in general. But in relation to the latter, liturgical law has certain special features. Rather than in ordinances and decrees, it is expressed in the liturgical books which also give the text of prayer formulas and the description of actions and gestures that constitute the official prayer of the Church. Contrary to general law it was never the object of any complete codification,[2] which made its study and interpretation more delicate and demanded an extensive knowledge of history. Destined to regulate sacred actions, it very rarely offered matter for jurisprudence; on the contrary it often had to take account of local customs.

Although liturgical law is expressed in a more complex and less categorical fashion, its binding force is no less stringent than that of the general law of the Church; in fact it is even more stringent at times. It frequently translates into practice the demands of divine law, as for example in the administration of the sacraments. Even aside from such instances, its observation is imposed by the very nature of its object, which is the prayer of the *Church*. For this prayer to be truly that of the Church, it is necessary that the Church recognize it as her own.

Liturgical law is not liturgy, as was pointed out earlier,[3] but it is a precondition for the existence and authenticity of the liturgy. To disregard its laws compromises, more or less severely, this authenticity and threatens the right of the Christian people to the riches they should derive from the prayer of the Church (can. 682).

[2]The *Codex Rubricarum* of 1960 has in fact a limited object: it replaces only the *rubricae generales* of the missal and breviary without touching on other documents.

[3]See above, ch. 1.

2 Competent legislative authority

I THE UNIQUE POWER OF THE HIERARCHY

Christian worship is the expression of a people at prayer, but it is not the people who preside. As we shall see later, the liturgical assembly has a president who holds his power and his authority not from the people but from Christ, through the bishop who has conferred ordination on him and has given him his mission. It was to the apostles, and through them to the episcopal college, that Christ entrusted the sacraments. The hierarchy, and it alone, has the assistance of the Holy Spirit to develop the rites and to determine how the sacraments are to be celebrated. Hence the unchangeable permanence of the tradition received from the Lord and the rich variety according to time and place.[4]

The ordering of the liturgy depends therefore on the power that the Church received from Christ to legislate, but much more is involved: it is also the work of the power by which the Church exercises the *priesthood* of Christ. Moreover since liturgical prayer is the expression par excellence of the faith of the Church and is the place where the faithful take nourishment, it must receive, in its entirety and in its every detail, the guarantee of the magisterium's approval.

For this reason, "no other person, even if he be a priest, may add, remove, or change anything in the liturgy on his own authority."[5] Hence in the exercise of worship, sacred ministers depend on their ecclesiastical superiors and exclusively on them (can. 1260).

It is true that some liturgical decisions in ancient times and in the early Middle Ages were the work of temporal sovereigns: the *Novellae* of Justinian, the capitularies of the Frankish kings, and others. It was Charlemagne who brought about the liturgical unification of his empire according to the usage of Rome. But such decisions drew their value only from the acknowledgment or the express consent of the hierarchy, in the framework of a society where Church and state were closely united.

II LITURGICAL LAW BEFORE THE COUNCIL OF TRENT

Liturgical law must therefore always assure both the universality of the Church's prayer, the radication of this prayer in the life, customs and culture of the various peoples. But it must do so according

---

[4]Council of Trent, sess. 21, ch. 2; Denz. 1728; CSL 21, 37, 38.

[5]CSL 22, 2; cf. 26; MD 58. See also Council of Trent, sess. 7, can. 13; Denz. 1613; cf. L. Beauduin, "Normes pratiques pour les réformes liturgiques" in LMD 1 (1945) 9-15.

to a synthesis which varies with the demands of each period.[6]

In effect, up to the Council of Trent much liberty was left to the bishops to compile their own liturgical books and to regulate divine worship. Liturgy was performed according to the customs of the local church, whence a great variety of usages. This had been the practice from antiquity; the differences, far from astonishing, were a manifestation of the spiritual richness of the Church and they enhanced the unity of the Church. The authenticity of the liturgy was assured by the local bishop, whose prerogative St Ignatius of Antioch, at the beginning of the second century, clearly expressed: "That Eucharist alone is to be regarded as legitimate which is performed under the leadership of the bishop or of him whom he has designated. Where the bishop is, there is the Church universal."[7]

Nevertheless the initiative of the bishops in liturgical matters was limited in practice by apostolic tradition: it is remarkable how often liturgical usages of the first Christian centuries were presented as "apostolic". Even the liberty of improvising formularies was exercised within precise bounds, to the point that different liturgies have very deep resemblances to one another. Moreover the controversies, at times very bitter, about questions of liturgical discipline among the churches, such as the date of Easter, underlined the necessity of adopting some unanimity. From the second century, with the decision of Pope Victor, the inherent right of the bishop of Rome to legislate for the liturgy of the entire Church is recognized: throughout the world Christians celebrate the same mystery of the Lord on the same day.[8] The general councils from the fourth century on almost always included in their acts some canons of liturgical discipline. On the regional level, the councils of Gaul, and especially those of the Visigothic kingdom, proved the necessity of further unifying the liturgical usages.[9] This need made itself felt especially at times when the unity of the Church or the certainty of her doctrine was troubled; hence the decisions of the African councils at the end of the fourth century putting an end to improvisation,[10] and the desire expressed by the Fathers of Trent for liturgical reform.[11]

[6]On this point see C. Callewaert, *op. cit.*, pp. 100 and 103.

[7]St Ignatius of Antioch, *Letter to the Smyrnaeans* 8, 1-2 (Roberts-Donaldson ed., *The Apostolic Fathers* 1, Edinburgh: Clark, 1870 [ANF 1] pp. 248-9).

[8]According to a remark made by St Leo the Great (fifth century); texts collected by M. B. de Soos, *Le mystère liturgique d'après saint Léon le Grand* (Münster: Aschendorff, 1958) pp. 31-4.

[9]Fourth Council of Toledo, 633, can. 2; H. Bruns, *Canones . . . selecti* 1 (Berlin, 1839) pp. 221-2.

[10]See above, ch. 3, **1**.

[11]See above, ch. 3, **2**.

III FROM TRENT TO VATICAN II (1563–1963)

BIBLIOGRAPHY

D. Bouix, *Tractatus de jure liturgico*, 4th ed. (Périsse, 1886).
C. Callewaert, *De sacra liturgia universim*, 4th ed. (Bruges: Beyaert, 1944) pp. 3-5; 123-47.
F. Cimetier, "La liturgie et le droit canonique" in R. Aigrain, *Liturgia* (Paris: Bloud et Gay, 1935) pp. 29-58.
M. Noirot, "Liturgique (droit)" in *Dictionnaire de droit canonique* 6 (Paris: Letouzey et Ané, 1957) col. 535-95 (this issue appeared in 1955).
P. Oppenheim, *Tractatus de jure liturgico*, 3 vols. (Turin: Marietti, 1939–40; *Institutiones systematico-historicae in sacram liturgiam* 2-4).

According to the desires and mind of the Council of Trent, Popes Pius V, Clement VIII and Paul V took upon themselves the unification and standardization of the liturgy, taking from local bishops the power which they had exercised before. The discipline which resulted is succinctly summed up by canon 1257 of the code of 1917: "It belongs to the Apostolic See alone both to compile and to approve liturgical books."[12] Evidently this implied the ordinary exercise of the supreme power; the prerogatives of a general council remained intact. But only one general council took place during this long period, the First Vatican Council (1869–70); it did not have time to treat the liturgical problems which were indirectly on its agenda.

All the treatises of rubricists were based on this discipline which remained intact until the Second Vatican Council. The liturgical law which this discipline created stays generally in force, until the liturgical reform promoted by the Second Vatican Council on December 4, 1963, is fully implemented; for this reason we will give a detailed description of it.

It should be pointed out that unification accomplished since the fifteenth century in no way led to total uniformity; it did not affect the Eastern liturgies, which the popes had unanimously admired and encouraged, and whose restoration they had promoted. Even in the Latin church, the communities with books or usages over two hundred years old were invited to retain them; and the Ritual of Paul V was never really imposed, strictly speaking. Finally the general practice retained its variety and distinctive nuances because of local Propers approved by law, by special indults and by the local customs respected by law.

---

[12]See MD 58: "It follows from this that the Sovereign Pontiff alone enjoys the right to recognize and establish any practice touching the worship of God, to introduce and approve new rites, as also to modify those he judges to require modification."

1 *Sources of written liturgical law,* 1563–1963

(a) The liturgical legislation which has been in force for these four hundred years is found above all in the liturgical books whose publication was entrusted to the Apostolic See by the Council of Trent. Its official editions appeared rather frequently and constituted the most normal and important mode of promulgation for the liturgical decisions of the supreme power. But there are others.

(b) The codes of canon law, both that of 1917 regarding the Latin church as well as the already promulgated parts of the oriental legislation, contain liturgical prescriptions; indeed, these prescriptions are quite numerous in the code of 1917.[13] However, they are the exception: general law as such abstains from legislating for the individual rites and lets them be governed by their own laws.[14]

(c) The popes, especially since Benedict xiv, have sometimes enacted liturgical legislation by constitutions, encyclicals or motu proprios. But in these cases, they usually lay down general principles, the application of which are spelled out by the competent Roman congregation which publishes annexed instructions. The popes can also appoint a delegate who uses their authority to make authoritative decisions affecting particular areas. Thus, in France and Belgium a decree of Cardinal Caprara, April 9, 1804, ruled on the external solemnities and the dates of certain liturgical feasts. The popes can also grant favors orally at the request of a cardinal who can then cite the authority of *oraculum vivae vocis.*

(d) The most common procedure is through the several Roman congregations by which the popes of modern times have legislated. This is done either by letting these ecclesiastical bodies exercise the usual powers delegated to them by the popes or by a special mandate asking them to submit a decree which the pope will then confirm. The Congregation for the Doctrine of the Faith (formerly the Holy Office), because of its duty to safeguard the deposit of faith, has competence to judge everything which refers to the validity of the sacraments. The Congregation for the Doctrine of the Faith

---

[13]The greatest number is found in the sections concerning the holy oils and the sacraments (can. 731-1143), the sacramentals (can. 1144-53); sacred places and times (can. 1154-1254); divine cult (general principles, can. 1255-64); eucharistic reservation and cult (can. 1265-75); cult of the saints, of images, of relics (can. 1276-89); processions (can. 1290-95); furnishings, vestments, linen, and sacred vessels (can. 1296-1306); to those can be added can. 98 which requires each of the faithful to belong to one rite; can. 239-40, 337, 349, 435, which concern the use of pontificals, and can. 2378 which prescribes serious punishment for clerics culpable of negligence in liturgical matters. The Roman ritual, from the time of the typical edition of 1925, included in its rubrics the prescriptions corresponding to the code of canon law.

[14]CIC, can. 2.

can also decide on rites which directly express a doctrinal affirmation.[15] By the same right, it at times recalls the essential norms of liturgical discipline[16] and the principles of sacred art;[17] Pope Pius XII had reserved for himself all decisions regarding the use of the vernacular in the Mass.[18] The rites of the papal chapels and the ceremonies for cardinals belong as such to the Congregation of Ceremonies (can. 254). Unaffected by the changes which the reform of the Roman Curia, announced by Pope Paul VI, can bring, the Oriental Congregation takes charge of everything regarding the oriental liturgies. For various reasons, other congregations can indirectly decide on ritual matters.[19] With these reservations, it is the Congregation of Rites which has direct and exclusive competence for everything that concerns the liturgy of the Latin rites.

2 The Congregation of Rites and its decrees

BIBLIOGRAPHY

A. Frutaz, *La Sezione storica della Sacra Congregazione dei Riti, origini e metodo di lavoro* (Vatican City: Tipografia poliglotta, 1963).
F. R. McManus, *The Congregation of Sacred Rites* (Washington: The Catholic University Press, 1954; *The Catholic University of America Canon Law Studies* 352).

Founded as a distinct Congregation by Sixtus V (by the bull *Immensa* of January 22, 1588), it functions today according to the rules laid down by St Pius X in the constitution *Sapienti Consilio* of June 29, 1908, summarized in canon 253. By his motu proprio *Già da qualche tempo* (February 6, 1930), Pius XI created a historical section whose influence, during the pontificate of Pius XII, determined the organization of a commission for general liturgical

---

[15]In this case the Holy Office intervened to prescribe a gesture of adoration for the celebrant of the Byzantine rite after the singing of the words of consecration, February 12, 1951; similarly it dealt with concelebration, May 23, 1957.

[16]For instance, *Commonitio* of February 14, 1958.

[17]Instruction of June 30, 1952.

[18]For instance, the letter of the cardinal secretary to the Prefect of Rites, April 29, 1955, about the chant in German at sung Masses; also the indult for the double proclamation of the readings granted to the dioceses of France, October 17, 1956.

[19]For the territories under its jurisdiction, the Congregation for the Propagation of the Faith can grant certain privileges or dispensations in the sphere of worship; so too the Congregation for Religious, though in a more restricted way. The Congregation of the Council treats of liturgical matters only incidentally, for example through the obligations of clerics or beneficiaries (can. 250). Liturgical law also contains some prescriptions from the Congregation for the Discipline of the Sacraments, especially the instructions of March 26, 1929, May 26, 1938, and October 1, 1949, about the Eucharist.

F

reform (*Pontificia commissio pro generali liturgica instauratione constituta*).[20]

The Congregation of Rites has gathered a certain number of its decrees and responses into an official collection published at the Propaganda Press: *Decreta authentica Congregationis sacrorum rituum ex actis eiusdem collecta*. The first three volumes, appearing in 1889–1900, bring together 4,051 documents dating from 1588 to 1900; the fourth volume, published in 1900, contains the instruction of Clement XI for the Forty Hours, together with added decrees and commentaries; the fifth volume (1901) is a general table of contents. This collection was promulgated under Pope Leo XIII (February 16, 1898); all the previous decrees not republished were abrogated.[21] Since then two appendices, equally official, have been added to it: volume 6 (appendix I), printed by the Vatican Press in 1912, and volume 7 (appendix II) in 1927, containing the decrees n. 4052 to 4404 (1900–1926).[22]

Decrees and responses become public when they are inserted in this collection. They are divided into general and particular; the particular decrees are obligatory only in the measure that they constitute an interpretation of the general law which is not limited by circumstances of time and place. But a considerable number of the decrees of the collection have become dead letter, either by the reforms of St Pius X, Pius XII, and John XXIII, or as a consequence of the great change of perspective promoted since then by the Second Vatican Council.

3 Custom in liturgical law

In the general law of the Church, custom has a privileged place, highlighted by the writings of the Fathers, the acts of the councils and the decisions of the popes. It constitutes an "unwritten law"; a good number of ecclesiastical laws had been purely customary for a long time before being formulated in writing.

Custom is the consistent practice not of one cleric nor of one or a few of the faithful but of a more or less vast portion of the Christian

[20]It is the official name given to it by the instruction of September 3, 1958.

[21]As regards the history of the dicastery, it would be of interest to publish its entire collection of decrees and responses even if they do not have juridical value any longer. Some of them are found in the collection which L. Gardellini published under the same title (Rome, 1808-1816), 5 vols., reprinted in 7 vols. (1824-1826) and in 5 vols. (1856-1888).

[22]For the decrees after this date, if they are not general and therefore published in the AAS, we must refer to the non-official publication *Collectio decretorum ad sacram liturgiam spectantium ab anno 1927 ad annum 1946* (Rome: Ed. liturgiche, 1947) or to the *Ephemerides liturgicae*, also non-official.

people (can. 26) who can be the subject of law: the whole Church, a group of local churches, a diocese, or even in certain cases a parish.[23] In order to have the force of law, the custom must have the acknowledgment of the lawgiver, who alone is capable of giving it validity (can. 25).

(a) *Consuetudo est optima legis interpres.* This formula originated with the jurist Paulus; it passed into the Code of Justinian, and from there into the *Sextus* of Boniface VIII and the code of 1917 (can. 29). It is particularly verified in liturgical law: living practice preceded the editing of the rubrics and continues to clarify their meaning. It makes up for their lacunae and obscurities, it decides their differences.

(b) A number of rubricists formerly held that custom could never prevail against the rubrics and decrees of the Congregation of Rites.[24] This opinion has been rejected by modern authors; this ideal of rigid uniformity is now clearly discarded.[25] But a custom must be legitimate and reasonable, and must have existed for a prescribed length of time.

Custom could indeed be abuse, routine, negligence. To be reasonable, custom must be justified by the good that it brings, by the alleviation of a real inconvenience. It has to promote the primary objectives of the liturgy: praise of God and sanctification of men. Therefore customs must be subject to critical judgment, and in the last analysis only the bishop is competent for that by virtue of liturgical responsibilities proper to him, as we shall see later. Also, a custom can be reasonable in one place and at one time and not be so in others, and vice versa.[26]

The span of time necessary for a custom to have force of law contrary to an existing law varies according to the case. According to the law of 1917, if the custom is opposed to a law which tends to annul every contrary custom for the future, this custom can only meet the time-requirement if it is centenary or immemorial. This is

---

[23]M. Noirot, *Revue de droit canonique* 3 (1953) 99-101.

[24]The defenders of this opinion and their arguments are cited in C. Callewaert, *op. cit.*, pp. 141-3; P. Oppenheim, *op. cit.*, 3, pp. 141-59. See the refutations of L. Stercky, *Manuel de liturgie et cérémonial* . . . , 17th ed., 1 (Paris: Gabalda, 1940) pp. 21-2; M. Noirot, "Liturgique (droit)" in *Dictionnaire de droit canonique* 6 (1957) (=1955) col. 535-57 and 563-91.

[25]CSL 37.

[26]The customs explicitly disapproved by the code of 1917 (can. 2), were judged unreasonable by the legislator and consequently they could not become acceptable by prescription no matter how long a time lapsed; such was the case (can. 818) regarding rubrics of his rite ignored by the celebrant of Mass or the addition of ceremonies and prayers on his own initiative.—M. Noirot, "La 'Rationabilitas' des usages contraires aux lois liturgiques depuis la promulgation du Code de droit canonique" in *Année canonique* 1 (1952) 129-40.

the case also of the customs which existed in 1918 and which were contrary to the prescriptions of the new code (can. 5). The time-requirement for other customs is about 40 years. The time stops if the Holy See or the bishop of the diocese opposes the usage in question before the expiration of the required time (can. 27).

IV LITURGICAL LAW CREATED BY VATICAN II

The Constitution on the Sacred Liturgy of the Second Vatican Council promulgated on December 4, 1963, introduced considerable changes in liturgical law, even before the carrying out of the reforms for which the constitution defined the *altiora principia*. It reinforces the authority of the diocesan bishop regarding liturgical matters; it states the principle of a certain decentralization and, to insure effectiveness, it gives powers to the "territorial episcopal conferences." Finally, in order to put reforms into practice, it presupposes the creation of an executive commission, which Pope Paul VI effectively organized in January 1964.

1 *The authority of the diocesan bishop*

"Regulation of the sacred liturgy depends solely on the authority of the Church, that is, on the Apostolic See and, as laws may determine, on the bishop."[27]

This principle of itself does not allow any change in relation to the preceding law: by no means is it a question of returning to the liturgical freedom as it was before the Council of Trent, especially in our time of world unity and the expansion of international organizations. But the proper authority of the local bishop is reaffirmed, given more precision and enlarged:

The bishop is to be considered the high priest of his flock. In a certain sense it is from him that the faithful who are under his care derive and maintain their life in Christ. . . . But because it is impossible for the bishop always and everywhere to preside over the whole flock in his church, he cannot do other than establish lesser groupings of the faithful. Among these, parishes set up locally under a pastor who takes the place of the bishop are the most important: for in a certain way they represent the visible Church as it is established throughout the world.[28]

It is only in the place of the bishop and united to him that the priests celebrate the sacred rites. This is why priests closely depend on him in liturgical matters, even if otherwise they enjoy a privilege of exemption. According to the law of 1917, the bishop had to make the canonical visitation of the churches of exempt religious and of nuns (can. 517), and in certain cases of regulars (can. 1261); if he

[27]CSL 22,1.   [28]CSL 41-2.

made decisions, if he prescribed or forbade something concerning divine worship, everyone, without exception, was subject to it (same canon). Finally, there are the important and delicate reforms which the Council places under his authority: "The regulation, however, of the discipline of concelebration in the diocese pertains to the bishop."[29] In certain cases it now belongs to the bishop to judge whether communion under both species is appropriate.[30]

Thus the bishop must see to it that no abuses creep into the administration of the sacraments and sacramentals, into devotion to the saints, and the word of God.[31] This vigilance must be directed not only to abuses dangerous to the faith but also to the liturgical laws and the tradition of the Church.[32] It is on this basis that the bishop judges the legitimacy of customs.

Even this vigilance of the bishop is not enough: he is also to foster pastoral renewal, to promote the liturgical movement (*actionem pastoralem liturgicam fovendam*),[33] to encourage and regulate the participation of the faithful in the liturgy, to promote the beauty of holy things[34] and the progress of sacred music. To accomplish this, the bishop shall form a liturgical commission and, if possible, a commission on sacred music, and another on sacred art. He may judge it fitting to unite all three of them into one commission; according to circumstances, several dioceses can set up one inter-diocesan commission.[35] The bishops make their decisions known by the promulgation of ordinances, directories and manuals or diocesan formularies.

The regulation of the *pia populi christiani exercitia* depends entirely on the bishops: they approve or prescribe the prayers, make them obligatory or limit them, keep watch over their practice;[36] "devotions proper to individual churches also have a special dignity if they are conducted by mandate of the bishops in accord with customs or books lawfully approved."[37]

Older liturgical law conceded to the bishops certain faculties, such as to imperate prayers or processions, to order the celebration of votive masses of second class, to structure the major and minor

[29]CSL 57, 2, 1°.
[30]CSL 55; cf. *Ritus servandus in distribuenda communione sub utraque specie*, n. 1.
[31]CIC, can. 336, 2.
[32]CIC, can. 1261, 1.
[33]CSL 43.
[34]This point is especially emphasized in CSL 124-7.
[35]CSL 45-6.
[36]CIC, can. 1259, 1; SRC, instruction of September 3, 1958, n. 12, 52-3.
[37]CSL 13.

litanies.[38] According to the new liturgical law it belongs also to the bishops to organize the catechumenate for adults, and to allow laymen to administer some sacramentals.[39] They have wide powers of dispensation from several general liturgical laws and of delegation for solemn acts which do not demand the episcopal character.[40]

2 *The national conferences of bishops*

While emphasizing the necessity to maintain and reinforce unity in essentials, the conciliar debates insisted on the need for decentralization, not only on the diocesan level, but according to larger geographical areas. From a liturgical viewpoint such diversification is demanded by the different civilizations, cultures, languages and traditions, whether in view of the difficulties peculiar to each region, or to adjust liturgical rites to the genius of each people and admit into the liturgy elements of national culture. As the ancient Church expressed her worship in forms which today make up the different liturgies of the West and of the East, so in the future, "the substantial unity of the Roman rite" can adjust itself to the diversity of different regions and peoples, especially in mission countries, with legitimate differences and adaptations.[41]

Concerning these local conditions, only the bishops can formulate a final judgment. In the past they exercised it by means of provincial, regional or national councils, the most famous examples of which were those of Gaul and Visigothic Spain. The Second Vatican Council authorized a much less rigid institution: the episcopal conferences, whose statutes were promulgated on October 28, 1965, in the Decree *Christus Domini,* which made the episcopal conferences an official organization within the Church (n. 37–38). These episcopal conferences are in principle the national assemblies of bishops, but can also cover a larger geographical area. They were already mentioned in the Constitution on the Sacred Liturgy: *competentes varii generis territoriales episcoporum coetus legitime constituti.*[42] In 1964 the Apostolic See had established temporary norms for its functioning in view of liturgical decisions regarding questions of the vernacular in the liturgy.[43]

Above all, decisions concerning the use of modern languages in

[38]NRC 80-90, 358, 371, 454.

[39]CSL 64, 79.

[40]CSL 97, 101; motu proprio *Pastorale Munus,* November 30, 1963.

[41]CSL 37-40, 54, 63b, 65, 77, 81, 107, 110, 111, 119, 123.

[42]CSL 22, 2; cf. 36, 3.

[43]Motu proprio *Sacram Liturgiam,* January 25, 1964; SRC, instruction of September 26, 1964, n. 23-31.

the liturgy will now be entrusted to these episcopal conferences. These will be true decisions (*statuere*), not simply petitions or proposals; but these decisions, as well as those of plenary or provincial councils, will be presented to the Holy See to be approved and confirmed (*probata seu confirmata*).[44] The national episcopal conferences were also charged to prepare rituals, especially for matrimony. In future, liturgical books must allow a wider margin for adaptations to local circumstances, on which the regional episcopal conferences can also rule.[45]

When a more radical adaptation of the liturgy or of discipline is proposed, especially if it concerns the introduction of local customs, the episcopal conference will not have the power to make final decisions: its proposals must then be submitted to the Holy See. If the Holy See requests that experimentations first be made, the episcopal conference has the responsibility to carry them out.[46]

There are therefore two levels of liturgical adaptation for the episcopal conferences: in certain cases they can decide matters for themselves, and in other cases they are restricted to submitting proposals to the Holy See.

In order to direct pastoral liturgy according to the faculties given to them, and to promote the necessary investigation and experimentation, the episcopal conferences will institute a liturgical commission. It will have the cooperation of experts in liturgical science, music, sacred art and the pastoral ministry. If possible, this commission is to be helped by an institute of pastoral liturgy, consisting of members among whom will be, if it seems well, laymen competent in the matter.[47]

3 *The executive council (Consilium ad exsequendam Constitutionem)*

For new liturgical books, the Constitution on the Sacred Liturgy foresaw the need for the collaboration of experts and consultations of bishops from different parts of the world.[48] To put this conciliar decision into effect, Pope Paul VI established a commission—the first of the postconciliar commissions—named the *Consilium ad*

---

[44]CSL 36, 3. This formula, resulting from the conciliar debates, should be interpreted in their light and according to the official commentary which the relator of the text, Bishop C. J. Calewaert of Ghent, submitted to the Fathers of the Council for their approval: *Emendationes* IV, pp. 14-15. Other articles of the Constitution on the Sacred Liturgy concerning liturgical language: 54, 63a, 76, 101.

[45]CSL 38, 63b, 77, 110, 119, 120, 128.

[46]CSL 39, 40, 65, 81, 107.

[47]CSL 44.

[48]CSL 25.

exsequendam Constitutionem de Sacra Liturgia. He announced its
scope in the motu proprio *Sacram Liturgiam* (January 25, 1964)
and entrusted to it, in a letter of the secretary of state dated January
29, the task of interpreting and applying the Constitution on the
Sacred Liturgy in "its spirit and letter." The *Consilium* is composed
of 50 bishops chosen from the various national episcopates. There
are also 300 experts who assist the bishops and assume the adminis-
trative tasks of a dicastery, but its main duty is to supervise the
general reform of the liturgy. The first results have been promulgated
by the Congregation of Rites in the form of instructions and typical
editions.

3 The liturgical books

The liturgical books constitute the fundamental source of liturgical
law. Their history is given elsewhere;[49] the evolution of the Oriental
books is entirely distinct from that of the Latin books, and they are
not subject to the same juridical statutes.

I LITURGICAL BOOKS OF THE ORIENTAL RITES

In general, in the Oriental rites the books are divided according
to the liturgical functions, as was true of the Latin books in ancient
times and in the early Middle Ages: books for the celebrant (*euchologion*) and for the deacon, lectionaries, collections of chants, the
common of the office (*horologion*), the psalter, and so on. Some of
them have been printed only in very recent times, hence the use of
manuscript books in certain churches up to the present.

From the juridical point of view, there is a definite trend, especially
in the churches united to Rome, to place the publication of these
texts under the care and responsibility of the patriarchs. For the
rest, the Sacred Congregation for the Oriental Church at present
supervises the preparation of liturgical texts, revised according to
scientific criteria in such a way as to guarantee the rites their own
genius and their original purity. But we cannot speak of *editiones
typicae* in the sense in which the term is used in Western legislation.[50]

II RULES FOR THE EDITION OF LATIN LITURGICAL BOOKS

In order to guarantee the authenticity of liturgical texts while

---

[49]For an overall view see above, ch. 1, 2; the history of the missal and of the
ceremonial, the ritual, pontifical, martyrology and breviary will all be treated in
greater detail in subsequent volumes of the present work.
[50]A. Raes, "Livres liturgiques des églises orientales" in *Dictionnaire de droit
canonique* 6 (1957) col. 606-10.

giving commercial publishers complete liberty[51] to reproduce them, canon 1390 requires that the local bishop compare them with the official text and attest to their exactness (*concordat cum originali*).

The official text itself, if it is a book of general Roman usage, must be the latest *editio typica*. The "typical edition" was, according to former law, the one which the Congregation of Rites had printed under its surveillance and which had been promulgated by decree.[52] The publication of books of chant was subject to special legislation.[53]

The Second Vatican Council asked for a complete revision of the Roman liturgical books, and this task was entrusted to the executive council created for this purpose in January 1964.[54]

The translations in the vernacular of the different countries, foreseen by article 36, §4 of the Constitution on the Sacred Liturgy, have been prepared and promulgated under the responsibility of the competent territorial authority.

If it is a matter of books of a special rite or of the local supplements to the Roman Rite, the official text to which the entire edition must conform is, depending on the case, the traditional book or the copy approved by the Apostolic See, or, for the rituals, the book published by the competent regional episcopal authority.[55]

III LITURGICAL BOOKS IN FORCE AT PRESENT FOR THE WHOLE ROMAN RITE

1. *Breviarium Romanum ex decreto sacrosancti Concilii Tridentini restitutum* . . ., promulgated by Pius V in the bull *Quoad Nobis,* July 9, 1568, reformed by St Pius X, then by Pius XII, and finally by John XXIII. The last typical edition was that of April 5, 1961.

2. *Missale Romanum ex decreto Sacrosancti Concilii Tridentini restitutum* . . ., promulgated by St Pius V in the bull *Quod primum,* July 14, 1570; last typical edition, June 23, 1962. The *Ordo Missae* and the *Ritus servandus* were modified and published separately in the typical edition of January 27, 1965. It is necessary to add the *Variationes* published on May 18, 1967 and the *Cantus qui in Missali Romano desiderantur* (typical edition, December 14, 1964).

---

[51]In fact this freedom is limited by the obligation imposed on the editor by the decree of August 10, 1946 (AAS 371); it demands a contract with the Administration of the Goods of the Holy See for the rights of authorship.

[52]SRC, decree n. 4266, May 17, 1911.

[53]SRC, instruction of September 3, 1958, n. 57-9; Martimort-Picard, *Liturgie et musique* (Paris: Ed. du Cerf, 1959) pp. 135-7.

[54]CSL 25, 31, etc.

[55]CSL 63b, which specifies: *actis ab Apostolica sede recognitis.*

3. *Ritus servandus in concelebratione missae et Ritus communionis sub utraque specie,* typical edition, March 7, 1965.

4. *Ordo Hebdomadae sanctae instauratus,* published by the decree of November 30, 1955. The new editions of the breviary and the missal have incorporated its changes, but further corrections are contained in the *Variationes . . .* published on March 7, 1965.

5. *Martyrologium Romanum,* published by order of Gregory XIII in the constitution *Emendato jam,* January 14, 1584; the last typical edition is that of St Pius X in 1914.[56]

6. *Pontificale Romanum,* published by order of Clement VIII in the brief *Ex quo in Ecclesia,* February 10, 1596; Pius XII and John XXIII introduced important changes: the second part was completely revised, and published by a decree of April 13, 1961; the first and the third part were simply revised in the typical edition of February 28, 1962.

7. *Caeremoniale episcoporum,* published by order of Clement VIII in the brief *Cum novissime,* July 14, 1600; Leo XIII issued the last typical edition in 1886. It should be corrected by the following book.

8. *Ritus pontificalis ordinis hebdomadae sanctae instaurati,* published by a decree of February 15, 1957.

9. *Rituale Romanum,* published by order of Paul V in the brief *Apostolicae sedi,* June 17, 1614; the last typical edition was published during the pontificate of Pius XII, and approved by a decree of the Congregation of Rites, January 25, 1952.[57]

10. *Ordo baptismi adultorum per gradus catechumenatus dispositus,* published by a decree of April 16, 1962.

11. *Memoriale rituum pro aliquibus praestantioribus sacris functionibus persolvendis in minoribus ecclesiis,* published by order of Benedict XIII in 1725; the last typical edition was the one by Benedict XV, promulgated by decree of the Congregation of Rites on January 14, 1920. Only parts one and two of this book are still in force.

12. *Ritus simplex ordinis hebdomadae sanctae instaurati,* published by a decree of February 5, 1957. It replaces parts three to six of the *Memoriale rituum.*

13. *Graduale sacrosanctae Romanae ecclesiae,* promulgated by a decree of August 7, 1907, n. 4203, which has to be supplemented by the *Cantus Gregoriani ad "Ordinem hebdomadae sanctae instaura-*

[56]The latest edition is the *quarta post typicam* of 1956; just as former editions, it reproduces, with only the addition of new notices, the *prima post typicam* approved by the Congregation of Rites on January 11, 1922 and justly criticized by historians.

[57]There has appeared an *editio prima post typicam* approved by a decree of November 21, 1953.

tum" pertinentes, published by a decree of February 11, 1956, and corrected by the *Variationes* of May 27, 1961.

14. *Kyriale simplex,* issued on December 14, 1964 to implement the Constitution on the Sacred Liturgy of the Second Vatican Council.

15. *Cantus historiae Passionis Domini nostri Jesu Christi . . . iuxta Ordinem hebdomadae sanctae instauratum,* published by a decree of January 16, 1957 and replacing the *Cantus Passionis* of July 12, 1916.

16. *Antiphonale sacrosanctae Romanae ecclesiae pro diurnis horis,* promulgated by decree n. 4298 of December 8, 1912; a second edition, made necessary by the changes in the breviary from 1912 to 1914, was published as the typical edition by a decree of October 28, 1919, but it must now be corrected by the *Cantus Gregoriani ad "Ordinem hebdomadae sanctae instauratum" pertinentes* (February 11, 1956) and by the books that follow; there are further corrections in the *Variationes in cantu,* May 27, 1961.

17. *Officium pro defunctis,* promulgated by a decree of May 12, 1909 and comprising the night office, vespers, the absolution and burial of the dead.

18. *Officium et missae in Nativitate Domini* (May 27, 1926).

19. *Officium hebdomadae sanctae et octavae Paschae cum cantu,* published on January 28, 1959, and replacing the one which had been published by a decree of February 22, 1922.[58]

IV LOCAL LITURGICAL BOOKS AND RITES OF THE LATIN
CHURCH, 1563–1963

A certain number of churches of the West and some religious orders who fulfilled the required conditions have preserved their own

---

[58]To be complete, it would be necessary to add: (a) the *Caeremoniale sacrae Romanae ecclesiae,* which has never been the object of promulgation nor of an official edition, but to which some legislative acts refer, such as the constitution *Vacante sede apostolica* of Pius XII, December 8, 1945; (b) the *Instructio Clementina pro expositione SS. Sacramenti occasione orationis XL horarum*; its official edition with commentaries occupies the fourth volume of the *Decreta authentica S. Congregationis Sacrorum Rituum* (Rome, 1900; the decrees of April 27, 1927 and January 11, 1928 should also be consulted); it has force of law only for the diocese of Rome, and it is not a liturgical book properly speaking, although considered as such by some decrees of the SRC. Neither is the *Canon Missae ad usum episcoporum* a liturgical book, but only an authorized adaptation of extracts from the missal. The *De oratione communi seu fidelium* published on January 13, 1965 is normative only for decisions of episcopal conferences.—We have omitted from this list the books which are no longer of any use, either because liturgical reforms have made them obsolete or because they have been incorporated into other liturgical books.

liturgical books or have obtained their restoration. At times it involves the whole of a proper liturgy, so that they do not use any Roman books at all, for example the church of Milan and the Cistercian Order; at times their privilege is limited to only one book such as the breviary, ceremonial or ritual. Since the ritual of Paul V has never been made obligatory, it is certainly legitimate for the churches and orders which have never adopted it to retain their own ritual, as for example the churches of the Spanish-speaking lands.[59]

There are also certain churches which celebrate the Roman liturgy but in a language other than Latin; such is the case of certain churches in Dalmatia. These translated Roman books must be considered books of particular liturgies; each is governed by its own statutes.[60]

On the other hand, the bilingual rituals, according to the law before 1963, do not take the place of the Roman ritual; they are only a local adaptation of it.

Some dioceses and religious orders which use the books of the Roman rite have preserved some rites of their own—it is unfortunate that they have not been more careful in preserving these spiritual treasures—the celebration of local feasts, especially feasts of saints. For these feasts they submit to the Apostolic See supplements or appendices corresponding to the Roman books, called "Propers" (*propria*).[61] Their use is obligatory, as is also the local calendar.[62] Along with the propers of the missal and breviary, the importance of propers of the ritual and books of chant should be noted. The propers of the ritual have allowed churches which have adopted the Roman Ritual to preserve ancient usages and adapt them to local needs.[63] The propers of the books of chant contain local and regional melodies whose disappearance would be a great loss.[64]

[59]M. Noirot, "Les rituels diocésains, leur position juridique actuelle" in *Revue de droit canonique* 2 (1952) 433-8; F. Miranda and the Junta Nacional de Apostolado Litúrgico, *Estudios sobre el Ritual* (Silos: Liturgia, 1958).

[60]C. Korolevskij, *Living Languages in Catholic Worship* (London: Longmans, 1957) pp. 73-114.

[61]The rules which have to guide the reform of the propers were determined by the *Instructio de calendariis particularibus et officiorum ac missarum propriis ad normam et mentem codicis rubricarum* of February 14, 1961; AAS 53 (1961) 168-80.

[62]NRC 48-58.

[63]The German *Collectio Rituum* of 1950 is a kind of proper, an appendix to the Roman ritual.

[64]Decrees of SRC, n. 4166, August 11, 1905, paragraph 5; n. 4234, March 24, 1909, 1.

V RESPECT DUE TO THE LITURGICAL BOOKS

Some liturgical books contain scriptural excerpts, especially gospel pericopes; hence the missal, for example, receives at Mass honors which are given to the book of gospels. Tradition has made all the liturgical books an object of veneration and thoughtful care; illuminations, bindings, cases, etc. have shown them as precious objects. They contain the text of the Church's prayer by which the grace of the sacraments is extended and divine praise given. Hence their appearance and preservation should always be a matter of concern.[65]

VI RUBRICS: THEIR OBLIGATION AND INTERPRETATION

Besides the texts of readings, chants and prayers, liturgical books contain notes more or less frequent and detailed on the postures, gestures and ceremonies to be observed, as well as on the choice and use of texts. At first short and few in number, these notes were written into the body of the texts; later on, in order to distinguish them better, they were written in coloured ink while the text was written in black; since the eleventh and twelfth centuries, they generally were written or printed in red, whence the name "rubrics."[66] Since the end of the Middle Ages, introductions to an entire book (missal, breviary) or to collections of ceremonies (pontifical, ritual) were added. Finally some books bore no text at all, but only ritual prescriptions (*Caeremoniale*, and the like). It is to all of these notes contained in liturgical books that the general term "rubrics" is given.

To decide how obligatory their prescriptions are and to ascertain their meaning is not always easy. The different liturgical books necessary for the same ceremony can present divergent rubrics because they have a different historical and literary origin. The interpretation of a given rubric can at times only be attained by finding once more the source from which the editor has drawn it, for the rubrics of the same ceremony of the pontifical, for example, come from different times and sources.

For this reason, the lawgiver himself is sometimes obliged to interpret a rubric; these *authentic* interpretations are given mainly by the Congregation of Rites. Without the intervention of the lawgiver, custom and usage offer the best and truly authentic interpreta-

---

[65]See src, instruction of September 26, 1964, n. 40.

[66]But the term was used in Roman law to designate the headings placed at the beginning of documents in a collection.

tion,[67] when the usage has not been artifiically tampered with. The commentaries of rubricists (a *doctrinal* intrepretation, which does not have official status), must now take into consideration two factors which can lead to a renewal of the study of rubrics: the progress in the history of the liturgy—especially work on the critical editions of liturgical books—and the growing consciousness of modern problems in pastoral liturgy.

[67]See above, "Custom in liturgical law."

CHAPTER FIVE

The Assembly

BIBLIOGRAPHY

L. Beauduin, "Essai de manuel fondamental . . ." in QLP 5 (1920) 219-28 (reproduced in *Mélanges liturgiques* . . . [Louvain: Mont César, 1954] pp. 81-91).

H. Chirat, *L'assemblée chrétienne à l'âge apostolique* (Paris: Ed. du Cerf, 1949; *Lex Orandi* 10).

I. H. Dalmais, *Introduction to the Liturgy* (Baltimore: Helicon; London: Chapman, 1961) pp. 27-55.

G. Dix, *The Shape of the Liturgy*, 2nd ed. (Westminster: Dacre Press, 1952) pp. 12-35.

C. Floristan, *The Parish Eucharistic Community* (Notre Dame, Indiana: Fides, 1964),

J. A. Jungmann, *Liturgical Worship—a Historical Inquiry into its Fundamental Principles* (New York: Pustet, 1941) pp. 30-46, 107-24. A new revised edition of this work has appeared with the title *The Liturgy of the Word* (London: Burns and Oates, 1966); cf. pp. 11-21, 56-64.

A. Kirchgaessner, *Unto the Altar—the Practice of Catholic Worship* (Freiburg: Herder; Montreal: Palm Publishers, 1963) pp. 119-46.

R. Lechner, "The People of God in Assembly" in *Worship* (May 1965) 259-64.

J. Lécuyer, "The Liturgical Assembly: Biblical and Patristic Foundations" in *Concilium* 2 (1966) 3-11.

A. G. Martimort, "L'assemblée liturgique" in LMD 20 (1949) 153-75.

A. G. Martimort, "L'assemblée liturgique, mystère du Christ" in LMD 40 (1954) 5-29.

A. G. Martimort, "Précisions sur l'assemblée" in LMD 60 (1959) 7-34.

C. Vagaggini, *Theological Dimensions of the Liturgy* 1 (Collegeville, Minnesota: Liturgical Press, 1959) pp. 151-65.

1 Liturgy and the assembly

The term *liturgy,* in the sense in which the Latin Church has used it since the end of the sixteenth century, as well as the modern distinction between "liturgical actions" and *pia exercitia,*[1] were not known in antiquity; rather the only term then in common use was *assembly*. Since the third century, the specific Greek word was σύναξις which has continued in use,[2] though we do encounter the terms συνέλευσις and even συναγωγή before this.[3] The Latin *coetus* and

---

[1] See above, ch. 1, "Definitions."

[2] See the texts compiled by J. M. Hanssens, *Institutiones liturgicae de ritibus orientalibus* 2 (Rome: Gregorian University, 1930) pp. 24-34.

[3] Συνέλευσις: St Justin, *First Apology* 67; συναγωγή: James 2:2.

convocationes were terms used by Tertullian,[4] and we find *collecta*[5] in other authors. *Processio* is a less ancient designation, though Tertullian applied the technically liturgical meaning of "to gather together" to the verb *procedere*.[6] Moreover, since the first Christians were accustomed to a constant change of place for their gatherings, they preferred to use verbs which described this movement, such as: συνάγειν, συνέρχομαι, ἀθροίζομαι, *coire, convenire* and *congregari*.[7] These verbs were sometimes given greater precision by the addition of the phrase ἐπὶ τὸ αὐτό, *in unum*.[8] Finally, there is the word ἐκκλησία, which has such specifically biblical overtones that it was converted into the Latin without translation. Besides meaning the aggregate of Christians spread over the world, *ecclesia* also defined the occasional meetings of individual Christians for the Word of God and the Eucharist.[9] The assembly therefore appears to the historian as the first and the most basic liturgical reality.

The notion of assembly, however, does not coincide with that of liturgy.

I CERTAIN LITURGICAL ACTIONS EXCLUDE THE PRESENCE OF THE PEOPLE

Monastic prayer, which will be treated later,[10] became a liturgical prayer only in the course of time. Of itself, the monastery or the chapter does not convoke the assembly of the faithful—the latter are even excluded from the churches of religious orders devoted to the hermit's life—nor is it necessary that the monastic office be presided over by a member of the hierarchy.[11] However, by the will

---

[4]*Coimus in cœtum et congregationem*: Tertullian, *Apologeticum* 39, 2; CC 1, p. 150; *convocationes*: *id., Ad Uxorem* II, 4, 2, *ibid.*, p. 388.

[5]St Jerome, *Epist.* 108, 20; See especially "Actes des martyrs d'Abitène" in P. Franchi de' Cavalieri, *Note agiografiche* 8 (Vatican City, 1935; *Studi e Testi* 65) pp. 49-71.

[6]Tertullian, *Ad Uxorem* II, 4, 1: *si procedendum erit.*—For *processio*, see B. Botte, "Processionis Aditus" in *Miscellanea liturgica in honorem L. Cuniberti Mohlberg* 1 (Rome: Ed. liturgiche, 1948) pp. 127-33.

[7]We have collected a certain number of citations in LMD 57 (1959) 55-74.

[8]About ἐπὶ τὸ αὐτό in the Acts, cf. L. Cerfaux, "La première communauté chrétienne à Jérusalem" in *Ephemerides theologicae Lovanienses* 16 (1939) 5-31, and reprinted in *Recueil Lucien Cerfaux* 2 (1954) pp. 125-56, see especially pp. 143 and 152, n. 1.—The term is found many times in St Ignatius of Antioch: *Ephes.*, 5, 3 and 13, 1; *Philadelph.*, 6, 2 and 10, 1; *Magnes.*, 7, 1-2, P. Camelot ed. (SC 10) pp. 74, 82, 100, 146, 150.

[9]This is evidently the case in 1 Co 11-14, and in the term οἶκος ἐκκλησίας or *domus ecclesiae*.

[10]In a subsequent volume.

[11]This is even expressly forbidden for the office of cloistered nuns: SRC n. 3180.

of the Church, such an office is performed *in the name* of the Christian people (*vicaria vice*). Since the time when this understanding was reached, the monastic office has always been looked upon as an act of public worship rendered to God in the name of the Church. The same holds for the office recited outside choral celebration, and even individually by clerics *in sacris,* the solemnly professed and certain religious.[12]

II THE PRESENCE OF THE PEOPLE IS NOT DEMANDED FOR THE VALIDITY OF SACRAMENTAL RITES

Though the solemn celebration of most of the sacraments has traditionally taken place in the midst of the assembly, penance has lost its public ritual forms and is now administered only in private. Similarly, because of necessity or other reasons, sometimes other sacraments are performed with only the priest and the recipient present. This is sufficient for validity since the public and social character of the sacrament is assured by the action of the minister alone, whose act is an act of the Church.

Even the celebration of Mass by a priest alone is valid. Following the lead of the Council of Trent,[13] the Holy See has had to reaffirm this at different times, by saying that such a Mass is always a public and social act. In the person of the priest the entire Church is already present and the fruits of the sacrifice are meant for the whole Church. Moreover the Mass without the participation of the people is licit, provided it is celebrated according to the conditions laid down for time, place and the presence of a server. We are no longer to speak of a "private Mass," once the classical term for describing such a Mass, and no one really has the right to slight or overlook it.[14]

III NEVERTHELESS THE LITURGY IMPLIES ASSEMBLY

Although the liturgy can be celebrated validly and in many cases licitly without the presence of the assembly, it remains true that its celebration calls for the gathering of the faithful; it always assumes it present, and should therefore inspire all the necessary steps to bring it about.

Liturgical services, according to the Second Vatican Council, are not private functions, but are celebrations of the Church, which is the "sacrament of unity," namely, a holy people united and organized under their bishops . . .

[12]CSL 84-5, 95-6, 98;—MD 140-42.
[13]Session 22, ch. 6, can. 8; Denz. 1747 and 1758.
[14]CSL 27; MD 96-7; SRC, the instruction of September 3, 1958, n. 2; *Directoire pour la pastorale de la messe à l'usage des diocèses de France,* 2nd ed. (1960) n. 212-13.

G

It is to be stressed that whenever rites, according to their specific nature, make provision for communal celebration involving the presence and active participation of the faithful, this way of celebrating them is to be preferred, as far as possible, to a celebration that is individual and quasi-private.[15]

Liturgical formulas are expressed in the plural,[16] and they contain dialogue with and invitations to the people. The people are said to surround the altar (*circumstantes*); it is for them that the word of God is read. The priest celebrating the Mass designates them as offering with him the eucharistic sacrifice: *nos servi tui sed et plebs tua sancta*. Certain gestures of petition and blessing are performed for the people.[17]

2 The importance of the liturgical assembly in the tradition of the Church

The fact that the Christians assembled periodically for prayer was judged from the beginning of the Church as characteristic of their way of life by the authors who described it to the pagans.[18] With remarkable insistence the acts of the Apostles frequently refer to the community united at prayer.[19] In St Paul's letters, the assembly is the object of regulations and reproaches (1 Co 11 and 14).[20] Later on when the fervor of the first generation had passed, it was recalled to illustrate the obligation that Christians had to come to the assembly. Pastors did not content themselves with reprimanding those who had deserted the assembly;[21] they rather described the spiritual benefit which those who attended drew from it, and they based its need on the very economy of salvation and the will of the Lord.[22] St John Chrysostom has given in his preaching perhaps the

[15]CSL 26-7.—Cf. also CSL 41-2.

[16]With the exception of the biblical formulas and specifically private prayers as, at Mass, the *mea culpa*.

[17]This is further developed in C. Vagaggini, *op. cit.,* pp. 157-65; in J. Jungmann, *op. cit.,* pp. 56-64.

[18]Pliny the Younger, *Epistolarum*, bk. 10, ep. 96, M. Schuster ed. (Leipzig, 1933; *Bibl. Teubner.*) p. 363; St Justin, *First Apology* 67, Pautigny ed. (Picard, 1904; *Textes et documents*) p. 143; Philippe Bardesane, *Le livre des lois et des pays* 46, F. Nau ed., *Patr. syr.* 2 (Didot, 1907) col. 606-7; Tertullian, *Apologeticum* 39; CC 1, p. 150.—For all the texts alluded to in this paragraph, see A. G. Martimort, "Dimanche, assemblée et paroisse" in LMD 57 (1959) 55-67.

[19]L. Cerfaux, *art. cit.* in *Recueil Lucien Cerfaux* 2, pp. 125-56; *ibid.,* the table on pp. 72-3.

[20]Also, James 2:1-4.

[21]Heb 10:25; St Ignatius of Antioch, *Letter to the Ephesians* 5, 3; 2nd ed., Camelot (SC 10), p. 72.

[22]St Ignatius of Antioch, *Letter to the Magnesians* 7, 1, *op. cit.,* p. 100; St Cyprian, *De dominica oratione* 8, Hartel ed., 1, p. 272; St Ambrose, *De officiis ministrorum*, bk. 1, ch. 29, n. 142 in PL 16, col. 64-65.

greatest development to the catechesis of the assembly.[23] Ascetical and canonical treatises equally bear witness to the obligation imposed upon Christians to assemble: the *Didache,* the *Teaching of the Apostles* and the *Apostolic Constitutions.*[24] Though somewhat obscured in the course of the Middle Ages, the notion of the liturgical assembly has always remained the underlying reason for the formulation of the Sunday precept,[25] and it is particularly evident in the legislation concerning processions.[26] Restoring the assembly to its place of honor was one of the objectives of the liturgical renewal prior to Vatican II.[27]

The actual coming together of Christians shows forth the work of gathering together into unity the children of God achieved by Christ, whose grace is mysteriously present in every liturgical celebration. Without itself being a sacrament, the assembly is a sign, the meaning of which we shall now try to glean from biblical tradition.

3 The assembly is a sacred sign

BIBLIOGRAPHY

L. Bouyer, *Liturgical Piety* (Notre Dame University Press, 1950) pp. 23-37. Published in England as *Liturgy and Life* (London: Sheed and Ward, 1958).
K. L. Schmidt, "'Ἐκκλησία" in G. Kittel, *Theologisches Wörterbuch des neuen Testaments* 3 (Stuttgart: Kohlhammer, 1938) pp. 502-39.
P. Tena Garriga, *La palabra ekklesia, estudio histórico-teológico* (Barcelona: Ed. Casulleras, 1958; *Colectanea San Paciano,* ser. teol., vol. 6).

I THE ASSEMBLY OF THE PEOPLE OF GOD IN THE OLD TESTAMENT

The arrival of the Hebrews at the foot of Mount Sinai marked a decisive stage in their history. Until that moment, they were only a

---

[23]St John Chrysostom, "On the Obscurity of the Prophets," *Homil.* 2, 3-4, PG 56, col. 181-2; "On the Incomprehensiblity of God," *3rd Homily against the Anomians* 6, PG 48, col. 725; *2nd Homily against the Anomians* 3-4, *ibid.,* col. 801-2; "On the First Epistle to the Corinthians," *Homil.* 27, 1-3, PG 61, col. 223-8; *Homil.* 36, 6, *ibid.,* col. 315; "On the Second Epistle to the Corinthians," *Homil.* 18, 3, PG 61, col. 526-7; "On the 2nd Epistle to the Thessalonians," *Homil.* 4, 4, PG 62, col. 491; "On Genesis," *Sermon* 6, 1, PG 54, col. 605; *ibid.,* col. 669, etc.— Cf. LMD 57, 62-3.

[24]*Didache* 14, 1; *The Syriac Didascalia,* ch. 13, Connolly ed. (Oxford: Clarendon, 1929) pp. 124-9; *The Apostolic Constitutions* 2, 59-63, F. X. Funk ed. (Paderborn: Schöningh, 1905) pp. 171-81.

[25]LMD 60 (1959) 10-11; LMD 57 (1958) 74-82.

[26]CIC, can. 1290-92.

[27]*Directoire pour la pastorale de la messe à l'usage des diocèses de France,* 2nd ed. (1960) n. 104-11.—Cf. John XXIII, encyclical *Sacerdotii nostri primordia,* August 1, 1959, AAS 51 (1959) 563-4.

band of fugitives; as such, they did not form a people, although they had witnessed the wonders of God in Egypt and at the Red Sea. Now, however, at the foot of Sinai, Yahweh assembled all the children of Israel. They listened to his voice, received the law from him, and promised they would keep it: "I will count you," says Yahweh, "a kingdom of priests, a consecrated nation." The covenant was sealed with the blood of animals sacrificed by Moses, and from that time on the Hebrews were a people, the people of God (Ex 19-24). This primordial event would bear in the biblical tradition the name of "assembly of Yahweh," *Qahal Yahweh,* which the LXX translated ἐκκλησία κυρίου; it is "the day of the assembly!"[28] The choice of the Greek word ἐκκλησία points to the first characteristic note of this assembly: it is *convoked* by God himself.[29] Moreover, when the Israelites were assembled, God was present in their midst (Ex 19:17-18); God proclaimed his word (Dt 4:12-13); and the assembly was concluded with the sacrifice of the covenant.[30] These four elements will be found essentially in the later assemblies.

Among them all,[31] the assemblies especially demanding our attention are the dedication of the temple by Solomon (1 K 8 and 2 Ch 6-7), the great Passover at the restoration of worship under Hezekiah (2 Ch 29-30), the renewal of the covenant when the book of the covenant was "discovered" in the temple during the reign of Josiah (2 K 23), and, after the return from exile, the assembly that lasted eight consecutive days and inaugurated Judaism (Ne 8-9). Now the convocation was no longer made by Yahweh himself but in his name; his presence however was assured by signs—the cloud, the ark, the temple, or even simply the book of the Scriptures. The reading from the book took on a greater and greater solemnity; it was truly God himself speaking.

After the exile the seasons of the Jewish year would be marked by the anniversaries of these great assemblies of the past, celebrated at Jerusalem by the pilgrim-faithful. This occurred up to the very time when, with the crowds gathered for such a feast, a new assembly was

[28]Dt 4:10; 9:10; 18:16; cf. 23:1-8.

[29]The term ἐκκλησία was used in Greek cities to designate the assembly of those citizens who met regularly. So, Pauly-Wissowa, *Realencyclopädie der klassischen Altertumswissenschaft* 5, 2 (Stuttgart: Metzler, 1905) col. 2163-7.

[30]See J. Lécuyer, *Le sacrifice de la Nouvelle Alliance* (Le Puy: Mappus, 1962) pp. 9-51.

[31]Also, note the assembly for the consecration of Aaron and his sons (Lv 8:3) and that for the consecration of the Levites (Nb 8:9); the assembly at Mount Ebal under the direction of Joshua (Jos 8:30-35); and the assembly convoked by Jehoshaphat to beg God's protection against Moab and Ammon (2 Ch 20:5-14).

signalled by the coming of the Holy Spirit on the apostles—the assembly of Jesus.

II THE CHURCH OF CHRIST, THE ASSEMBLY OF THE NEW PEOPLE OF GOD

The mystery of salvation in Christ is in reality the constitution of the new people of God,[32] a gathering together in unity of all God's scattered sons (Jn 11:52), an assembly, the *Church* (Mt 16:18). This assembly is convoked by the heralds sent by Christ (Mt 28:18-20). Its unity is deeper than that of the former assemblies; it is a Body, a new temple, the spouse of Christ. The new covenant is sealed in blood: the blood of Christ poured out once and for all unto the remission of sins. Christ is always present to his Church, till the very end of time, when the liturgy of the assembly will gloriously attain its definitive completion in heaven.

III THE LITURGICAL ASSEMBLY MANIFESTS THE CHURCH

For this reason, the liturgical assembly is the most expressive manifestation on earth—a veritable "epiphany"—of the Church; it betokens and reveals the Church.[33] The assembly is so much the sign of the Church that the same word in St Paul means one and the same entity; and in the Acts, the Church from its first days seems almost a permanent assembly at prayer. The Fathers speak about particular liturgical assemblies as if they were the entire Church; an assembly is the Body of Christ, so much so that not to attend would amount to lessening the Body of Christ.[34] Christians are invited to meet "as at the one only temple of God."[35] The voice of the assembly

---

[32] 2 Co 6:14-16; Tt 2:14; Ep 1:14; Heb 8:6-11; 1 P 2:9-10; Rv 4:9-10; 21:3.— On the Church and the new covenant, J. Lécuyer, *op. cit.*, pp. 67-174; see especially chapter 2 in the constitution *De Ecclesia* promulgated by Vatican II on November 21, 1964.

[33] CSL 41.—The liturgical assembly is not the only visible manifestation; there is, in addition, the general council, the pilgrimage to Rome, the instruction given by pastors outside the assembly, the charitable services rendered by the community, especially the sending of missionaries to unbelievers; however, the liturgical assembly is the most common, ordinary and accessible manifestation of the Church.

[34] *The Syriac Didascalia*, ch. 13, Connolly ed., pp. 124-5;—cf. St John Chrysostom, "On 2 Cor.," *Homil.* 18, 3. In modern times, it has been chiefly due to the idea of the mystical Body that such precise development has been made with regard to the liturgy: L. Lahaise, "La liturgie est l'Église en prière" in SL 14 (1937) 57-62;—MD 5;—B. Capelle, "Théologie pastorale des encycliques *Mystici Corporis* et *Mediator Dei*" in LMD 47-48 (1956) 67-80;—CSL 26.

[35] St Ignatius of Antioch, *Letter to the Magnesians* 7, 2, 2nd ed. Camelot (SC 10) p. 100.

is the voice of the Church, the spouse of Christ; and the sacrifice offered in the assembly is the Mass, the memorial and the presence of the sacrifice of the cross which constitutes the Church.

Because it is the very expression of the Church, the assembly must at the same time be a gathering of brothers in unanimity and a structured body having distinct functions,[36] as we shall elaborate later on.

However, this sign, the assembly, is not so obvious that it cannot be misinterpreted; in order to see, one must have faith.

IV IT IS GOD WHO CONVOKES HIS PEOPLE

We must not lose sight of the fact that whatever human effort is made towards effecting the assembly, it is God who calls his people together; his initiative anticipates ours; the assembly is a gift of God to men. It is the sacrifice of Christ already accomplished on Calvary and made present again through the Mass, which established the Church and reunites all men in the assembly of the baptized. Further, the assembly is convened and presided over by the bishop or his priests, who have this power in the mission they have inherited through apostolic succession and by the priestly character which configures them to Christ the head.

V THE PRESENCE OF THE LORD IN THE ASSEMBLY

"Where two or three meet (συνηγμένοι) in my name, I shall be there with them." The Fathers, notably St John Chrysostom, applied these words of Jesus (Mt 18:20) to the liturgical assembly, asserting that it implies the presence of the Lord.[37] The presence of Christ is bound up with the sign composed by the meeting of the baptized in one place at prayer; for this reason it is customary at least in the monastic liturgy to pray facing one another. This presence, however, is not sacramental in the strict sense of the term. The assembly must hear the word of God, which brings about another presence of the Lord; the assembly is also orientated toward the sacraments, the acts of Christ, and above all toward the Eucharist which makes the glorious humanity of the Crucified really present.[38]

VI THE ASSEMBLY PREFIGURES HEAVEN

The assembly is the anticipated image of the Church in heaven,

---

[36]CSL 26.
[37]St John Chrysostom, "On Genesis," *Sermon* 6, 1; "On Anne," 5, *Sermon* 1.
[38]CSL 7; cf. 33; MD 19.—This will be further elaborated below, ch. 9.

perceived now only in the obscurity of faith. Hence St John, in the visions of the Apocalypse, depicts heaven as a liturgical assembly. There will be the very same gathering of God's people; there will be heard the same acclamations and the same canticles, particularly that of Moses. The earthly liturgy, in the likeness of the celestial, contemplates the resurrected One, the immolated Lamb; in him the liturgy sees reflected the glory of the Father, and it acclaims him under the glorious title of *Kyrios*. Like the heavenly assembly and united with it—*cum omni militia caelestis exercitus . . . memoriam sanctorum venerantes*—the earthly assembly is intent upon the divine praise. The presence of Christ is the pledge and the anticipation of his happy return; liturgical prayer gives intense expression to eschatological hope.[39]

4 The people of God in the assembly

I THE GATHERING OF ALL THE PEOPLE

The assembly is open to all who have received the faith of the Church and not denied it publicly, and have been baptized or at least are disposed for it through the catechumenate. The Church can however exclude persons from its assemblies and its worship by the penalty of excommunication or interdict. In the ancient usage of which certain liturgies still bear witness, catechumens and public penitents were sent away before the eucharistic celebration.

The assembly therefore is not reserved to a spiritual elite; it must gather together a people with all the coarseness, procrastination, mediocrity and limitation under which they suffer. Judging by the sermons of St Augustine, St John Chrysostom or St Caesarius, the early Church was quite aware of this. Even today considerable pastoral effort is required to lead the people at prayer during liturgical celebrations.

The members of the assembly are sinners who look for the mercy of God; hence the common prayer should make public avowal of the state of sin (for example in the *Confiteor*),[40] and it should contain an invocation of the Lord's mercy. The assembly is not the gathering of the perfect; its spiritual poverty can even at times be a scandal. The holiness of the Church can be obscured by the sinfulness of its members.

In the very first days of the Church, the liturgical assembly at

[39]CSL 8.—Cf. O. Rousseau, "Le prêtre et la louange divine" in LMD 21 (1950) 7-21; P. Prigent, *Apocalypse et liturgie* (Neuchâtel: Delachaux et Niestlé, 1964; *Cahiers théologiques* 52).

[40]Cf. *Didache* 14.

Jerusalem brought together the totality of Christ's faithful. But the Church was destined to spread over the whole world, and so liturgical assemblies had to be multiplied according to the limitations of human structures: thus we find the Church divided into regional units, then according to cities, and finally into parishes in towns or in sections of a city.[41] This crystallization of local assemblies, of the hierarchy, is indispensable; but neither the local church not the liturgical assembly coincides with the city or other human communities.[42] Nor can the assembly be closed in on itself or isolated; it prays for the absent,[43] and welcomes with joy the brethren who come from other churches and bear witness to it of the Church's catholicity;[44] it seeks without respite to gain new members through baptism. If some local diversification is necessary and traditional, it must enhance rather than obscure the deep unity of faith and of prayer of the Church spread over the world. All the faithful, even when away from home, should be able to participate in the liturgy at least partially.[45]

II A BROTHERLY UNION IN DIVERSITY

One of the essential laws of the economy of salvation is that the new people of God must unite men in spirit despite everything that humanly sets them at odds. Christ has reconciled Jews and pagans, destroying the barrier which kept them apart and suppressing hostility (Ep 2:14). The birth of the Church at Pentecost is the undoing of Babel: people of all countries hear the voice of the apostles (Ac 2:6-11). There is no longer circumcized and uncircumcized, neither Jew nor Gentile, neither Greek nor barbarian nor Scythian, neither stranger nor guest, neither slave nor freeman; but all the baptized are together one in Christ, who is the consummation. There is only one faith, one baptism, one Bread which we break, one cup of the Blood of Christ, one Body.[46] The liturgical assembly must manifest these divergent origins and this brotherly unity; it cannot accept the division of race, language, social status, or age. "The Church has been established not to divide those who gather within

---

[41]See N. Maurice-Denis Boulet, "Titres urbains et communauté dans la Rome chrétienne" in LMD 36 (1953) 14-32; E. Griffe, "Les paroisses rurales de la Gaule," *ibid.*, 33-62.—Cf. CSL 42.

[42]A. Chavasse, "Du peuple de Dieu à l'Église du Christ" in LMD 32 (1952) 50-52; A. G. Martimort, "L'assemblée liturgique, mystère du Christ" in LMD 40 (1954) 19; *id.*, "Précisions sur l'assemblée" in LMD 60 (1959) 32-3.

[43]LMD 20 (1949) 163-4.

[44]H. Chirat, *op. cit.*, pp. 18-21.

[45]LMD 60 (1959) 24 and 32; A. Chavasse, *art. cit.*—CSL 37-8, 54.

[46]Rm 10:12; 1 Co 12:13; Ga 3:28; Ep 2:19; Col 3:11. Cf. Rv 4:9.

it, but to unite those who are divided, for this is the meaning of assembly (σύνοδος)."[47]

The Church therefore must tend toward that union of hearts of which the early Church is the outstanding model[48] and whose unanimity in the form of prayer is its exterior expression.[49] This involves self-sacrifice, and demands from the Christian a constant asceticism to reconcile himself with his brothers before making his offering (Mt 5:23), and to abolish the scandalous differences of which St Paul (1 Co 11:21) and St James (Jm 2:1-4) complain. The assembly itself procures the grace of brotherly love and unity.

III ACTIVE AND ENLIGHTENED PARTICIPATION

BIBLIOGRAPHY

C. Callewaert, *De sacra liturgia universim* (1919), 4th ed. (Bruges: Beyaert, 1944) pp. 32-40.

J. B. O'Connell, *Active Sharing in Public Worship—A Commentary on the Chief Purpose of the Second Vatican Council's Constitution on the Sacred Liturgy* (London: Burns and Oates, 1964).

P. Oppenheim, *Notiones liturgiae fundamentales* (Turin: Marietti, 1941; *Institutiones systematico-historicae in sacram liturgiam* 6) pp. 184-213.

La participation active des fidèles au culte, SL 2 (Louvain, 1933; studies by B. Capelle, B. Botte, P. Charlier, A. Robeyns *et al.*).

A. M. Roguet, "Participation in the Mass: Theological Principles" in *Studies in Pastoral Liturgy* 2, V. Ryan ed. (Dublin: Gill, 1963) pp. 120-37. Bibliography on active participation, pp. 210-14.

Lived intensely by the Christians of antiquity and insisted on by the Fathers, the active participation of the people in the liturgy fell more or less completely out of use after the Middle Ages. The faithful were strangers to the liturgy, and even at times deprived of the sight of the altar by walls and rood-screens enclosing the choir—a condition worse than that of those "quiet spectators" of whom Pius XI complained.[50] St Pius X in 1903 took the initiative for a return to tradition, proposing "as the primary and indispensable source of the true Christian spirit, the active participation in the holy mysteries and the public and solemn prayer of the Church."[51] His challenge was taken up by Pius XI in 1928; it provided the impetus

---

[47]St John Chrysostom, "In 1 Cor.," *Homil.* 27, 3, PG 61, col. 228.

[48]Ac 1:13-14; 2:42-7; 4:33-7; 5:12.—See L. Cerfaux, *Recueil* . . . 2 (1954) pp. 129-30, 150-52.

[49]St Cyprian, *De dominica oratione*, Hartel ed. (CSEL 3) pp. 271-2.

[50]The constitution *Divini Cultus*, of December 20, 1928, n. 9; in A. Bugnini, *Documenta pontificia ad instaurationem liturgiam spectantia* (Rome: Edizioni Liturgiche, 1953) p. 65.

[51]*Tra le sollecitudini*, November 22, 1903; *ibid.*, pp. 12-13.

the liturgical movement needed and prepared the way for numerous doctrinal studies, ending with the teachings of the encyclical *Mediator Dei* and, above all, those of the Second Vatican Council.[52] Finally, pending the revision of the liturgical books,[53] diocesan and national directories[54] and the Congregation of Rites[55] have proposed concrete regulations with regard to active participation especially at Mass,[56] but also in all the other liturgical actions.

Active participation is comprised of bodily posture, gestures, offering the gifts and the collection, the responses to the celebrant, and in general entering into the chant or dialogue, the times of sacred silence, and, ultimately, sacramental communion at Mass.[57] These various elements will be studied in the course of the following chapters.

Active participation must moreover be intelligent, devout and interior.[58] Liturgical action is a sign through which the faith must attain the divine mystery which it accomplishes. It demands a religious attentiveness; the mind of the faithful must be in agreement with their voice when they chant or speak.[59] The faithful should make their own the prayer said by the celebrant whom they hear; they must listen to the word of God with docility.[60] All this requires on their part an understanding of the rites and texts, and on the part of the priest a whole ensemble of pastoral duties, including especially catechesis, the dissemination of suitable books, the use of commentaries and commentators, and, when the Church permits it, the translation of texts into the language of the people.[61]

The Christian people is a royal and priestly people, sharing in the

---

[52]MD 80-111; CSL 11, 14, 19, 21, 27, 28.

[53]CSL 31.

[54]On the directories, see LMD 37 (1954) 146-70; 51 (1957) 116-24, 125-6; 55 (1958) 171-5.—In the *Directoire pour la pastorale de la messe à l'usage des diocèses de France*, 2nd ed. (1960) n. 112-48.

[55]SRC, the instruction of September 3, 1958, n. 22-23, 45, 93b.

[56]This will be treated in a subsequent volume.

[57]CSL 30;—cf. SRC, *op. cit.*, n. 22 a, b, and c.

[58]CSL 11 (*scienter, actuose, fructuose*), 14 (*plenam, consciam atque actuosam*), 19 (*internam et externam*), 21 (*plena, actuosa, communitatis propria*), 48 (*per ritus et preces id bene intelligentes, sacram actionem conscie, pie et actuose participent*), 50 (*pia et actuosa*).—Cf. Pius XII, "Discourse to the Congress at Assisi" on September 22, 1956, *The Assisi Papers* (Collegeville, Minnesota: Liturgical Press, 1957) pp. 223-36.

[59]*Sic stemus ad psallendum, ut mens nostra concordet voci nostrae*: St Benedict, *Regula Monachorum*, 19.—Cf. CSL 11.

[60]CSL 33.

[61]CSL 35-6.

priesthood of Christ.[62] The right and duty which the faithful have
of taking an active part in the liturgy is founded on the sacrament of
baptism, whose character, according to St Thomas' teaching, deputes
one for divine worship.[63]

It follows that Christian worship possesses an originality distinguishing it so much from the pagan cults of antiquity that its celebration requires a totally different style of building. The liturgical
assembly is not a meeting as that of spectators in a theatre; there
are no spectators: there are only participants. And the assembly
attains an interior and manifest unanimity which, far from alienating
the freedom of each member, is its fruit under the impulse of the
Holy Spirit.[64]

IV A FESTIVE PEOPLE

Speaking in paradox, St Jerome maintained that it is not the feast
which convokes the assembly, but the assembly which creates the
feast: "Everyone sees in his neighbor the source of greater joy."[65]
And St John Chrysostom in a talk about Pentecost elaborates this:

> Even if the fiftieth day has passed, the feast has not. The assembly is always a
> feast. How can we prove this? The very words of Christ: "Where two or three
> are gathered in my name, there am I in the midst of them." When Christ is
> among the assembled faithful, what greater proof do you wish that it is a
> feast?[66]

The assembly meets above all to celebrate in the joy of thanksgiving the events of the mystery of salvation. It is also convened for
rites of penitence, such as litanies, ember days, Lenten stations,
vigils; but these penitential rites are almost always a preparation for
a feast.

The feast surpasses the limits of the liturgical assembly. It gladly
prolongs itself in prayer and extra-liturgical ceremonies, the *pia
exercitia,* which can at times attain a very high quality of expression

---

[62]CSL 14: . . . *actuosam . . . participationem . . . quae ab ipsius Liturgiae natura
postulatur, et ad quam populus christianus "genus electum, regale sacerdotium,
gens sancta, populus adquisitionis" vi baptismatis ius habet et officium.*

[63]St Thomas, *Summa Theol.,* III, q. 63, a. 6; C. Vagaggini, *op. cit.,* pp. 74-7.—J.
Lécuyer, *Le sacerdoce dans le mystère du Christ* (Paris: Ed. du Cerf, 1957; *Lex
Orandi* 24) pp. 171-228.

[64]An analysis of the liturgical assembly as a form of social life appears in M.
Festugière, *La liturgie catholique, Essai de synthèse* (Maredsous, 1913) pp. 61-8.

[65]*Non quo celebrior sit dies illa qua convenimus, sed quo, quacumque die convenien-
dum sit, ex conspectu mutuo laetitia maior oriatur: Comment. in epist. ad Galat.,*
bk. 2, ch. 4; PL 26, col. 378.

[66]*5th Sermon on Anne* 1; PG 54, col. 669.

and constitute the cultural patrimony of a people. The feast has often inspired games or sacred dramas; it also awakens the joys of city and family. It naturally calls for leisure, cessation of work and "days off." This set of customs, even if profane, has very great pastoral value, provided that its bond with the liturgy stays firm or is renewed.[67]

5 The different functions of the assembly

BIBLIOGRAPHY

A. Kirchgaessner ed., *Unto the Altar* (Freiburg: Herder; Montreal: Palm Publishers, 1963) pp. 119-37.

LMD 60 (1959), "Les acteurs de la célébration liturgique selon l'Instruction de la Congrégation des Rites"; 61 (1960), "Les fonctions liturgiques d'après la Tradition."

A. G. Martimort and F. Picard, *Liturgie et musique* (Paris: Ed. du Cerf, 1959; *Lex Orandi* 28) pp. 177-201.

Although the assembly is the fraternal and single-minded meeting of a people, and the members are active participants, it calls for a division of functions. Not everyone can be doing everything, and this not simply by a decision of human wisdom for the sake of good order and convenience, but in consequence of the institution by Christ and the nature of the Church. The assembly has a president, the celebrant; between him and the people various other ministers function. This sharing of functions makes of the assembly an organic body, an expression of the mystical Body of Christ (1 Co 12:12-30), and of the liturgy a hierarchical act "each one playing his own role in the divinely-ordained harmony of the entire action."[68]

I THE CELEBRANT

"The priest presides over the assembly in the person of Christ."

---

[67]On not working on days of assembly, see H. Dumaine, "Dimanche" in DACL 4 (1920) col. 943-56. On the prolongation of the feast in all its aspects, see J. Leclerq, "Dévotion privée, piété populaire et liturgie au moyen âge" in *Études de pastorale liturgique* (Paris: Ed. du Cerf, 1944; *Lex Orandi* 1) pp 149-83.—O. Casel, "*La notion de jour de fête*" in LMD 1 (1945) 23-36.—M. H. Vicaire, "Célébration liturgique et joie de la cité" in LMD 22 (1950) 129-45.—M. Righetti, *Storia liturgica* 2 (2nd ed., Milan: Ancora, 1955) pp. 400-408.—K. Young, *The Drama of the Medieval Church* (Oxford, 1933) vol. 2.—R. Donovan, *The Liturgical Drama in Medieval Spain* (Toronto, 1958).—There is a good example of the secular prolongation of the liturgical feast in Ne 8:9-17.

[68]L. Bouyer, *Liturgical Piety* (Notre Dame University Press, 1955) p. 32.—See especially CSL 26 and 28; St Clement of Rome, *Letter to the Corinthians*, 40-41; Engl. tr., *Writings of Apostolic Fathers* (ANF) vol. 1, pp. 35-6.

This formula of the Second Vatican Council[69] sums up three traditional principles.

(1) The liturgical action has a president who directs and leads the entire community at prayer. In antiquity his role extended even to assigning the several functions, choosing the texts to be read or chanted, and giving the signal to begin and end the chants, and so on.[70]

(2) This president is the celebrant, i.e. he prays, performs the sacred actions, and breaks the bread of the Word of God and of the Eucharist for the people. He is not there simply to maintain good order.

(3) He is president and celebrant not by election by the assembly, nor because of his human qualities, but because his ordination has given him the priestly character of bishop or priest. Because of this character he fills the role of Christ (*in persona Christi*). It is through his identification with Christ the head and mediator that he represents the entire assembly and even the entire Church, and interprets their intentions,[71] whence the importance that the liturgy attributes to the prayer of the celebrant.[72] When he consecrates the Eucharist Christ is present in him.[73]

However, it is not enough for the celebrant to have received priestly ordination; he must also, within the unity of the Church, participate in the mission inherited from the apostles. Hence the celebrant is primarily and par excellence the local bishop, and no one can preside at a liturgical service without his order or permission.[74] St Ignatius of Antioch stressed this in his letters.[75] When the bishop is present, he presides, even if he is not the celebrant; his seat is placed in such a way that he is in the center and is seen by the entire assembly.[76]

In the place of the bishop and with his consent, it is a priest who

[69] . . . *A sacerdote, qui coetui in persona Christi praeest* . . . CSL, 33; cf. SRC, the instruction of September 3, 1958, n. 93.

[70] This aspect of the president's duties is well considered in St Augustine's sermons, and later, in the eighth century, in the OR 1, Andrieu OR 2, pp. 67-108.

[71] MD 40, 84, 93.

[72] On the prayer of the celebrant, see above, ch. 3.

[73] CSL 7; MD 19-20.

[74] CSL 26 and 41. The liturgical movement has always insisted upon the right of the bishops concerning the liturgy. G. Lefebvre, *Liturgia* (Saint-André-lez-Bruges, n.d.), 2nd ed., pp. 53-60.

[75] *To the Magnesians* 3-4 and 6, Camelot ed. (SC 10) pp. 96-8; *To the Trallians* 2-3, *ibid.*, pp. 112-13; *To the Romans* 9, *ibid.*, pp. 136-7; *To the Philadelphians* 4, *ibid.*, pp. 142-5; *To the Smyrnians* 8-9, *ibid.*, pp. 162-3.

[76] See above, ch. 4.

presides at the assembly,[77] but he may not perform certain rites reserved to the bishop either by divine or ecclesiastical law.

Sometimes several bishops or priests celebrate together, concelebrate, by sharing efficaciously in truly sacerdotal actions under the presidency of one. Thus, episcopal consecration is conferred by three bishops concelebrating;[78] Mass can be concelebrated in certain cases;[79] and the anointing of the sick is sometimes conferred in the East by several priests at once.[80] The gathering of priests around their bishop for pontifical celebrations, above all on Holy Thursday and at ordinations to the priesthood, is a traditional practice which manifests the unity of the priesthood, of which the source is the bishop.[81]

Some rites can in the absence of priests be presided over and celebrated by a deacon, notably solemn baptism and burial.[82]

The dignity of the celebrant is recalled to the minds of the faithful by the vestments which he wears, by the place he occupies—whether sitting or at the altar—by the ministers who serve him, by the procession which accompanies him, and by the marks of respect accorded him. At his arrival and departure, the faithful should rise, as also when he greets them.

II MINISTERIAL SERVICE IN GENERAL

Among ministers of the liturgy, there are those who are ministers of the word of God, charged with the public readings; others are ministers of the celebrant whom they assist and serve; still others are more directly concerned with the service of the people whom they lead and attend.

Certain of these functions are strictly reserved to those who have received a sacred ordination, even to the extent that no one could fulfil them except those who are of the same or a higher ministerial order. Other functions can be fulfilled by lower clerics or even by unordained men; the latter receive each time a special deputation. In carrying out their various functions clerics exercise a *ministerial service which is proper and direct,* in virtue of their ordination or at least in relation to their clerical state. Laymen, when fulfilling the functions for which they have been deputized, exercise a *direct*

[77]CSL 42.

[78]To be treated in a subsequent volume.

[79]To be treated in a subsequent volume.

[80]Among the Byzantines, Copts and Armenians.

[81]On concelebration, see LMD 35 (1953).

[82]CIC, can. 741, 845, 2; RR, tit. 7, ch. 3, n. 19.

ministerial service, but one which is *delegated;* hence they are not *ministri,* but *ministrantes.*[83]

Women do not receive deputation for any ministerial service properly so-called; based on 1 Co 14:34, this has been the tradition. However, in the past, widows and deaconesses were set apart by the Church, which made them members of something similar to an *ordo* by giving them a sacred blessing. These women exercised an apostolate of charity in the community, and they assisted the hierarchy at certain functions, such as at the baptism of women.[84]

Deacons are ministers par excellence, as their name, διάκονοι, indicates. Principally assistants to the bishop, they likewise serve priests at the liturgical celebration. Especially in the Eastern tradition, they are also charged with guiding the people in their participation by indicating to them the external and internal attitudes they were to assume, and by suggesting to them the prayer intentions during the litanies. The deacons come and go from the celebrant to the people, which occasioned a comparison of them, in the Byzantine traditions, to the angels in Jacob's vision ascending and descending the ladder which reached to heaven.[85] They prepare the gifts for the Eucharist and help in distributing communion; in most of the rites it is their special task to offer the chalice.[86] Finally, deacons were responsible for certain readings in the assembly, though, since the time of Gregory the Great, in the Roman rite their function has been limited chiefly to the reading of the gospel.[87]

III LECTORS

Since the reading of the Word of God occupies an important place

[83]csl 28-9;—cf. src, the instruction of September 3, 1958, n. 93 a and c, 113.

[84]Andrieu or 4, pp. 140-47; J. Daniélou, "Le ministère des femmes dans l'Église ancienne" in lmd 61 (1960) 70-96.

[85]On the diaconate in general: Hippolytus of Rome, *The Apostolic Tradition* 8, Boote ed. and French tr. (lqf 39) pp. 22-5; Dix ed. and English tr., *The Treatise on the Apostolic Tradition* (spck, 1937), vol. 1, pp. 15-18; *The Apostolic Constitutions* 8, 10, Funk ed., 1, pp. 488f, etc.; Nicetus of Remesiana, *Opusc. de psalmodiae bono,* ch. 3, pl 68, col. 376; *De septem ordinibus ecclesiae,* Kalff ed., p. 40; St Isidore, *De eccles. officiis,* bk. 2, ch. 8, pl 83, col. 789; Yves de Chartres, *De excellentia eccl. ordinum,* pl 162, col. 517.—The Oriental tradition has been studied particularly by S. Salaville and G. Nowack, *Le rôle du diacre dans la liturgie orientale* (Athens. The French Institute of Byzantine Studies, 1962).— M. Hayer, "*Le ministère diaconal dans l'Église maronite*" in *Orient syrien* 9 (1964) 291-322.

[86]St Ambrose, *De officiis* 1, 204, pl 16, col. 84; Cf. J. Brinktrine, "Mysterium Fidei" in el 44 (1930) 493-500.

[87]*The Apostolic Constitutions* 2, 57, 7, Funk ed., 1, p. 161; St Gregory the Great, the Synod of 595, *Registrum,* P. Ewald ed., 1, p. 363.

in the liturgical assembly, from the very beginning there were *lectors,* distinct from the celebrant, as had been also the custom in the synagogue. But this office very quickly yielded to a permanent minister ordained by the blessing of the bishop.[88] Lectors in the true sense of the word gradually withdrew from the proclamation of the more revered texts out of respect for the higher hierarchical orders. Hence in the Roman usage the gospel is reserved to the deacon, as we have remarked, or, in his absence, to the celebrant. The epistle is read preferably by a subdeacon. Except for the gospel, the reading of the texts, when there is no cleric present, can be assigned to a layman, who may wear the cleric's garb.[89]

IV MINISTERS TO THE CELEBRANT

In the solemn celebration of the Roman rite, the celebrating bishop is assisted by at least one priest, several deacons, and at least one subdeacon. They accompany him, serve him and aid him in the performance of the rites. Another subdeacon carries the processional cross, the acolytes carry candlesticks with burning candles and help with the preparation of the offerings at the Mass by presenting the wine and water to the subdeacon; a cleric (the thurifer) holds the thurible with burning coals, while others accompany the bishop with the miter, the crozier, the book, the bugia, the pitcher for the washing of the hands, and the gremial veil.

When the celebrant is not a bishop, Roman usage prescribes for his assistance one deacon and one subdeacon (except in the chant of the office), two acolytes and a cleric thurifer; sometimes a cleric or a subdeacon carries the processional cross. When the celebration is not solemn, two acolytes suffice, or even one at a read Mass.[90]

The direction of the ceremonies is entrusted in the East primarily to the deacons; in the West lower clerics perform this function, except at the liturgy of the bishop, where at least one of the masters

[88]In St Justin's description of the liturgy in the *First Apology* 67, there is already mention of ὁ ἀναγινώσκων, as distinct from προεστώς and the deacons in the edition by L. Pautigny, p. 142; this was already a permanent office in Hippolytus, *The Apostolic Tradition* 11: "The reader is appointed by the bishop's handing to him the book. For he does not have hands laid upon him" (Dix ed., p. 21); an ordination properly so-called was practised in Carthage by the time of St Cyprian: *Ep.* 29, Bayart ed. (the Budé collection) 1, pp. 70-1; *Ep.* 38, *ibid.,* pp. 95-6; *Ep.* 39, *ibid.,* pp. 97-100.

[89]*Ritus Servandus . . .* of March 7, 1965, n. 44; cf. SRC, the instruction of September 26, 1964, p. 50.

[90]These last-mentioned services are often entrusted to children; their spiritual formation should be of more concern than their technical training: MD 200. Cf. J. König, "Serving at the Altar" in *Unto the Altar,* A. Kirchgaessner ed. (Freiburg: Herder, 1963) pp. 138-46.

MAXIMIANVS

Vesture
Emperor Justinian and Bishop Maximian
Mosaic in the Church of S Vitale, Ravenna, 537

Photo Alinari

of ceremonies is a priest (though he is not vested in the garb of his rank).[91]

V MINISTERS AT THE SERVICE OF THE PEOPLE

The deacons, as we have noted, also exercise their ministry among the people, less so in the West than in the East. In Western usage this function is limited to a few brief biddings to the people.[92]

The instruction of September 3, 1958, has made official under the title of "commentator" a minister whose office has seemed particularly necessary in our era, but which is in fact an adaptation of the role once performed by the deacon. He should make the service more understandable for the faithful by explaining the rites, by readings and prayers. He directs the participation of the faithful in their responses, prayers and singing. The function of the commentator is filled by a priest (or deacon) or at least a cleric; lacking these, it can be entrusted to laymen, just as the other functions. The commentary should blend harmoniously with the rhythm of the celebration and stress the preeminence of the celebrant.[93] The commentator is not to be confused with the lector.

The early Church had need of *porters* in charge of welcoming and seating the faithful, keeping out those who had no right to participate, and maintaining good order in the assembly, especially at the moment of eucharistic communion. This service was sometimes entrusted to deacons. In Rome clerics received the order of porter for several centuries, but these duties have in the end been transferred to lay ushers. Today they are again endowed with a position of honor through the progress of pastoral liturgy.[94]

VI THE SCHOLA CANTORUM

Liturgical tradition has known and practised from the beginning the singing of psalms by a soloist; the psalms, just as the other readings, were meant to be heard for their own sake. The same minister was entrusted with both the chants and the readings,[95]

---

[91]*Caer. ep.,* bk. 1, ch. 5.

[92]Details are given in the following chapter.

[93]SRC, the instruction of September 3, 1958, n. 96; cf. CSL 35, 3.—A. M. Roguet, "Le commentateur" in LMD 60 (1959) 80-98.

[94]The history of the office of porter will be treated in a subsequent volume.—For the actual functions of this office, see the *Directoire pour la pastorale de la messe à l'usage des diocèses de France,* 2nd ed. (1960) n. 96 and 106.

[95]Such was the case of the lector mentioned by Victor of Vitus in *De persecutione Vandal.* 1, 13, PL 58, col. 197. On the Roman deacons until St. Gregory the Great withdrew them from the readings that needed more musical competence, see the Synod of 595, *loc. cit.*

H

except in the region around Antioch where psalmists were given a blessing distinct from that of the lector.[96]

Of a completely divergent nature and origin is the group of cantors, distinct from the rest of the assembly, to who m was entrusted the chants meant to accompany an action, or those chants too difficult for the people to sing. This group was called in medieval Rome the *schola cantorum*.[97] Its origins are far from clear, although recent historians have discarded numberless legends about it.[98]

Whatever it might have been in the past, the Roman liturgy at present requires for its solemn performance a choir or *schola cantorum*, which fulfils in the conditions prescribed by law a collective ministerial service;[99] hence in the recruitment and formation of its members, both technical competence and spiritual quality are to be sought.[100] Normally the schola stands near the altar, but in such a manner as not to distract the people.[101]

In the years of liturgical decadence, the cantors and schola tended to encroach upon the role of the people; the hierarchy has often had to warn against abuses of this kind.[102]

---

[96]The psalmists (ψάλτοι, ψαλτῳδοί) or cantors (ᾠδοί) both appear in the *Apostolic Constitutions* 2, 28, 5; 3, 11, 1 and 3; 6, 17, 2 etc.; we also find them mentioned in the pseudo-council of Laodicea, canons 15, 23, 24. The tradition is maintained in the two Antiochian rites; the Western Syriac pontifical has a formula for the blessing of the psalmists which today is confused with that for tonsure. The Maronites now (since the Synod of Lebanon in 1736) clearly distinguish the order of cantors as the first minor order. However, among the Byzantines the traces of this "order" seem to be rather precarious, as, for example, in the Euchology of Barberini 390; J. Morin, *Commentarius de sacris ecclesiae ordinationibus*, 2nd ed. (Amsterdam, 1965) pp. 85-6; A. Michel, "Ordre" in DTC 11, col. 1393.—In the West, despite the *Statuta ecclesiae antiqua* and the influence which they have had upon authors and liturgical books, psalmists have never come into existence; B. Botte, "Le rituel d'ordination des *Statuta ecclesiae antiqua*" in RTAM 11 (1939) 229, 237-40; cf., also, Andrieu OR 3, 524.

[97]Amalaire, *Liber Officialis*, bk. 3, ch. 3, J. M. Hanssens ed., 2, pp. 265-9, speaks of the *chorus cantorum*.

[98]On the Roman *schola cantorum*, see M. Andrieu, "Les ordres mineurs dans l'ancien rit romain" in RevSR 5 (1925) 233-9; E. Josi, "Lectores, schola cantorum, clerici" in EL 44 (1930) 282-90.

[99]SRC, the instruction of September 3, 1958, n. 93 and 99; the instruction of March 5, 1967, n. 19-22; cf. CSL 29.

[100]SRC, the instruction of September 3, 1958, n. 98c and 100-101; the instruction of March 5, 1967, n. 24.

[101]Cf. *ibid.*, n. 23.

[102]Pius XI, *Divini Cultus* 9, December 20, 1928; MD 187; CSR 114; SRC, the instruction of September 3, 1958, n. 25; the instruction of March 5, 1967, n. 7, 9, 15, etc.

VII THE ORGANIST AND MUSICIANS

Liturgical celebration allows for musical instruments in certain cases and under specified conditions.[103] Musicians are at the service of the liturgy in which they participate in a direct manner, although this function cannot be classified as a true ministerial service. They must obey certain laws, hence they must know what the law is, and they must engage in the spiritual effort which their participation presupposes.[104]

The role of the organist is particularly delicate and important; he accompanies the chants, he often plays solo and must contribute to the unity and the harmonious movement of the celebration, above all with his improvisations. Therefore he needs to be competent both in the liturgy and in music.[105]

6 Vestments and liturgical insignia

BIBLIOGRAPHY

M. Andrieu, *Ordo Romanus*, especially vol. 2, pp. 234-5, 310-22; vol. 4, pp. 129-84.

P. Batiffol, "Le costume liturgique romain" in *Études de liturgie et d'archéologie chrétienne* (Gabalda and Picard, 1919) pp. 30-83.

J. Braun, *Die liturgische Gewandung im Occident und Orient* (Freiburg: Herder, 1907).

L. Duchesne, *Origines du culte chrétien . . .* , 5th ed. (E. de Boccard, 1920) pp. 399-419. Engl.tr., *Christian Worship—its Origin and Evolution* (London: SPCK, 1931) pp. 379-98.

R. Lesage, *Vestments and Church Furniture* (London: Burns and Oates, 1960; *Faith and Fact* 113).

M. Righetti, *Manuale di Storia Liturgical* 1, 3rd ed. (Milan: Ancora, 1964) pp. 584-642.

P. Salmon, *Étude sur les insignes du pontife dans le rit romain* (Rome: Officium Libri Catholici, 1955).

During the first centuries the celebration of the liturgy did not require clothing distinct from that worn in ordinary life, nor did it assign distinctive insignia to the different hierarchical orders or to diverse functions. It was uniquely the position or the place (τόπος) which they occupied in the assembly,[106] and of course the part that

[103]SRC, the instruction of March 5, 1967, n. 62-7.

[104]*ibid.*, n. 67.

[105]*ibid.*, n. 64-5; cf. CSL 120; A. Deprez, "La musique d'orgue et les organistes" in SL (1912) 188-207; J. Kreps, *Le rôle unificateur de l'organiste liturgique* (Louvain: Mont César, 1921).

[106]St Clement of Rome, *Epistle to the Corinthians* 40, 5; H. Hemmer ed. (Picard, 1926) p. 84; Engl. tr., *The Apostolic Fathers* (ANF 1) pp. 35-6.—In the era of the *Ordines Romani,* the place occupied in the assembly is so characteristic of the order received that mention is made in the account of the ordination ritual of the accession of the newly-ordained to the place which he should thereafter

they took in the celebration, which distinguished the members of the hierarchy from the faithful and the ranks of the hierarchy from each other.

However, some prescriptions concerning deportment were given to the faithful, and several of these principles have been preserved even up to our time.

I THE DEPORTMENT OF THE FAITHFUL IN THE ASSEMBLY

Article 1262 of the code of canon law prescribes the following:

§1 It is desirable that, according to the ancient discipline, men and women should be separated in the churches into two groups.

§2 Men, when they are present at the sacred services, both in the church building or outside, must leave their heads uncovered, unless this is contrary to local customs or they are prevented from doing so by particular circumstances; women must cover their heads and be modestly attired, above all when they approach the sacred table.[107]

The separation of men and women in the assembly was required by the *Apostolic Tradition,* which explains the prescription in relation to the kiss of peace.[108] Though the latter custom eventually fell into disuse almost everywhere, the separation of men and women is still maintained in some places.

The obligation for men to leave their heads uncovered during the sacred services, and for women to keep their heads covered, was stated by St Paul in his letter to the Corinthians as a general custom of the Christian assemblies and as an expression of the harmonious ordering which characterizes the Church (1 Co 11:5-10).[109]

But there was one instance where the faithful were clothed with a distinctive liturgical dress, and that was at the time of their Christian initiation. After their baptism they were invested in a white robe, the style of which was left to custom. The neophyte kept it on for the confirmation and the Mass which followed immediately after baptism. In the early Church, this garment was not laid aside until the Saturday after Easter, or a week after baptism.[110]

---

occupy: *dum vero consecratus fuerit (diaconus), dat osculum episcopo et sacerdotibus et stat ad dexteram episcoporum . . . et stat (presbyter) in ordine presbyterii . . . et tunc iubet eum (episcopum) domnus apostolicus super omnes episcopos sedere* (OR 34, n. 10, 12, 42).

[107]See also the prescriptions of the Congregation of the Council, January 12, 1930, AAS 22 (1930) 26.

[108]In the edition of B. Botte (LQF 39) n. 18, pp. 40-41.

[109]J. Huby, *Saint Paul, Première épître aux Corinthiens* (Paris: Beauchesne, 1946; *Verbum Salutis* 13) pp. 239-54.

[110]To be treated in a subsequent volume.

II VESTMENTS AND INSIGNIA IN THE PRESENT DISCIPLINE OF THE ROMAN RITE

Pending the reforms considered by the Council,[111] the prescriptions in force concerning liturgical vestments and insignia in the Roman rite are found in the *Caeremoniale Episcoporum*, the *Codex Rubricarum* of 1960 and in several places in the pontifical and ritual.[112]

1 *The choir dress and the vestments of minor ministers*

All ministers, even the laity who fulfil a properly liturgical function, and all who approach the altar must in principle be clothed in a long robe reaching to the heels (*vestis talaris*), either the cassock or the religious habit. Over the cassock, a shorter white linen garment, called the surplice (*superpelliceum*) is worn, or, in accordance with the usage of certain churches, an alb similar to that of the sacred ministers. The cantors traditionally are attired in a cape, which can be worn also by certain ministers of lower rank than a bishop.

Both secular and regular clerics who participate in a liturgical action without carrying out any particular function wear the "choir dress," a garment worn over the longer robes and generally[113] reserved to times of prayer: the surplice for the cleric, the cowl for the monk, the cape for canons regular, the rochet and the mozetta, the small mantle or cape for prelates and secular canons, etc.[114]

But in certain circumstances an ancient usage has reappeared in that each member of the hierarchy participates in a celebration with the distinctive vestments of his own rank. Such would be the case with cardinals at the solemn services presided over by the pope; canons at solemn services when the bishop presides; or the clergy taking part in the Corpus Christi procession, etc. Over the surplice or rochet they would wear the amice and then the tunic, the dalmatic, the chasuble or the cape.[115]

2 *The vestments of sacred ministers and the celebrant*

The sacred ministers—deacon and subdeacon[116]—as well as the celebrant at solemn liturgical actions, with the exception of the office, wear the amice, the alb and the cord over the cassock or

---

[111]CSL 128.—Since then, SRC, the instruction of May 4, 1967, n. 25-27.

[112]To these should be added OHS, and especially the papal ceremonial.

[113]We say "generally", because the choir dress was often worn outside the times for prayer, and even, according to an old custom, all the time by canons regular and bishops.

[114]On all these usages, see A. Gréa, *La sainte liturgie* (Paris: Bonne Presse, 1909) pp. 79-119.

[115]*Caer. Ep.*, bk. 1, ch. 15, n. 6; ch. 8, n. 4, etc.

[116]The subdeacon of the Mass as well as the one who carries the cross.

religious habit. The *amice* is like a cowl, which monks and certain regulars have maintained in its original form by wearing it about the neck. The *alb* is a long, graceful robe of white linen, with sleeves; the *cord* or *cincture* is used to gather the alb at the waist. The alb is the only vestment which has a biblical symbolism, as we shall see. It is deplorable that embroidery, lace and frills have obscured its true nature.

The *maniple,* a strip of silk draped over the left forearm, was, until 1967, worn at Mass by the subdeacon, deacon and celebrant; this usage is now considered optional.

The subdeacon is attired for most liturgical actions[117] with the *tunicle* (sometimes called a dalmatic), a silken vestment reaching to the knees and fitted with wide sleeves.

The deacon wears, slung over the left shoulder and reaching to the right side of the waist, a long silk sash called the *stole*; over this he wears the *dalmatic,* a wider and more ornamented vestment than the subdeacon's tunicle, though of the same shape and worn on the same occasions.

Priest-celebrants likewise wear a *stole,* but they put it around the back of the neck and cross it on the breast.[118] For Mass they also put on the *chasuble* (*planeta*), a broad and sleeveless vestment, which, according to the ceremonial, folds down over the arms and reaches at least to the knees. In present practice, for other liturgical services the celebrant wears, instead of the chasuble, the *cope* (*pluviale*), a silk vestment open at the front and with a more or less modified cowl.

3 *The liturgical vestments and insignia of the bishop*

The bishop always wears a *ring*; when he celebrates solemnly he wears a more precious one. When he is completely vested, he wears over the alb and hung from the neck by a cord a metal cross called the *pectoral cross*; he covers his head with the *miter,*[119] and, within the limits determined by legislation, he carries the *crozier* or *staff*. The cope which he wears is fastened by a precious clasp, called *formal* or *pectoral*.

[117]Not all of them, since in certain circumstances he wears only the alb.

[118]For some less solemn liturgical actions, when the priest does not wear the alb he puts on the stole over the surplice; in this case he lets the two ends of the stole hang loosely without crossing them.—The stole is not allowed to be used by an ordinary priest when presiding over the divine office.

[119]There are three types of miters in use according to the regulations prescribed in the *Caer. Ep.*: the precious miter, made of white silk, with ornamentation in embroidery and even with gems;—the gold-covered or gold-thread miter;—the simple miter made of white linen and without any decoration.

When the bishop celebrates a solemn Mass, besides the vestments which are used by all priests he wears stockings and sandals, a tunic and dalmatic, both of light silk, and gloves, all of the color required for the Mass of the day.

Archbishops and certain bishops have the privilege of wearing over the chasuble, on specific days and within the boundaries of their own jurisdiction, the *pallium*, presented to them by the pope. It is a narrow white woolen band marked with black crosses; it rests on the shoulders and is fixed with pins in such a way that it circles the neck, with a pendant in front and another in back.[120]

Even if they are not bishops, cardinals celebrate Mass in the same manner as bishops; they are attired in the same vestments and have the right to use the same insignia. The use of "pontificals" formerly granted to abbots and other prelates will henceforth be more strictly reserved to bishops or to those who exercise a certain jurisdiction.[121]

III HISTORICAL DEVELOPMENT

The origins of liturgical vestments and insignia are very divergent. When writing a history of them, besides recourse to the usual documents, notably the *Ordines Romani,* the pontificals and liturgical tracts dating from the Middle Ages, great importance must be attached to works of art: mosaics, frescoes, ivories, manuscript miniatures, and other works and artifacts preserved in museums and private collections.

The early practice of not distinguishing members of the hierarchy by garb or insignia was apparently still in vogue at Rome in 428, according to the witness of Pope St Celestine I.[122] But in the East, by the fifth century the deacon was already fitted out with the *orarion,* more or less resembling the modern stole.[123] The garb of celebrants and ministers was like that worn by Roman citizens of good means in ordinary civil life, according to the laws enacted in Rome in 382 and 397 requiring a robe of white linen, the *tunica,* and

---

[120]Today the pallium is so sewn that there is no chance of its falling out of place. On the use of the pallium, see *Caer. Ep.,* bk. 1, ch. 16; PR, part 1, *De Pallio.*

[121]CSL 130; apostolic letter, *Pontificalia insignia,* June 21, 1968.

[122]St Celestine I, *Epistola ad episcopos per Viennensem et Narbonensem Provincias;* Jaffe-Wattenbach, *Regesta* . . . , n. 369; PL 50, col. 431; see other witnesses, such as St Augustine, in P. Batiffol, *op. cit.,* pp. 30-34.

[123]The pseudo-council of Laodicea, can. 22-23, prohibited the ὡράριον to be used by lower clerics: Bruns 1, 76.—The term *orarion* is known in the West with a number of meanings: Andrieu OR 2; pp. 235, 312; OR 4, pp. 134-7, 148; P. Batiffol, *op. cit.,* pp. 79-83.

an undergarment, the *paenula* or *byrrhus*;[124] military attire and work clothes were not mentioned. However, before long the clergy adopted clothing which was different from that worn in day-to-day life, though the difference was only with regard to the purpose of the garment and the quality of the fabric.[125] These clothes evolved into, in church nomenclature, the *linea,* our present alb, and the *planeta,* our present chasuble.[126] In addition to these, the bishop and the Roman deacons were attired in the *dalmatica,* a shorter robe though more dear and ornate, worn over the *linea* and under the *planeta.* It was an honorific dress doubtless corresponding to the senators' *colobus*; this is why, among other reasons, the popes very reluctantly conferred the privilege of wearing it upon other deacons.[127] The *campagi,* or ornate buskins, and the *pallium* were courtly paraphernalia bestowed upon the popes by emperors.[128] A further insigne adopted was the *mappula,* which the consuls used to wave to signal the opening of the public games.[129] All this is exactly the apparel which the *Ordo Romanus* 1, toward the beginning of the eighth century, describes, in addition to the *anagolaium* or hood, and the *cingulum,*[130] both of which were probably of monastic derivation.[131]

---

[124]P. Batiffol, *op. cit.,* pp. 35-47; L. Duchesne, *op. cit.,* pp. 399-402; M. Righetti, *op. cit.,* pp. 587-90.

[125]Already perhaps in the time of Origen, *Homilies on Leviticus* 4, 6, PG 12, col. 441; other texts are cited by M. Righetti, *op. cit.,* pp. 585-6; P. Salmon, pp, 34-5; cf. OR 1, 29: *mutent vestimenta sua: ibid.,* 33: *mutat vestimenta solemnia.*

[126]The *planeta* was at first an outdoor garment of dark color, a "raincoat", and was worn by all ministers at the time of OR 1, but they removed it during the services; it was the origin of the "folded chasuble", which has been in use up to our time. Nevertheless the pope, other bishops and priests wore a *planeta* which they were given at ordination as a mark of their dignity: OR 34, n. 11 and 37; it was not only an outdoor garment, but an honorific vestment.

[127]P. Batiffol, *op. cit.,* pp. 40-42; L. Duchesne, *op. cit.,* pp. 402-03; Andrieu OR 4, pp. 132-4; P. Salmon, *op. cit.,* p. 24.

[128]On the *campagi*: L. Duchesne, *op. cit.,* p. 415; P. Salmon, *op. cit.,* pp. 21-3.— On the *pallium*: P. Batiffol, *op. cit.,* 57-71; L. Duchesne, *op. cit.,* 404-10; P. Salmon, *op. cit.,* pp. 21-23, 27, 36.

[129]The *mappula* is the origin of the *maniple.* See OR 1, n. 37-8; P. Batiffol, *op. cit.,* p. 55.—On the *mappula* of the Roman consuls, there is a very rich documentation provided in the consular diptychs, a list of which and some reproductions will be found in DACL 4, col. 1094-1145 (H. Leclerq).—Another ancestor of the maniple was the *pallea linostima* (LP 1, 225, cf. *ibid.,* pp. 171 and 189).

[130]OR 1, n. 34; Andrieu OR 2, p. 78.—In fact, the OR 1, n. 34 notes also a *linea dalmatica,* distinct from both the *linea* and the *maior dalmatica.*—In German countries the *anagolaium* was called the *humerale* and later the *amictus.*

[131]P. Batiffol, *op. cit.,* pp. 51-3; P. Salmon, *op. cit.,* p. 24.

The stole, at first unknown in Rome, was the sole distinctive mark of the deacon in Spain and Gaul, as was the practice in the East; priests also adopted the stole, but wore it in a different way.[132] The consolidation of the Roman liturgy with the Gallican during the Carolingian age saw the introduction of the stole into Roman liturgical raiment.[133] The Franco-germanic liturgy, which had a great influence upon the later Roman liturgy chiefly through the use of the pontifical, brought about a modification in terminology and style with the introduction of the cope (*cappa*), which in many ceremonies supplanted the chasuble.[134]

The crozier and the ring, already in use in Spain during the seventh century, were imported into Gaul and afterwards Germany, whence they were incorporated into the Roman books, although the crozier never was adopted in the papal liturgy.[135] The miter followed a reversed order in its introduction; under the name of *phrygium*, it first appeared in the non-liturgical apparel of the popes in the ninth or tenth centuries.[136] It was introduced about the end of the twelfth century into the rite for the consecration of bishops found in the Roman pontifical.[137] Later it took on different forms; rubrics in the fifteenth century listed the three types now in use. The stockings, the gloves, the double tunicle and a garment to put on underneath the alb (the *camicia*, the ancestor of the rochet), all seem to be of Frankish origin.[138]

From the twelfth century on, liturgical apparel changed very little. Its subsequent evolution was merely decorative: vestments

---

[132]L. Duchesne, *op. cit.*, pp. 411-12; Andrieu OR 4, pp. 129-31.

[133]OR 6, n. 11; OR 8, n. 1; cf. Andrieu OR 2, pp. 235, 312; 4, pp. 130-39.—Cf. L. Duchesne, *op. cit.*, pp. 413-15.

[134]Formerly, the term *casula* was a synonym of *cappa*: then later *casula* became synonymous with *planeta*. See Andrieu OR 4, pp. 149-53; also, OR 10, n. 2-8. Cf. also M. Righetti, *op. cit.*, pp. 607-11; P. Salmon, *op. cit.*, pp. 45-6.

[135]On the ring: P. Salmon, *op. cit.*, pp. 24, 26, 39, 41;—on the crozier; *ibid.*, pp. 24, 36-9, 43-5, 71; P. Salmon, "Aux origines de la crosse des évêques" in *Mélanges en l'honneur de Mgr Michel Andrieu* (Strasbourg: Palais universitaire, 1956) pp. 373-83.

[136]Andrieu OR 4, pp. 169-84; P. Salmon, *op. cit.*, pp. 27-8, 40-46, 72.

[137]The pontifical of Appamée, Andrieu PR 1, pp. 151-2.

[138]On the stockings, see Andrieu OR 2, pp. 311-12;—the double tunicle was perhaps already in existence in OR 1, n. 34; in any case, it was surely existing by the time of OR 8, n. 1 and 4.—The *camicia*, in OR 8; cf. the commentary by Andrieu, *op. cit.*, pp. 312-14.—The gloves: M. Righetti, *op. cit.*, pp. 611-12; P. Salmon, *op. cit.*, pp. 36, 39, 68, 72.—The pectoral cross appeared for the first time in the pontifical by Durandus: *ibid.*, pp. 68-72.—We might point out here the *rationale*, an ornament introduced by bishops in the Middle Ages, but not kept in use: *ibid.*, pp. 41, 44-5.

became "ornaments," *paramenta*; they were heavily laden with
embroidery, gold thread, precious gems, and even with legendary
and allegorical designs; they were stiffened and cut down so much
as to be hardly recognizable.[139] In our time, reversal has fortunately
taken place, motivated not by love of the archaic but by concern
for liturgical beauty, and with a view to rediscovering the real
meaning of the vestments.[140]

VI THE SIGNIFICANCE AND BLESSING OF LITURGICAL
VESTMENTS

Although the history of liturgical vestments evinces their rather
incidental nature, as to their origin, number and style, and often
their late introduction, and although certain simplifications are
desirable today, the Church assigns them a great significance. This
is shown by the detailed legislation concerning them (can. 1296-
1306), and by the general requirement that they be blessed; the
texts of these blessings are centuries old, and the vestments themselves are used as symbols during ordination rites to illustrate the
order being conferred.

1 *The deeper meaning of liturgical vestments*

The importance of liturgical vestments has been recognized by
Protestants—who cannot be accused of wanting to justify the
usages of the medieval Church—even if they reject a hierarchy of
orders. In its fullness, the liturgical vestment "submerges" the
individuality of the person wearing it, thereby manifesting in another
way his dignity and function. "It is only natural that the man who
officiates at the worship of the assembly should be attired in a way
which corresponds to the task assigned him, and visibly express
what he is doing; . . . the person who executes the function of
worship acts not as a private individual but as a minister of the
Church."[141] Indeed, the Catholic faith teaches us to discern in the
person of the bishop, the priest and the deacon an invisible and
inalienable likeness to Christ; and it is only logical that in the

---

[139]See M. Righetti, *op. cit.*, pp. 596-605.

[140]After a long period of caution, the SRC has permitted local ordinaries to put
this reform into effect at their own discretion: declaration of August 20, 1957,
AAS 49 (1957) 762. Otherwise, from now on the episcopal conferences have
complete competence "*quoad materiam et formam sacrae supellectilis et indu-
mentorum*" (CSL 128).

[141]R. Paquier, *Traité de liturgique* (Neuchâtel: Delachaux et Niestlé, 1954)
p. 122; cf. pp. 120-29.—From the Catholic viewpoint, although he does not
write within the perspective of liturgical vesture: E. Peterson, *Pour une théologie
du vêtement* (Lyons: L'abeille, 1943).

performance of their ministry—in the deepest sense of the term: *in persona Christi*—they don a garment which reminds others as well as themselves who they are and what they should appear to them. The long white robe called the alb first of all signifies a break with the bustle of ordinary life, but above all it reminds us of the royal and sacerdotal vestment of the heavenly liturgy, where our Lord reigns with the angels and the elect.

2 *Medieval allegorizations*

The Middle Ages saw a multiplication of allegorical literature on liturgical vestments and insignia.[142] Reference was often made to supposed relationships with the Levitical liturgy. Such explanations were very artificial, although even St Paul did not refrain from such comparisons.[143] It is not therefore surprising that the liturgy has retained specific elements of these in three instances, namely in the words pronounced by the bishop while investing the newly ordained,[144] in the prayers said by the bishop and priest preparing for Mass,[145] and in the blessings of vestments in the pontifical.

3 *The blessing of liturgical vestments and insignia*

It is not certain that the false decretals of Stephen I[146] prove that the custom of blessing liturgical vestments dates from the second half of the ninth century. The first formulas appeared in the tenth century, in the ritual for the dedication of churches (where before that there could be found blessings for various objects used at worship) and in the ritual for ordinations.[147] There has not been much modification in the formularies up to our time; from the Romano-germanic pontifical they passed into the Roman pontifical of the twelfth century,[148] or were adopted by Durandus of Mende.[149] The entire collection is found almost complete, though abridged,

[142]P. Salmon, *op. cit.,* pp. 9, 15, 19.

[143]When he described the combat equipment of the Christian in Ep 5:11-17.

[144]To be treated in a subsequent volume.

[145]These two types of prayers are found in the MR after the *Praeparatio ad Missam* (where there is also given a third form, *quando pontifex celebrat private,* but which borrows everything from the other two formulas).

[146]Included in the decree of Gratian, *De consecr.,* dist. 1, ch. 42; Friedberg, col. 1305.

[147]They are found in the ritual for dedications in PRG 40, 79-82, vol. 1, pp. 152-4, or in the *Pontificale Lanaletense,* Doble ed. (HBS 74) p. 15, or in Rheims 340; in the ritual for ordinations in the pontifical called that of Egbert, W. Greenwell ed. (*Surtees Society* 27, 1853) pp. 16-17.

[148]Andrieu PR 1, p. 201; cf. PR 2, pp. 451-2.

[149]Andrieu PR 3, pp. 520-21.

in the present Roman pontifical and in the ritual.[150] Moreover, in the *ordo* for the consecration of a bishop, we find the formulas for the blessing of the crozier, the ring, the miter and the gloves.[151]

V THE LITURGICAL COLORS

Although the Eastern rites do not attach much importance to the colors of liturgical vestments, the Roman rite distinguishes five colors: white, red, green, violet and black. However, indications of the number of colors and the principles governing their use in different places are rather vague. It was probably not until the twelfth century that much attention was paid to colors;[152] but we can say that it was normal in outdoor processions to wear vestments with dark colors. Only white was inspired by biblical symbolism: it is the color of Christ's transfigured garments, of the angelic apparitions, and of the redeemed in the Apocalypse.[153] Still, the variety of colors, especially as marking the different seasons of the liturgical year, has definite pastoral advantages.[154] In mission countries where the local culture attaches to colors meanings incompatible with liturgical practice, the episcopal conferences have the right to modify them to suit the needs of the people.[155]

[150]PR, part 2; RR, tit. 9, ch. 1-2.

[151]To be treated in a subsequent volume.

[152]See M. Righetti, *op. cit.*, pp. 613-15, and especially, J. Braun, *op. cit.*, pp. 728-60.

[153]E. B. Allo, *L'Apocalypse*, 2nd ed. (Paris: Gabalda: 1921; *Études bibliques*) pp. 48-50.

[154]Cf. R. Paquier, *op. cit.*, pp. 127-9.

[155]NRC, n. 117. SRC, the instruction of May 4, 1967, n. 23.

CHAPTER SIX

The Dialogue between God and his People

Both present-day liturgical formularies and those of the past show a very great variety of style and literary genre. For this reason most commentators have tried to enumerate the various forms, to discover their origins, and to sift and classify the laws governing their composition. This is by no means an unimportant work: it has brought out the richness of liturgical prayer, it has often led to a more objective interpretation of the texts, and has drawn attention to the importance of certain forms, such as the acclamation, the litany, or the biddings.

However, to limit oneself to this aspect alone would be to run the risk of forgetting that these formularies were intended to be the concrete and living prayer of the Church, and that the liturgy, in its concrete expression, is a dialogue between God and his people. In his analysis of the divine office, Dom Gréa describes it as the uninterrupted colloquy between the Bridegroom and the Bride: "In her song of praise, the Bride, that is the Church, speaks to her Beloved and delights to tell of all his loveliness; in the readings, the Beloved speaks in turn to her and gladdens her with the sound of his voice; finally, in the prayers, the Bride, who has found the Bridegroom, . . . who has recognized his presence and heard his voice, speaks to him in her turn, confiding to him her desires, her sorrows and joys, her needs and gratitude."[1]

Dom Gréa's intuition has been confirmed by the Constitution *De sacra Liturgia* of the Second Vatican Council; it reiterates his thoughts almost word for word and on several occasions emphasizes the idea: "In the liturgy God speaks to his people and Christ is still proclaiming his gospel. And the people reply to God by both song and prayer."[2]

Some historians of the liturgy thought they could make out the same sequence of parts as the basic pattern for every liturgical celebration, a sequence which is "neither arbitrary nor random, but corresponds to the profound nature of the economy of salvation." In the first place, they say, we hear the *Word of God* in the readings from Scripture. The word in turn comes down and "awakens in the

[1]A. Gréa, *La sainte liturgie* (Paris: Bonne Presse, 1909) p. 2.
[2]CSL 33; cf. 7, 84.

people's hearts an echo which is expressed in song." Then finally there is the *prayer of the assembly*, which is fittingly divided into two stages: first, the prayer of the people themselves; then, in the name of the people, the prayer of the celebrant.

This structure cannot be applied to each and every liturgical action. Even in the primitive Church it is not verified as precisely as has been supposed, especially with regard to "the echo of song"; but it can be admitted that it is a "true expression of the life of the Church."[3]

1 The Word of God in the assembly

The liturgical assembly, just as the "Qahal Yahweh" of the Old Testament, is called together in the first place to hear God speaking to it: "If only you would listen to him today, 'Do not harden your hearts as at Meribah . . .' " (Ps 95:7-8). As was the case in the worship of the synagogue, one of the most essential characteristics of Christian worship is that in it there is no important liturgical action in which the Word of God is not proclaimed, and above all by the reading of Sacred Scripture. It is this that explains the insistence with which the liturgy Constitution of the Second Vatican Council underlines it.[4]

I THE READING OF THE BIBLE IN THE LITURGY

BIBLIOGRAPHY

A. Baumstark, *Liturgie comparée*, 3rd ed. (Chevetogne, 1953) pp. 123-43; Engl. tr., *Comparative Liturgy* (Westminster, Maryland: Newman Press; London: Mowbray, 1958).

A. Bea, "The Pastoral Value of the Word of God in the Sacred Liturgy" in *The Assisi Papers* (Collegeville, Minnesota: Liturgical Press, 1957) pp. 74-90.

H. Chirat, *L'assemblée chrétienne à l'âge apostolique* (Paris: Ed. du Cerf, 1949; *Lex Orandi* 10) pp. 87-95.

I. Herwegen, "L'Écriture sainte dans la liturgie in LMD 5 (1946) 7-20.

P. Jounel, "The Bible in the Liturgy" in *The Liturgy and the Word of God*, papers of the 3rd National Congress of the C.P.L., Strasbourg (Collegeville, Minnesota: Liturgical Press, 1959) pp. 1-20.

[3]J. A. Jungmann, *The Liturgy of the Word* (London: Burns and Oates, 1966) p. 35. The proof in favor of this schema as given in chap. 4 does not wholly convince; but see in the same line, H. Chirat, "Les éléments fondamentaux de la célébration du culte" in LMD 20 (1949) 13-32; J. Rabau, *La messe, notes doctrinales* (Tournai: Centre diocésain de documentation, 1959) pp. 46-64. This last author, who gives the first part of the Mass the title, "The dialogue between God and his people," will surely pardon us for using this title as the heading for the present chapter.—Cf. also, A. Baumstark, *Liturgie comparée,* 3rd ed. (Chevetogne, 1953) pp. 49-52; Engl. tr., *Comparative Liturgy* (Westminster, Maryland: Newman Press, 1958).

[4]CSL 6, 7, 24, 33, 35, 51, 56, 78, 90, 106.

1 *The important place of biblical readings in the liturgy*

The Christian liturgy has in fact inherited from the synagogue the practice of reading at each prayer gathering some passages from the inspired books (Lk 4:16-21; Ac 13:27), but it has given this reading a new meaning: the risen Christ, on the road to Emmaus, "explained to them the passages throughout the scriptures that were about himself," before making himself known in the breaking of bread (Lk 24:27, 31). Similarly he explained to the apostles that everything written about him in the law of Moses, the prophets, and the psalms must be fulfilled (Lk 24:44). This is why the Church has never ceased to make use of the texts of the Old Testament, defending it against those who would make little of it. But to these texts she joins "the teaching of the apostles," to which the first Christians "remained faithful" (Ac 2:42), and above all the very words of Jesus in the gospel.

It seems that these readings were already a traditional and essential part of the Sunday assembly at the time of St Justin: "The memoirs of the apostles and the writings of the prophets, he says, are read in so far as time permits."[5] Perhaps they became the daily practice in the third century, at least in certain places,[6] and the liturgical development which took place in the fourth century gave them an even more important place, which they have retained up to the present day.

It is thus that in some churches the Mass has three or four and up to six readings;[7] the "greater vespers" or vigils very frequently take on the form of the paschal vigil as a prolonged meditation of the Scriptures;[8] the administration of the sacraments is quite often enshrined in a Bible service.[9]

The Roman rite, on the other hand, up to 1963 only offered a very

---

[5]*First Apology* 67, L. Pautigny ed. (*Textes et documents*) pp. 142-3; Engl. tr., ANF 2, pp. 65-6.

[6]Hippolytus, *The Apostolic Tradition,* c. 39 and 41, B. Botte ed. (LQF 39) pp. 86-9, would seem to suggest so.

[7]In the West, the Milanese liturgy has three readings. In the East, the Armenian rite has three (prophet, apostle, and gospel); the Nestorian rite has four (law, prophets, apostles, and gospel) as has also the Coptic rite (*paulos, catholica, praxis,* and gospel); and finally the Syrian rite has six (law, wisdom, prophets, acts, apostle, and gospel). But the Catholics have an annoying tendency to reduce their number; A. Raes, *Introductio in liturgiam orientalem* (Rome: Istituto orientale, 1947) pp. 76-9.

[8]This is the case with the Byzantine μεγάλοι ἑσπερινοί (Christmas, Epiphany, Annunciation, etc.) and with the Milanese vespers of Christmas Eve, the vigil of the Epiphany, and that of Pentecost.

[9]P. Jounel, *op. cit.,* pp. 11-12.

impoverished reduction of this traditional practice. The paschal
vigil has no more than four Old Testament readings, where formerly
there were ten and even twelve.[10] The Mass, with the exception of
some privileged ferias, includes only two readings: an extract from
the Gospels, preceded by another passage from the New or Old
Testament. It was only on the Ember Saturdays that there was to be
found a vigil with five readings preceding the usual two readings of
the Mass: since 1960, there has been available an abridged formulary,
which may be used at non-conventual Masses.[11] Readings rarely
occur in the Roman ritual; they are found particularly in the rite for
visiting the sick and in the *Ordo commendationis*.[12] It is true however
that the reading of Holy Scripture is given more place in the Roman
office than in the office of the Eastern rites: over and above the
lessons of matins, it is taken up again under the form of "little
chapters" or short lessons at other hours of the day.[13]

The Second Vatican Council expressed the wish that, as regards
both the Mass and the office, the treasures of Sacred Scripture be
opened more generously, to provide a plentiful and varied choice of
biblical passages.[14] This wish has already been partially fulfilled by
the use of new weekday lectionaries, which should result in having
the entire New Testament and long extracts of the Old read within
a cycle of one or several years.

2 *The significance of biblical readings in the liturgy*

The readings are intended to be listened to—"*sedentes auscultant*,"
as the rubric of the *Ordo hebdomadae sanctae* puts it—and then to be
meditated on in prayer. Read by a lector or higher minister, these
texts have for the attentive faithful the value of a word spoken here
and now, today, by the prophet or apostle, or by the Lord himself.
This is brought out by the prayers, acclamations, or chants which,
in the various Eastern rites, accompany the readings.[15] It is shown
with even more solemnity in the ceremony which surrounds the
proclamation of the gospel, as well as by the reverence with which
the gospel-book itself is kept and carried in procession.[16] The

[10]To be treated in a subsequent volume.
[11]To be treated in a subsequent volume.
[12]To be treated in a subsequent volume.
[13]To be treated in a subsequent volume.
[14]CSL 35, 1; 51; 78; 92a.
[15]See, for example, *Petit paroissien des liturgies orientales* (Harissa: Impr. Saint-Paul, 1941) pp. 99, 191-5, 297-302, 365-7, 451-9.
[16]P. Jounel, *op. cit.*, p. 43-6.

apostle is present, the Lord is present;[17] the reading brings it about that *today* a saving event takes place.[18]

3 Laws governing biblical readings in the liturgy

BIBLIOGRAPHY

G. Kunze, *Die gottesdienstliche Schriftlesung* 1 (Göttingen: Vandenhoeck & Ruprecht, 1947).
P. Oppenheim, *Tractatus de textibus liturgicis* (Rome: Officium libri catholici, 1945) pp. 115-200.

Because all the books of the Bible can be read, in their entirety, in public assembly, liturgical usage is the clearest indication of the biblical canon of each local church. Hence the practice of *continuous reading* (*lectio continua*), used by the synagogue and adopted by the early liturgies. This consisted in taking up the reading of a biblical book at each assembly at the point at which it had been interrupted the previous time. At Mass, the *lectio continua* generally distributed both the cycle of the gospel readings and the cycle of readings of the other parts of the New Testament over a whole year. The Byzantine liturgy has retained or at least reintroduced this practice,[19] and traces of it can still be seen in the Roman missal. In Rome itself, at the night office, both the liturgy of St Peter's and that of the Lateran made use of the *lectio continua* of the Old Testament;[20] the cycle they followed forms, in an abbreviated version, the basis of the present distribution of "current Scripture" (*Scriptura occurrens*) in the breviary.

The practice of continuous reading was arranged in such a way that certain books of the Bible were assigned to a particular period of the year, thus giving it a special character. For example, in almost every liturgy the reading of the Gospel of St John, as well as of the Acts of the Apostles and in some places of the Apocalypse, is one of the characteristics of Paschaltide. In the Roman rite, Isaiah is read in

---

[17]"He is present in his word, since it is he himself who speaks when the holy scriptures are read in church," CSL 7; cf. 33. Cf. St Germanus of Constantinople, in N. Borgia, *Il commentario liturgico di san Germano* . . . (Grottaferrata, 1912) p. 26-7; A. M. Roguet, "La présence active du Christ dans la Parole de Dieu" in LMD 82 (1965) 8-28.

[18]Cf. the characteristic texts of St Leo in M. B. de Soos, *Le mystère liturgique d'après saint Léon le Grand* (Münster: Aschendorff, 1958; LQF 34) pp. 52ff.

[19]The complete table of the distribution of the passages for the readings is given in A. Couturier, *Cours de liturgie grecque-melkite* 1 (Ed. Gabalda, 1912) p. 48*-88*.

[20]OR 14 (probably a practice in St Peter's in the second half of the seventh century), Andrieu OR 3, pp. 39-41; OR 13 A (a practice in the Lateran in the first half of the eighth century), Andrieu OR 2, pp. 481-8.

I

the office of Advent. Many churches began the reading of the Penta-
teuch in Lent.[21]

Even where it had always been the practice, continuous reading
gave way at times to another system, that of reading selected
passages. It happened first, of course, on feast days and during Holy
Week, to commemorate certain events by the reading of their
scriptural account. Similarly we find it in the catechetical gatherings
for catechumens. The choice of texts adapted to an event was, as
early as the end of the fourth century, one of the characteristics of
the liturgy at Jerusalem which aroused the admiration of the pilgrim
Egeria.[22] We frequently find parallels made between passages of
different books of the New Testament, or especially between the
Old and New Testament, so as to clarify one by the other and to
show the development of revelation in the different phases of the
economy of salvation.[23] At times however, because it was only an
historical accident that brought texts together in a fixed series of
readings, it would be useless to seek an intrinsic correlation.[24] One
must likewise be careful not to attribute, without explicit evidence,
the choice of texts to topographical or archeological circumstances,
whose influence was, we feel, exaggerated by the commentators of the
early twentieth century.[25]

Because it is question of an inspired text, the liturgy on principle
gives the text of a passage in its entirety, without abridgement or
modification. There are however exceptions to this strict rule: the
beginning and end of the reading may have initial or concluding
formulas such as *"In diebus illis,"* *"In illo tempore,"* *"Carissimi,"*
"Dicit Dominus omnipotens," *"In Christo Iesu Domino nostro,"* etc.
More rarely some intermediary verses are suppressed with a view to
stressing the closeness of certain texts to one another or underlining
some particular aspect.[26] Finally, various types of "centonism" are

---

[21]A. Baumstark, *Liturgie comparée,* pp. 136-42.

[22]Egeria, *Peregrinatio,* H. Pétré ed. (SC 21) pp. 204, 218, 220, etc.

[23]P. Jounel, *op. cit.,* pp. 24-5. See the many examples noted by A. Chavasse, "La
structure du carême et les lectures des messes quadragésimales dans la liturgie
romaine" in LMD 31 (1952) 76-119.

[24]R. Hesbert, *Les séries d'évangiles des dimanches après la Pentecôte,* LMD 46,
pp. 35-59, and especially A. Chavasse, *Les plus anciens types du lectionnaire et
de l'antiphonaire romains de la messe,* RB 62 (1952) 3-94.

[25]In particular by C. Callewaert, *De sacra liturgia universim,* 4th ed. (Bruges:
Beyaert, 1944) pp. 161-3; A. Coelho, *Cours de liturgie romaine* 1 (Lophem-
lez-Bruges, 1928) pp. 66-9; and especially I. Schuster, *Liber sacramentorum* 3
(Brussels: Vromant, 1929).

[26]C. Callewaert, *op. cit.,* pp. 166-7; P. Oppenheim, *Notiones liturgiae fundamentales*
(Turin: Marietti, 1941) pp. 371-3.

used, joining together in one text extracts from different books. This is still found today in the responsories, which in fact are not strictly readings but chants.[27] As regards the gospel, this practice was intended to suppress the doublets and form a gospel harmony. It is thus that various churches compiled *diatessarons*; because of the serious criticisms to which they lend themselves, they are no longer used anywhere.[28]

The reading of the Bible necessitated translations. At first made orally by interpreters, translations were later undertaken in a systematic way and codified, with a view to ensuring the literary and, even more, the doctrinal exactitude of the texts to be read. Versions which were too exclusively erudite scarcely ever found their way into the liturgy.[29]

Originally it was the Bible itself that was used by the reader, the passage (or at least its conclusion) being indicated by the celebrant. As the usage became more and more fixed, manuscripts appeared indicating in the margin the beginning and the end of the readings. Later, tables of passages were compiled, and finally books presenting biblical excerpts in the order in which they were used in the liturgy.[30]

II THE COMMENTARY ON THE BIBLICAL READING

The reading of the sacred text is followed, at least in important liturgical functions, by the celebrant's commentary, the *homily*. It is the application of what has just been read to the concrete circumstances of the moment and to the needs of the people present. It is a pastoral act, since it consists in breaking the bread that is the Word of God; and it is a truly liturgical act, since it forms a unit

[27]See C. Marbach, *Carmina scripturarum* . . . (Strasbourg: Le Roux, 1907); P. Alfonzo, *I responsori biblici* . . . (Rome: Lateranum, 1936).

[28]P. Salmon, *Le lectionnaire de Luxeuil* (Rome: Abbaye de Saint-Jérôme, 1944; *Collectanea biblica latina* 7) pp. lxx-lxxiii; A. S. Marmadji, *Diatessaron de Tatien,* texte arabe établi et trad. en français . . . (Beirut, 1935); C. Peters, "Das Diatessaron Tatians" in *Orientalia christiana analecta* 123 (1939); J. Leloir, "Le Diatessaron de Tatien" in *Orient syrien* 1 (1956) 208-31, 313-34.

[29]This is the case with the Greek translations of Aquila and Symmachus, with the Hexapla translation of Origen, and with the *Psalterium iuxta Hebraeos* of St Jerome: *Richesses et déficiences des anciens psautiers latins* (Rome: Abbaye de Saint-Jérôme, 1959; *Colectanea biblica latina* 13) pp. 101-2.

[30]There is no recent synthesis on this topic; one might consult especially P. Salmon, *op. cit.*; A. Mundó, "El commicus palimpsest Paris Lat. 2269" in *Liturgica I, Cardinali* . . . *Schuster in memoriam* (Montserrat, 1956; *Scripta et documenta* 7) pp. 151-275; T. Klauser, *Das römische Capitulare evangeliorum* (Münster; Aschendorff, 1935; LQF 28); A. Baumstark, *Nicht-evangelische syrische Perikopenordnungen* . . . , *ibid.,* 1921 (LQF 15); A. Chavasse, *art. cit.*, note 23.

with the readings, whose efficacy it prolongs, and is expressly provided for in the liturgical books. If the celebrant cannot give the homily himself, another priest or a deacon supplies it, in which case care must be taken not to weaken the bond between this preaching and the liturgical action.[31] As is already witnessed by St Justin,[32] the giving of a homily was the practice in all the ancient churches at the Sunday assembly or even more often, and it is the homily that has given us most of the biblical commentaries that we have from the Fathers.[33]

In the absence of the living word of the celebrant, certain churches, and especially monasteries, were content at times to have the writings of the Fathers read, even during their lifetime, as was the case with the commentaries of St Gregory the Great. It is principally at the night office that the custom of reading the Fathers has been developed and preserved.[34]

III THE INFLUENCE OF THE BIBLE ON THE ENTIRE LITURGY

BIBLIOGRAPHY

J. Daniélou, "The Sacraments and the History of Salvation" in *The Liturgy and the Word of God* (Collegeville, Minnesota: Liturgical Press, 1959) pp. 21-32.

P. Jounel, "The Bible in the Liturgy," *ibid.*, pp. 1-20.

C. Vagaggini, *Initiation théologique à la liturgie* 2 (Bruges: Abbaye Saint-André, 1963) pp. 12-45 (vol. 2 of this work not available in English).

Not only is the Bible read and commented upon, but its influence is felt throughout the whole liturgy, as is stressed by the Second Vatican Council.[35] It will be seen further on that it frequently

---

[31]CSL 24, 35, 52.—Cf. J. Leclercq, "Le sermon, acte liturgique" in LMD 8 (1946) 27-46; G. Chevrot, "Réflexions à la suite de quelques essais de prédication liturgique" LMD 5 (1946) 34-59.

[32]St Justin, *First Apology*, 67, *op. cit.*, pp. 142-3: "When the reader has finished, the president gives a discourse to draw attention to and to urge the imitation of this lofty teaching."—The homily formed part of the synagogue service as can be seen from Lk 4:20-21.—H. Chirat, *L'assemblée chrétienne à l'âge apostolique* (Ed. du Cerf, 1949) pp. 95-117.

[33]A. Bea, "Valeur pastorale de la parole de Dieu dans la liturgie" in LMD 47-48 (1956) 133-5.

[34]St Benedict, *Regula monachorum*, 9, P. Schmitz ed. (Maredsous, 1946) p. 31; St Gregory the Great, *Registrum epistolarum* 12, 6, Ewald ed., 2, p. 352; St Caesarius of Arles, *Admonitio* or *Serm.* 1, 15, CC 103, p. 11.—Cf. P. Bayart, *Les divins offices* (Paris: Bloud et Gay, 1948) pp. 181-208.

[35]"Sacred Scripture is of the greatest importance in the celebration of the liturgy· For it is from holy Scripture that lessons are read and explained in the homily, and psalms are sung; the prayers, collects and liturgical songs are scriptural in their inspiration; and it is from the Scriptures that actions and signs derive their meaning . . ." (CSL 24).

furnishes the reply which the assembly gives to the reading it has just heard. The signs used by the liturgy are principally biblical. The prayer of the celebrant, if not simply a meditation on the readings which have preceded it, at least takes its style and inspiration from the Bible.[36] The sacraments are understood in reference to the biblical types which figure prominently in the great consecratory prayers and which serve then as a point of departure for catechesis.[37] The Bible and the liturgy show the same basic attitude to God, the same world outlook, the same interpretation of history. In fact, there can be no real liturgical life without initiation into the Bible; the liturgy in turn offers a living commentary on the Bible, giving to it the fullness of its meaning.[38] But it must not be lost sight of that this pervading spiritual atmosphere, before being that of the liturgy, is primarily that of the whole New Testament. The centuries during which this biblical sense had been lost did not produce any durable liturgical creations, but strayed into artificial allegories and accommodated interpretations, whose persistence causes a certain embarrassment today.

IV NON-BIBLICAL READINGS IN THE LITURGY

BIBLIOGRAPHY

B. de Gaiffier, "La lecture des actes des martyrs dans la prière liturgique en Occident" in *Analecta Bollandiana* 72 (1954) 134-66.

H. Urner, *Die ausserbiblische Lesung im christlichen Gottesdienst* (Göttingen: Vandenhoeck & Ruprecht, 1952).

The early liturgies sometimes permitted non-biblical readings in the assemblies. These were intended to be listened to for their own authority—as distinct from the sermons of the Fathers, of which we have just spoken, which were simply a commentary on the sacred text as a substitute for the homily of the celebrant. Putting aside the biblical apocrypha, erroneously accepted here and there as authentic Scripture but quickly enough rejected,[39] two kinds of texts have been given this honor: the letters of eminent bishops, especially the

---

[36]This is also the case with the collects of the paschal vigil in the Roman usage; but is was more constant in the early liturgies. Each reading and even each psalm was followed by a period of silence which the celebrant closed with a collect. See L. Brou, *The Psalter Collects* (London, 1949; HBS 83).

[37]J. Daniélou, *Bible et liturgie* (Ed. du Cerf, 1951; *Lex orandi* 11). Engl. tr., *The Bible and the Liturgy* (Notre Dame University Press, 1956; *Liturgical Studies* 3).

[38]P. Oppenheim, *Notiones liturgiae fundamentales . . .*, p. 378-83.

[39]However, we will see further on that the liturgical chants have, by way of contrast with the readings, readily retained certain apocryphal texts, when they resembled centos of authentic texts.

bishops of Rome,[40] and the Acts of the martyrs. These latter were read in certain Western churches at Mass on the anniversary day,[41] a fact which has saved them from oblivion or the falsifications to which they fell victim elsewhere.

The Roman liturgy includes these non-biblical readings only in the night office of the breviary. They comprise the acts of the popes, such as encyclicals, and *"legendae"*, i.e. hagiographical readings.[42]

2 Song

The Word of God calls for reply. This reply sometimes takes the form of *song*, and in fact, after the readings, it is the chants which have most firmly established themselves in the Christian liturgy.

I SONG AS THE ASSEMBLY'S RESPONSE TO THE READINGS

BIBLIOGRAPHY

H. Chirat, "Les éléments fondamentaux de la célébration du culte" in LMD 20 (1949) 13-32.

J. Jungmann, *The Liturgy of the Word* (London: Burns and Oates, 1966) pp. 46-55.

The saying of St Augustine, *"Legenti respondentes cantavimus,"* "We have sung in reply to the reader,"[43] is often quoted. In context it refers to the reading of a psalm,[44] to which the people replied with a refrain taken from the same psalm, i.e. a responsorial type of psalmody. The Fathers, especially St Augustine and St Leo, considered the psalm which follows the epistle of the Mass as a true reading; this was a single psalm, whatever the number of other readings. With regard to the biblical canticles of the paschal vigil, they were the continuation of the readings, chanted by the reader, and not responses of the schola or of the people. But in the liturgies of the West the reading tends to call for the response of chant, whether it

---

[40]This was the case with the Epistle of St Clement, read at Corinth from time immemorial according to the testimony of the bishop Dionysius, who besides had read in the Sunday assembly a letter received by him from Pope St Soter (third quarter of the second century): Eusebius, *Hist. eccl., IV,* 23, 11; G. Bardy ed., 1 (SC 31) p. 205.

[41]P. Salmon, *Lectionnaire de Luxeuil,* 1944, pp. 181-3 (=PL 72, col. 208);—B. de Gaiffier, *art. cit.,* has gathered the essential documentation on this subject.

[42]To be treated in a subsequent volume.

[43]*In psalmum* 40 *enarratio, Sermo ad plebem* 1; CC 38, p. 447; PL 36, col. 453.

[44]Tertullian had already thus described the sequence of the rites at the Sunday assembly: "Prout Scripturae leguntur, aut psalmi canuntur, aut allocutiones proferuntur aut petitiones delegantur" (*De anima* 9, 4; CC 2, p. 792).

be a simple acclamation, a poetic composition, or psalmody: a biblical canticle, responsorial psalm, gradual, responsory, short responsory, or simple versicle. In the Roman usage this principle holds above all in the office. At certain solemnities in the Visigothic rite there occurs what seems to be an intended correspondence between the text of the reading and that of the *psallendum*.[45]

II THE GENERAL PLACE OF SONG IN THE LITURGY

BIBLIOGRAPHY

R. Aigrain, *La musique religieuse* (Paris: Bloud et Gay, 1929; *Bibliothèque catholique des Sciences religieuses*).

Le Chant liturgique après Vatican II, Semaine d'études internationales, Fribourg, 1965 (Paris: Fleurus, 1966; *Kinnor* 6).

J. Gelineau, "Commentaire du chapitre VI de la Constitution conciliaire sur la liturgie" in LMD 77 (1964) 193-210.

J. Gelineau, *Voices and Instruments in Christian Worship* (Collegeville, Minnesota: Liturgical Press, 1964).

T. Gérold, *Les Pères de l'Église et la musique* (Alcan, 1931; *Études d'histoire et de philosophie religieuse* 25).

H. Hucke, "Musical Requirements of the Liturgical Reform" in *Concilium* 2 (1966) 26-41.

J. Jungmann, "Liturgy and Congregational Singing" in *Pastoral Liturgy* (London: Challoner, 1962) pp. 345-56.

J. Quasten, *Musik und Gesang in den Kulten der heidnischen Antike und christlichen Frühzeit* (Münster: Aschendorff, 1930; LQF 25) 78-157.

Christian antiquity had only to follow the advice of the Apostle Paul, continuing the biblical tradition, in order to make of song a normal mode of expression for liturgical prayer: "With gratitude in your hearts sing psalms and hymns and inspired songs to God" (Col 3:16); "Sing the words and tunes of the psalms and hymns when you are together, and go on singing and chanting to the Lord in your hearts" (Ep 5:19). In the church at Corinth, as St Paul also bears witness, there may even have appeared charismatic improvisations (1 Co 14:26); his epistles contain precious fragments of liturgical chants of the early community.[46] Here singing appears as a sign of joy particularly adapted to the sentiment of thanksgiving, as is in turn suggested in Jm 5:13: "If anyone is feeling happy, he should sing a psalm." And in the same way the Apocalypse shows

---

[45]L. Brou, "Le 'psallendum' de la messe . . ." in EL 61 (1947) pp. 20-21. But this is not the original usage.—It is only with much reserve that we accept the conclusions proposed by the authors cited above in the bibliography for this paragraph.

[46]This is certainly the case with Ep 5:14 and 1 Tm 3:16; and perhaps also 1 Tm 6:15-16; Ep 1:4-14; Col 1:15-20.

the Church in heaven expressing in song her acknowledgment of the redemption and her praise of the Lord (Rv 4:8, 11; 5:9-10; 14:3; 15:3-4; 19:1-8, etc.).[47]

Song is also regarded as a means of expressing unanimity of feeling, since its rhythm and melody give rise to such a merging of voices as to make it seem as though there were only one;[48] in fact it is only song that affords an expression of cohesion as soon as the assembly exceeds the dimensions of a small group. The Fathers likewise emphasize that song gives to words a greater force and intelligibility, thus making it possible to adhere to them more closely and to meditate on them.[49] Finally music, whether vocal or instrumental, can create a festive atmosphere and give to certain occasions a ring of triumph; it was in this way that it entered into the great moments of the liturgy of Israel.[50]

But it is difficult for song and music to keep always to the strictly functional role which is theirs and not go beyond their purpose. This explains the frequent hesitation of bishops and theologians to approve of certain forms of art and the lurking temptation to the faithful to stop at esthetic emotion without going on to the text itself, which the music should help them appreciate.[51]

---

[47]A. Hamman, *La prière*, (I) *Nouveau Testament* (Tournai: Desclée, 1959) pp. 351-71.

[48]Cf. Rm 15:6; St Clement, *Epistle to the Corinthians*, 34, 7: "We also, brought together in community of feeling in the unity of one body, cry out to him insistently as with one mouth"; St Ignatius, *Epistle to the Ephesians*, 4, 1-2; St John Chrysostom, *Homil.* 36 *in* 1 *Cor.*, n. 6, PG 61, col. 315;—cf. J. Quasten, *op. cit.*, pp. 91-100.

[49]For example, St Augustine, *Confess.* 9, vi, 14, P. de Labriolle ed. (Coll. *Budé*) 2, 1926, p. 220; 10, xxxiii, 49-50, *ibid.*, p. 276-8. Pope St Pius X, *Tra le sollecitudini*, I, 1: "Siccome suo officio principale è di rivestire con acconcia melodia il testo liturgico che viene proposto all' intelligenza dei fedeli, così il suo proprio fine è di aggiungere maggiore efficacia al testo medesimo, affinchè i fedeli con tale mezzo siano più facilmente eccitati alla devozione," in A. Bugnini, *Documenta pontificia ad instaurationem liturgicam spectantia . . .* (Rome: Edizioni liturgiche, 1953) p. 14.

[50]After the crossing of the Red Sea, Ex 15:1-20; for the entry of the ark into Jerusalem, 2 S 6:5; for the dedication of the temple of Solomon, 2 Ch 5:12.— A comprehensive view of these doctrinal perspectives is to be found in the encyclical *Musicae sacrae* of Pius XII, December 25, 1955, n. 2-3 and 11-15, AAS 48 (1956) pp. 6-7, 11-13; the Council summed it up in CSL 112-13.

[51]Already in the fourth and fifth centuries there were sharp controversies over sacred music; cf. St Augustine, *Confess.* 10, xxxiii, 49-50; St Basil, *Epistle* 207; Nicetas of Remesiana, *De psalmodiae bono*, JTS 24 (1923) 225-52. In the Middle Ages, St Thomas had a certain difficulty in defending liturgical chant: II-II, q. 91, a. 2.—See J. Jungmann, *Des lois de la célébration . . .*, pp. 122-36.

III THE BIBLICAL CHANTS

1 *The privileged place of the psalms in the liturgy*[52]

BIBLIOGRAPHY

J. Daniélou, "Les psaumes dans la liturgie de l'Ascension" in LMD 21 (1950) 40-56; Engl. tr., "The Ascension" in *The Bible and the Liturgy* (Notre Dame University Press, 1956) pp. 303-18.

B. Fischer, *Die Psalmenfrömmigkeit der Märtyrerkirche* (Freiburg, 1949); enlarged in French ed., "Le Christ dans les psaumes, La dévotion aux psaumes dans l'Église des martyrs" in LMD 27 (1951) 86-113.

P. Salmon, *Les "tituli psalmorum" des manuscrits latins* (Paris: Ed. du Cerf, 1959; *Études liturgiques* 3) pp. 10-37.

L. Walsh, "The Christian Prayer of the Psalms according to the 'Tituli Psalmorum' of the Latin Manuscripts" in *Studies in Pastoral Liturgy* 3, P. Murray ed. (Dublin: Gill, 1967) pp. 29-73.

It seems that in the very first centuries the psalms only appeared in the liturgy in the form of readings, on the same level as the other books of the Bible. But from the time of the persecutions there grew up a tendency in favor of the singing of the psalms, a tendency that was further developed by the Fathers of the late fourth century and by monasticism. From then on fidelity to the psalter has been the mark of all liturgical renewal. Only the Syrians have abandoned psalmody in the office in favor of non-biblical chants.

The psalter, distributed over a cycle which permits it to be sung in its totality within a certain period of time, constitutes the essential basis of prayer for monks and clergy. In both Jewish and Christian tradition, some psalms are more particularly linked with a certain hour of the day or day of the week.

Over and above this, the psalms frequently furnish the response to the reading, whether they be sung in their entirety (for example in the Roman-rite Mass of the first Sunday of Lent), or whether they be reduced to some verses (gradual, responsory) or even to a single verse (after the chapter of the minor hours in the monastic office).

They form the traditional processional prayer in the Roman liturgy: at Mass they make up the entrance, offertory, and communion chants; in the ritual they are sung at burials and at thanksgiving processions, and their use has been restored for the Palm Sunday procession. At the dedication of churches they accompany the performance of almost all the actions. The prayer of the psalms likewise occupies an important place in the care of the sick and dying.

[52]To be treated in greater detail in a subsequent volume.

The Roman liturgy makes use of three versions of the psalter: for the ornate chants of the Mass and office it has generally preserved the so-called "Roman" psalter, which preceded St Jerome's revision; for psalmody apart from this it allows a choice between the psalter revised by St Jerome, the "Gallican Psalter," and a translation published by the Pontifical Biblical Institute in 1945 on the orders of Pius XII.[53] The Second Vatican Council has ordered the preparation of a new version taking better account of various specified factors.[54]

2 The biblical canticles

BIBLIOGRAPHY

F. Cabrol, *Cantiques* in DACL 2 (1910) col. 1978-94.
W. S. Porter, "Cantica mozarabici officii" in EL 49 (1935) 126-45.
O. Rousseau, "La plus ancienne liste des cantiques liturgiques tirés de l'Écriture" in RechSR 35 (1948) 120-29.
H. Schneider, *Die altlateinischen biblischen Cantica* (Beuron, 1938; TA 29/30).
H. Schneider, "Die biblischen Oden . . . " in *Biblica* 30 (1949) 28-65, 239-72, 433-52, 479-500.

Like the psalms, there are other lyrical passages of the Bible which have gained a privileged position in liturgical life. The paschal vigil and the morning prayer (*orthros* or *laudes*) traditionally include the singing of biblical canticles. They have also been given a place in the Mass[55] and in the other hours of the office (the canticles in the third nocturn of feasts in the Benedictine usage, the canticle of Mary at vespers, the canticle of Zachary at lauds, the canticle of Simeon at compline in the Roman office).

From early times eight canticles in particular have been chosen from the Old Testament which, together with the three from the New Testament, occur in most manuscripts and in liturgical usage.[56] While the East sang them all in succession, the Roman Church distributed them throughout the entire week, and, since the time of Pius X, has added a new series which constitutes the "first schema" of lauds. Already in the Apocalypse we have evidence of the predilection of the Christians for the canticle of Moses (15:3).

---

[53]Cf. A. G. Martimort in LMD 59, pp. 167-73 for a summary of studies on the psalter, together with bibliographical notes.

[54]". . . and is to take into account the style of Christian Latin, the liturgical use of psalms also when they are to be sung, and the entire tradition of the Latin Church" (CSL 91).

[55]L. Brou, "Les 'benedictiones' ou cantique des trois enfants dans l'ancienne messe espagnole" in *Hispania sacra* 1 (1948) pp. 21-33.

[56]To be treated in a subsequent volume.

3 *Other biblical chants*

BIBLIOGRAPHY

P. Alfonzo, *I responsori biblici dell'ufficio romano* (Rome: Lateranum, 1936).
C. Marbach, *Carmina scripturarum* . . . (Strasbourg: Le Roux, 1907).
P. Pietschmann, "Die nicht dem Psalter entnommenen Messgesangstücke auf ihre Textgestalt untersucht" in JL 12 (1932) 87-144.

Along with the psalms and canticles, there are other liturgical chants taken from the Bible, the most important and universal being the *Sanctus* (Is 6:3). This is similarly the case with the greater part of the acclamations. A special place of importance should be given to the non-psalmodic antiphons (particularly certain Roman offertories and certain communion antiphons), and especially to the responsories which accompany the readings of current Scripture: the choice of texts and the way in which they are woven together make them genuine masterpieces. Some responsories and antiphons are taken from the Prayer of Manasseh and from the Third and Fourth Book of Esdras.[57] These apocrypha have had a lasting success, because they are made up of centos of inspired texts and express authentic biblical themes.

4 *The various types of psalmody*

The psalms, as we have already seen, were sometimes treated as simple readings, which were listened to in silence. However, the *responsorial psalmody*, as described by St Augustine or St Athanasius, very quickly came into use: a reader chanted the psalm alone, the assembly taking up by way of refrain or acclamation some words taken from the psalm. This is, in a word, the method we have retained for the *Benedictus es* in the Masses of the Ember Days and which the East has also retained to some extent.

The great bishops of the fourth century devised a more attractive method of psalmody which was called antiphonal chant; light has not yet been sufficiently shed on the exact meaning of this innovation. In any case the West mainly practised yet another method: psalmody alternating between two choirs, with almost always an *antiphon* serving as introduction and conclusion to the chant.[58] The oldest

---

[57]A list is given in C. Marbach, *op. cit.,* pp. 537-8; to these must be added the *Improperia* of Good Friday, and texts indicated in M. Righetti, *Manuale di storia liturgica* 1, 3rd ed. (Milan: Ancora, 1964) p. 198; see also D. de Bruyne, "Fragments d'une apocalypse perdue" in RB 33 (1921) 97-109.

[58]The antiphons were, in certain circumstances, repeated during the psalm, as is still prescribed in the pontifical for a number of rites.—Since L. Petit, "Antiphone dans la liturgie grecque" in DACL 1 (1907) col. 2461-88, these difficult problems in connection with the original forms of psalmody have only been tackled again in a scientific way by A. Baumstark, *Nocturna laus* (Münster: Aschendorff, 1927; LQF 32) pp. 124-43.

lists of antiphons, both for the psalms at Mass and for those of the office, testify to an extraordinary knowledge of the psalter on the part of their authors: sometimes they simply help one to pray the psalm, and sometimes they clarify it in the light of the action which is being performed (offertory, communion) or of the mystery being celebrated on a particular day.[59]

The *responsory* is a psalmodic form in which the text is reduced to a selection of verses. Sometimes it is given a very ornate melody (gradual, responsories at the nocturns), at other times it takes the form of a "short responsory" sung immediately after an abridged reading (chapter).

Are the *versicles* the ultimate abridgement of the responsory? Their place after the short readings would lead one to believe so. But in fact the versicles are used in other ways, particularly where a group of them are combined to make up a type of litany equivalent to the diaconal litanies which will be examined a little further on.

IV NON-BIBLICAL CHANTS

BIBLIOGRAPHY

A. Baumstark, *Liturgie comparée* . . . , pp. 102-22 (for early liturgical poetic composition); Engl. tr., *Comparative Liturgy* (Westminster, Maryland: Newman Press, 1958).

G. Del Ton, G. Schirò and A. Raes, "Innografia" in *Enciclopedia cattolica* 7 (Vatican City, 1951) col. 28-29 (the best current overall view).

O. Heiming, *Syrische 'Eniânê und griechische Kanones* . . . (Münster, Aschendorff, 1932; LQF 26).

M. Righetti, *Manuale di storia liturgica* 1, p. 670-78 (for the compositions of the Latin Middle Ages).

E. Wellesz, *A History of Byzantine Music and Hymnography*, 2nd ed. (Oxford: University Press, 1961).

Before the biblical chants occupied the fundamental place in the liturgy which we have just observed, it seems that certain new poetic compositions, fragments of which we find in the epistles of St Paul, were already being sung. Such creations were not without some danger: heretical movements have always made use of them as a means of propaganda; in the years of liturgical decline they show a great indigence, distorting the celebration of worship and supplanting original elements such as biblical psalmody. From this stems the reaction against them which takes place every so often. As early as the third century, chants savoring of Gnosticism were eliminated; in the fourth century one had to be on the defense

---

[59]For some examples (restricted to Psalms 20-24) see P. Blanchard, "Le psautier dans la liturgie" in *Richesses et déficiences des anciens psautiers latins* (Rome: Abbaye de Saint-Jérôme, 1959; *Collectanea biblica* 13) pp. 231-48.

against Arian canticles; in the sixteenth century the greater part of the medieval compositions had to be rejected.

These abuses should not, however, cause every non-biblical composition to be banned from the liturgy, as the French demanded in an excess of severity in the eighteenth century. On the contrary, the Church has always welcomed hymnography: St Ambrose wanted to fight against the Arians with their own weapons and popularize the liturgy. Magnificent masterpieces have thus been created, which deserve to be kept alive in the Church's prayer more because of their spiritual content and depth of contemplation than because of their literary perfection.

The oldest type in use was psalmodic in form. They were non-biblical psalms, ψαλμοί ἰοδιοτιχοί, similar in structure to the biblical ones. Most famous among these are the Odes of Solomon,[60] and especially the *Gloria in excelsis* and the *Te Deum*,[61] which are still sung.

In the East, hymnography blossomed from the fourth century onward in Palestine and Syria; St Ephrem is the best known poet, while certain compositions are attributed also to Severus of Antioch.[62] But it is the Byzantine liturgy that has provided the framework for the finest developments under the form of *kontakia* and *canons*; the greatest names are those of Romanus Melodus, Andrew of Crete, and St John Damascene.[63] On the other hand, the troparions (a type of antiphon) constitute one of the attractions of the Greek liturgy, even if they occupy an almost inordinate place today. The singing of the *Acathist hymn* in honour of the Virgin is celebrated with particular solemnity.[64]

In the West, the hymns of St Ambrose, accepted by St Benedict into his monastic office, have served as models for other composi-

---

[60]French translation and historical introduction: J. Labourt and P. Batiffol, *Les Odes de Salomon, une oeuvre chrétienne des environs de l'an* 100-120 (Paris: Gabalda, 1911; it first appeared in *R vue biblique* 21 [1910] pp. 483-500, and 22 [1911] pp. 5-59, 161-97).

[61] On the *Gloria in excelsis*: B. Capelle, "Le text du Gloria in excelsis" in RHE 44 (1949) 439-57; this article appeared again in *Travaux liturgiques* 2 (Louvain: Mont César 1962) pp. 176-91.—On the *Te Deum*: A. Baumstark, "Te Deum und eine Gruppe griechischer Abendhymnen" in OC 34 (1937) 1-26.

[62]See the bibliography previous to 1948, prepared by A. Raes in *Miscellanea in honorem L. C. Mohlberg* 1 (Rome: Ed. liturgiche, 1948) pp. 342-3.

[63]R. Aigrain, *La musique religieuse* (Bloud et Gay, 1929) pp. 86-94.—P. Maas and C. Trypanis, *Sancti Romani Melodi cantica genuina* (Oxford: Clarendon, 1963); ed. with translation, J. Grosdidier de Matons, 1 (SC 99), 1964; 2 (SC 110), 1965; 3 (SC 114), 1965; 4 (SC 128), 1967.

[64]Greek text, translation and introduction by G. Meersseman (Fribourg: Editions universitaires, 1958).

tions. They are used principally in the office, though some strophes from them occur also in processions and sometimes in certain chants of the Mass in place of psalm texts. Along with Sedulius and Prudentius, the masters of the classical epoch, one could also count some great Frankish poets.[65] The Middle Ages saw the development of more mediocre types of hymn: sequences, tropes, etc., of which the liturgy has retained only very few examples;[66] yet this period also inspired the wonderful marian antiphons, which we still sing after compline.

Mention should also be made of the non-poetic compositions which have merited a permanent place in the liturgy; prominent among these are the antiphons and responsories taken from the legends of the saints, especially as in the office of St Laurence, St Agnes, and St Martin.

Happily, though at a fairly late date, the creeds or professions of faith became liturgical chants. In the earliest times they were "handed over" to the candidates at baptism, then "given back" by them, but they were only used in private prayer. The creed of Nicaea-Constantinople, however, was introduced into the liturgy of the Mass, at first in the East, then in the West; and another creed, long attributed to St Athanasius, has been used in psalmodic form in the office.[67]

Since the Middle Ages there has been built up, more or less on the fringe of the liturgy, a repertory of "canticles" in modern languages, reflecting the peculiar genius of each country. The encyclical *Musicae sacrae* of 1958 and the instruction of September 3, 1958, while taking care that they should not encroach on the authentic chants, underlined their importance and specified the place they could occupy at the periphery of worship.[68]

V DOXOLOGIES AND ACCLAMATIONS

Among the chants attention must also be drawn to two forms,

[65]To be treated in a subsequent volume.

[66]M. Righetti, *loc. cit.*, gives the principal bibliographical references; by glancing through U. Chevalier, *Repertorium hymnologicum.* . . . (Louvain: Bollandistes, 1892-1919), 6 vols., one will get some idea of the extraordinary wealth of the medieval repertory.

[67]M. Righetti, *op. cit.*, pp. 225-35.

[68]An essential study: H. Anglés, *La música de las Cantigas de santa Maria del Rey Alfonso el sabio* 3 (Barcelona: Biblioteca central, 1958);—cf. also A. Gastoué, *Le cantique populaire en France, ses sources, son histoire* (Lyons: Ed. Janin, 1924);—MD 189;—Pius XII, encyclical *Musicae sacrae* in *Musique et liturgie*, 1956, p. 21, n. 9; p. 26, n. 34-6; pp. 31-2, n. 59-64; SRC, instruction of September 3, 1958, n. 9, 13-15, 19, 33, 51-3.

partly of biblical origin and partly of free composition, which give a very distinctive aspect to liturgical celebration: the doxologies and the acclamations.

1 *Doxologies*

BIBLIOGRAPHY

B. Botte, "In unitate Spiritus sancti" in Botte-Mohrmann, *L'ordinaire de la messe*" (Paris: Ed. du Cerf, 1953; *Études liturgiques* 2) pp. 133-9.
A. Stuiber, "Doxologie" in RAC 4 (1958) col. 210-26.
C. Vagaggini, *Theological Dimensions of the Liturgy* 1 (Collegeville, Minnesota: Liturgical Press, 1959) pp. 122-5.

The frequent recurrence of doxologies underlines the extent to which the liturgy is the worship of the Blessed Trinity. The doxologies, simple phrases of praise and adoration of God in Jewish prayer, for example at the conclusion of each of the books of the psalter, became more developed and clearly trinitarian in the Epistles and in the Apocalypse.[69] They very quickly formed the conclusion of the great Christian prayers. The formula *Gloria Patri*[70] was already a chant of the assembly in the fourth century. It was all the more widespread as its text became the affirmation of Nicene orthodoxy against Arianism. Shortly after this the *Gloria* became the final verse of all developed psalmody.[71] Other doxologies are genuine hymns, for example the *Te decet laus*, which, though of great antiquity, is confined today to the monastic night office on feast days.[72] The *Gloria in excelsis* and the *Te Deum* have also been regarded as doxologies. Finally, it has become almost universal practice to conclude hymns with a strophe of praise to the Blessed Trinity.

2 *Acclamations*

BIBLIOGRAPHY

A. Baumstark, *Liturgie comparée*, pp. 80-101.
T. Klauser, "Akklamation" in RAC 1 (1950) col. 216-33.
M. Righetti, *op. cit.*, pp. 208-16.

The acclamations give evidence of the popular and almost spontaneous style of liturgical celebration.[73] They are short formulas,

[69]Rm 9:5; 11:36; 16:25-27 (at least in most MSS); Ga 1:5; Ep 3:20-21; Ph 4:20; 1 Tm 1:17; 6:16; 2 Tm 4:18; Heb 13:21; 1 P 4:11; 2 P 3:18; Jude 25; Rv 1:6; 5:13; 7:12.
[70]On the history and variants of the formula, see J. Gaillard in *Catholicisme* 5, 1957, col. 59-61.
[71]St Benedict, *Regula monachorum*, c. 9, 11, 13, 43, etc.
[72]In can be found, in Greek, in the *Apostolic Constitutions*, VII, 98, 3, Funk ed., pp. 456-8.
[73]See the remarks of C. Rauch, "La prière du peuple" in LMD 20 (1949) 127-9.

easy to sing from memory and in unison, which are used either to express acceptance of the Word of God, faith, or concurrence in a prayer, or to form as it were a cry of triumph at the passing of the Lord taking place under the signs of the gospel and the Eucharist. The most important acclamation, judging by the insistence with which it is described and commented on by the Fathers, is the *Amen*, which has passed untranslated from the Jewish liturgy into the New Testament[74] and the Christian liturgy. In the first centuries it is characteristic of the active participation of the faithful at Mass; it proclaims their faith in the Eucharist and ratifies the prayer and desires that have been enunciated.[75] The *Alleluia*, used as the refrain to certain psalms, is similarly a biblical acclamation—according to the Apocalypse a chant of heaven.[76] Its usage in the liturgy has been made the object of peculiar rules,[77] which vary according to the different churches, and which have caused fierce opposition between these churches.

Mention must also be made of the *Kyrie eleison*, a formula of the people's response to the diaconal litanies or a continuously repeated prayer, and of the *Deo gratias*, the *Gloria tibi Domine*, the *Δόξα σοι κύριε*, the *Agios o Theos*, and the Gallican *Laus tibi Christe*.[78] The acclamations are frequently by way of reply to the greetings of the celebrant or to invitations to prayer and make up a dialogue with them: *Et cum spiritu tuo*, *Habemus ad Dominum*, *Dignum et iustum est*. Some of these formulas are in fact a heritage from the synagogue. The Fathers of the Church have likewise laid great stress on these responses and made them the object of their commentaries.[79]

---

[74]Dt 27:15-26 (each time: "And all the people shall answer saying: Amen"); 1 Ch 16:36 ("And let all the people say, 'Amen!' Alleluia!"); Ne 8:6; Ps 40:14; 71:19; 88:53; 105:48; 1 Co 14:16; 2 Co 1:20; Rv 3:14; 5:14; 7:12; 19:4.

[75]St Justin, *First Apology* 65, 67 (the manuscript translation of the second text is less sure); St Dionysius of Alexandria, quoted by Eusebius, *Hist. eccl.*, VII, 9, Bardy ed. (SC 41) 2, p. 175; St Ambrose, *De sacramentis* 5, 25; St Augustine, *Sermons* 272, 334, 362; PL 38, col. 1247, 1469, 1632, etc.—I. Cecchetti, *L'Amen nella Scrittura e nella liturgia* (Tipografia Vaticana, 1942).

[76]Psalms 104-06, 110-17, 134-5, 145-50; Rv 19:1-6; —many of the sermons of St Augustine comment on the *Alleluia*: 254, 256, 262.—The monastic rules made provision for the singing of the *Alleluia* straight through the psalms on certain days or at certain hours.

[77]For example, St Benedict, *Regula monachorum*, 15.—Many Mass liturgies make use of the *Alleluia* as an acclamation during the gospel or offertory processions. For the use of the *Alleluia*, cf. H. Engberding, "Alleluia" in RAC 1 (1950) col. 293-9.

[78]The Spanish liturgy had a unique form of acclamation, used on certain occasions: the *clamor*; see L. Brou, "Le psallendum de la messe . . ." in EL 61 (1947) 45-54.

[79]To be treated in a subsequent volume.

3 The prayer of the people

BIBLIOGRAPHY

J. A. Jungmann, *The Liturgy of the Word* (London: Burns and Oates, 1966) ch. 6, "The People's Prayer," pp. 56-64.
C. Rauch, "La prière du peuple" in LMD 20 (1949) 127-32.

The liturgical chants, such as those whose characteristics we have just delineated, are intended sometimes to create an atmosphere of festivity or of recollection. Yet for the most part they are essentially a prayer, a prayer of the people, and even in a more special way a prayer of praise. It is a prayer which appears to be spontaneous. There are certain moments during the celebration, especially after the readings and chants, which are times of more intense prayer. The people are expressly invited to pray; they express their prayer in different ways, after which the celebrant generally says a priestly prayer which sums up and concludes the prayer of the faithful. This prayer then, without ceasing to be contemplation and praise, becomes in a special way intense supplication. Such a form also complies with the instructions of the Apostle Paul[80] and was already confirmed in the first descriptions of the liturgical assembly.[81]

I THE CALL TO PRAYER

In the Latin liturgies it was quite often the celebrant who invited the people to pray. Even today each of the solemn prayers of Good Friday is preceded by a formal invitation said by the celebrant himself: *Oremus, fratres dilectissimi, Deum Patrem omnipotentem* . . . A more elaborate type of invitation to prayer is addressed by the bishop to the people who take part in the ordination ceremony, or in the consecration of a church, altar, or chalice. The *Pater Noster* of the Mass is likewise preceded by an invitatory addressed to the faithful: *Praeceptis salutaribus* . . . For the most part, however, the invitation to prayer is reduced to the simple word: *Oremus.* The Gallican liturgy prescribed an invitatory to be said by the celebrant before every priestly prayer; one of these, the *Praefatio Missae*, was

---

[80]Ph 4:6; 1 Tm 2:1-2.

[81]St Justin, *First Apology* 67, 5: "Then we stand up together and pray"; 65, 1-2: "we offer intense (εὐτόνως) prayers together, for (ὑπέρ) ourselves, the newly-baptized, and for all others everywhere, that, having received instruction in the truth, we may be worthy to be considered good administrators by reason of our works and our keeping of the commandments, and to receive eternal salvation" (the French translation of L. Pautigny, *op. cit.,* p. 139, is not very exact); Tertullian, *Apologeticum*, 39: "Oramus etiam pro imperatoribus, pro ministeriis eorum et potestatibus, pro statu saeculi, pro rerum quiete, pro mora finis," J. Waltzing ed. (Coll. *Budé*), p. 82; *De anima* 9, quoted above, note 44.

K

somewhat more developed, becoming almost a catechesis on the feast of the day.[82]

In the East it is the deacon who invites to prayer and guides the people by his "proclamations," as is seen already in the *Apostolic Constitutions*,[83] and as is in fact the practice today in the greater part of the Eastern churches. He directs the prayer of the people even more closely when he leads the litany, announcing the intentions one by one.

In the Visigothic liturgy we find side by side invitatories pronounced by the celebrant (the *missa*,[84] the invitatory to the *Pater Noster*, sometimes one for the *Credo*, etc.) and those pronounced by the deacon in the Eastern manner.[85]

It is in continuity with this tradition, though under a new and original form, that the instruction of September 3, 1958 and later the Second Vatican Council have allowed the intervention of a "commentator" in the Latin liturgical celebration.[86] Just as those contained in the early books, these interventions should be short and hieratic; they should guide the people in their prayer and not be a substitute for it, and above all they should lead the faithful to the prayer of the celebrant, certainly never covering it over or putting it into the background. They are not simply explanations or digressions halting the flow of the liturgical action, but an impetus enlivening the interior rhythm of the people's participation.[87]

---

[82]Cf. the ideas proposed in this respect by the Second Vatican Council, CSL 35, n. 3.

[83]Funk ed., pp. 478-86, 488-92, 514-16, 518, 546.—In 410 the Synod of Mar Isaac at Seleucia-Ctesiphon spoke several times of the "proclamations" which the deacons make from their *bêma* (*ambo*): can. 13 and 15; J. B. Chabot, *Synodicon orientale* (Paris: Imprimerie nationale, 1902) pp. 265-8. Could it have already been mentioned in can. 2 of the Council of Ancyra in 314: κηρύσσειν ?—On contemporary practice, see S. Salaville and G. Nowack, *Le rôle du diacre dans la liturgie orientale* (Athens: French Institute of Byzantine Studies, 1962; *Archives de l'Orient chrétien* 3).

[84]To observe the usual liturgical phraseology.

[85]For example, the *Liber ordinum*, M. Férotin ed. (Didot, 1904), col. 83, 145, 182, 217-23, to confine ourselves solely to the formulas which the rubrics of this book attribute expressly to the deacon. See also J. Pinell, "Una exhortación diaconal en el antiguo rito hispánico, la supplicatio" in *Analecta sacra Tarraconensia* 26 (1964) 3-25.

[86]See above, preceding chapter, 5.

[87]SRC, instruction of September 3, 1958, n. 96; Martimort-Picard, *Liturgie et musique* (Ed. du Cerf, 1959; *Lex orandi* 28) pp. 185-90; A. M. Roguet, "Le commentateur" in LMD 60 (1959) 80-98.—CSL 35, §3.

II SILENT PRAYER

BIBLIOGRAPHY

I. Cecchetti, "Tibi silentium laus" in *Miscellanea liturgica in honorem L. Cuniberti Mohlberg* 2 (Rome: Ed. liturgiche, 1949) pp. 521-70.
H. Chirat, *L'assemblée chrétienne à l'âge apostolique* (Paris: Ed. du Cerf, 1949) pp. 121-5.
A. G. Martimort, "Le sens du sacré" in LMD 25 (1951) 66-9.

After the invitation to prayer, the Roman liturgy makes provision for a period of silence; this is now the case at least following the *Flectamus genua: "omnes, flexis genibus, per aliquod temporis spatium in silentio orant."*[88] It is to be hoped that these rubrics will be observed, since they represent an ancient tradition and correspond to a deep need. In this way the uniformity of public prayer is harmoniously reconciled with the incommunicable individuality of personal prayer. The people are given an initiation into mental prayer: the silence permits of meditation on the Word of God. In the monasteries of ancient Egypt each psalm was followed by such a period of silence.[89]

Since our language is powerless to describe the perfections of the Lord, silence is also an expression of our wonderment, adoration, and consciousness of God. The liturgy of St James puts it thus: "Let all mortal flesh be silent, and stand with fear and trembling, and meditate nothing earthly within itself: for the King of kings and Lord of lords, Christ our God, comes forward to be sacrificed."[90]

That is why the episcopal directories insist on the place and quality which silence should have in the liturgy.[91] The instruction of September 3, 1958 urges a period of "sacred silence" from the consecration of the Mass up to the *Pater noster.*[92]

In the liturgy of the Apocalypse silence is also eschatological expectation (Rv 8:1-4).

III THE LITANY

BIBLIOGRAPHY

A. Baumstark, *Liturgie comparée* . . . , pp. 83-90.
E. Bishop, "Kyrie eleison" in *Liturgica historica* (Oxford: Clarendon, 1918) pp. 116-36.
H. Leclercq, "Litanie" in DACL 9 (1930) col. 1540-51.

[88]NRC, n. 440.
[89]John Cassian, *De institutis coenobiorum*, 2, 7 (M. Petschenig ed., 1888; CSEL 17, p. 23).
[90]Brightman, p. 41.
[91]*Directoire pour la pastorale de la messe à l'usage des diocèses de France*, 2nd ed., 1960, n. 140-42.
[92]SRC, instruction . . . , n. 14c, 27f.—CSL 30: "At the proper times all should observe a reverent silence."

There is a form of public prayer that is easier than silence: the litany. Its oldest expression is the diaconal litany, which is perhaps connected with the prayer of the synagogue. It seems at any rate to have originated in Syria and was in use in Antioch at the time of St John Chrysostom;[93] it always had a prominent (sometimes too prominent) position in the Eastern rites. The deacon enunciates one by one a series of prayer intentions which the people make their own with the supplication: *Kyrie eleison.*

It is under a somewhat similar form that the Prayer of the Faithful was reintroduced into the Roman Mass in 1965. Pope Gelasius (492-496) had adopted this litany type of prayer, of which only a few traces are subsequently found in the *Ordo missae*,[94] but it was always retained in the Milanese liturgy for the Sundays of Lent. The Spanish liturgy also practised it;[95] different versions are to be found in various early books.[96] The litany prayer still exists in the Benedictine office, and in the Roman office it has survived in the form of the ferial prayers. The litany of the saints, whose history is as yet only imperfectly known, takes up in its third section the style and themes of the early diaconal litanies, after the invocation of the saints and the enumeration of the mysteries of Christ.[97] It is the favorite prayer of the people in processions and during the great consecratory acts of the liturgy: ordinations, dedications, consecration of virgins, and at the Easter vigil. It is hardly necessary to emphasize the significance it has in the promotion of pastoral liturgy.

IV THE OUR FATHER

BIBLIOGRAPHY

J. A. Jungmann, in *Gewordene Liturgie* . . . (Innsbruck: Rauch, 1941) pp. 137-72.

[93]St John Chrysostom, texts collected by Brightman, p. 478, and *In 2 Cor.*, 18, 3; Egeria, *Peregrinatio*, Pétré ed. (sc 21) pp. 92-3; cf. *Apostolic Constitutions* VIII, 6, 4; 8, 6; Funk ed., pp. 479, 487.

[94]To be treated in a subsequent volume.

[95]See, for example, *Liber ordinum*, Férotin ed., col. 114-17.

[96]They have been collected by H. Leclercq, *op. cit.*, col. 1553-66, and by B. Capelle, "Le Kyrie de la messe et le pape Gélase" in RB 46 (1934) 128-39 (= *Travaux liturgiques* . . ., 2, pp. 116-34).

[97]On the history of the litany of the saints: E. Bishop, "The litany of saints in the Stowe missal", in *Liturgica historica* . . . , pp. 137-64; E. Moeller, "Litanies majeures et Rogations" in QLP 23 (1938) 80-86; M. Coens, "Anciennes litanies des saints" in *Analecta Bollandiana* 54 (1936) 5-37; 55 (1937) 49-69; 59 (1941) 272-98; 62 (1944) 126-68; E. Moeller, "Un cas d'abréviation de l'office romain au XIIIe siècle: les litanies du samedi saint" in *Miscellanea historica in honorem Leonis Van der Essen* (Brussels: Ed. Universitaires, 1947) pp. 329-43; M. Coens, "Les plus anciennes litanies de Stavelot" in *Analecta Bollandiana* 75 (1957) 5-16; B. Opfermann, "Litania italica, ein Beitrag zur Litaneigeschichte" in EL 72 (1958) 306-19.

The Lord's Prayer, which in the earliest times occupied an important place in baptismal catechesis and in spiritual treatises, was the private prayer *par excellence* of the faithful. The *Didache*, for example, recommends that it be said three times a day.[98] But since the *Pater noster* was not entrusted to those who were not baptized, the liturgy could allow it to be said publicly only when the catechumens were absent, i.e. during the eucharistic prayer proper. This is perhaps the origin of the practice in certain rites of saying the *Pater* in a low voice. It is preeminently the prayer of preparation for communion and was a common prayer at the conclusion of the hours of the office.

In the Eastern rites the *Pater* was sung by the people (at least in theory, since unfortunately a choir or some of the ministers often took the place of the people); in the Gallican liturgy the situation was the same.[99] The other Latin liturgies made it a prayer of the priest, restricting the participation of the people either to the final *Sed libera nos a malo*, or to the *Amen* said in answer to each of the petitions.[100] The instruction of September 3, 1958 allowed the *Pater* to be said by all the faithful at low Masses; the instruction of September 26, 1964 extended this permission to sung Masses, thus doing away with the divergence between Rome and the Eastern rites on this point.

4 The prayer of the celebrant

BIBLIOGRAPHY

B. Botte, "La prière du célébrant" in LMD 20 (1950) 133-41.
J. A. Jungmann, *The Liturgy of the Word*, pp. 65-74.

The practice of a liturgy which is not solemn, in particular of the private Mass, has frequently led the celebrant to play a substitute role in respect of functions which are not his own. Even in the prayers which are proper to him, there are good grounds for distinguishing between those which express his personal devotion and which remain in some way private prayers, and those where he truly acts as president of the assembly and where he exercises his role of mediator. The practice of solemn celebration and the study of the historical evolution of the rites make this distinction obvious. Furthermore, certain interventions of the priest, such as explanatory formulas and exorcisms, are not so much prayers as actions.

[98]*Didache*, 8, 2-3, Hemmer ed., pp. 16-17.—See J. Lebreton, "La prière dans l'Église primitive" in RechSR 14 (1924) 13-15.

[99]Gregory of Tours, *De virtutibus s. Martini*, II, 30, Arndt-Krusch ed. (MGH), p. 620.

[100]This last form occurs in the Mozarabic liturgy: *Missale mixtum*, PL 85, col. 559.

The important actions of the celebrant are generally preceded in all the liturgies by a *greeting addressed to the people*; St Augustine and St John Chrysostom vouch for this as a traditional practice. These salutations are biblical in character, composed from expressions taken from both the New and the Old Testament: "Peace be with you," "Peace be to all,"[101] "The Lord be with you,"[102] "The grace of the Lord Jesus Christ, the love of God and the fellowship of the Holy Spirit be with you all."[103] The reply of the people— "And with your spirit"—is likewise biblical.[104] This greeting has often become simply a calling to attention or an invitation to silence, in order to obtain a hearing for an exhortation or reading.

I THE GREAT PRIESTLY PRAYERS

Two forms of priestly prayer are distinguished by their solemnity, their function, and by their very style. They are the thanksgiving (preface, eucharistic prayer, anaphora, *contestatio, illatio*), and the collect, which in its present form is typically Western, but which has parallels in the Eastern rites.

1 *Thanksgiving prayers*

We include together under this category all the great constitutive consecratory prayers, even those which only took the form of a thanksgiving preface at a later date. In fact in the current Roman liturgy we find such prayers not only in the canon of the Mass but also in the consecration of bishops, priests, deacons, virgins, abbots, baptismal water, chrism, churches and altars, cemeteries, and in the formula for the reconciliation of penitents; formerly this was true also of the nuptial blessing. In their primitive state the older of these prayers included neither the introductory dialogue nor the opening *Vere dignum* . . . But the introduction of the thanksgiving style came about almost naturally, so much was it suggested by the basic pattern of the Mass, the spirit of liturgical tradition, and the heritage of the synagogue.[105]

---

[101]*Pax vobis* is, in the present Roman rite, the greeting of the bishop following on the singing of the *Gloria in excelsis*; it is the greeting of the risen Christ in Jn 20:19 and 26. Εἰρήνη πᾶσι recurs frequently in the course of the Byzantine liturgy.

[102]*Dominus vobiscum*: Rt 2:4; 2 Th 3:16.

[103]2 Co 13:13. Except for a few variants, it is the greeting said by the celebrant in the Eastern rites (the Copts excepted) before the eucharistic anaphora.

[104]Cf. 2 Tm 4:22. Cf. P. Milner, "Et cum spiritu tuo," in *Studies in Pastoral Liturgy* 3, P. Murray ed. (Dublin: Gill, 1967) pp. 202-10.

[105]A. Baumstark, *Liturgie comparée* . . . , pp. 53-8. But the blessing of the chrism has always been a thanksgiving formula.

Originally improvised on specific themes,[106] these prayers were the first to be fixed in writing both in the East and in the West, especially when they resulted from the literary genius of the great bishops of the fourth century. Their liturgical importance is underlined by the invitatories and the dialogue with the people which precede them as well as by their uniform style, but above all by their sacramental efficacy: for the Eucharist[107] and holy orders they constitute the sacramental word; the consecration of chrism is essential to the sign of confirmation; the consecration of baptismal water, though not required for the validity of the sacrament, expresses the symbolism of the water and is a preparation for the sacrament. The prefaces are the climax of the great sacramentals of the Church. They include contemplation of the divine perfections, proclamation of the economy of salvation, and the appeal to the sanctifying action of the Holy Spirit.

2 *The collect*

BIBLIOGRAPHY

B. Capelle, "Collecta" in RB 42 (1930) 197-204; reprinted in *Travaux liturgiques*
   . . . 2 (Louvain: Mont César, 1962) pp. 192-9.
M. P. Ellebracht, *Remarks on the Vocabulary of the Ancient Orations in the Missale Romanum* (Nijmegen-Utrecht: Dekker and Van de Vegt, 1963).

The other pre-eminent form of sacerdotal prayer did not take shape quite so early. Though it did not appear in the liturgy which St Augustine used at Hippo, it is to be found in the *Apostolic Constitutions*. Its earliest formulations in Rome could date from the time of St Leo.[108] Its literary forms vary greatly between East and West. The collect is the prayer said by the celebrant after the people have prayed, concluding either a diaconal litany or a period of silent prayer. When the prayer is in silence, the faithful formulate in the quiet of their hearts their praise and petitions; the contents of this prayer are varied and known only to God. It is the task of the celebrant to gather together these petitions into a single collection, giving them public expression as the unanimous prayer of the assembly; whence the name *collectio* or *collecta*. In the Roman tradition this type of prayer is written in a style of precise brevity devoid of all lyricism, and with a fulness of expression which makes

---

[106]B. Botte, *op. cit.,* pp. 133-6.

[107]Ignoring, for the moment, the fact that the consecratory prayer of the Mass today has lost its unity and that the preface is no more than the beginning of this prayer.

[108]With the exception, however, of the solemn collects of Good Friday, which constituted, perhaps as early as the fourth century, the Roman form of the "Prayer of the faithful": A. Baumstark, *Liturgie comparée* . . . , p. 87.

their translation into another language difficult; this is not the case
with the prayer formularies which have an identical function in the
other liturgies, even in the Latin ones.[109]

3 *Characteristics of the great priestly prayers*

The priestly prayer, whether "thanksgiving" or "collect," constitutes the climax of the celebration: even when it is not sacramental,
it gives form, so to speak, to the other elements of worship, so as to
make them truly liturgical. It shows the mediation which the priesthood of the bishop and priest exercises *in persona Christi* between
God and his people. That is why at these moments of prayer nothing
should be allowed to interfere with the voice of the celebrant.[110]
The faithful stand and make this prayer their own both by their
silent attention and by the *Amen* which they say at its conclusion.

That is also why the formulation of this prayer is purposely
stripped of every trace of individualism and emotional expression:
it is collective and universal.[111] The celebrant utters his prayer in
such a way as to be heard by all those taking part in the celebration.[112]
It is a solemn declaration and not really a chant, whose musical
setting could distract from the text. Nor should it make use of
poetic devices. It is prose in noble and dignified language; it is only
the prosaic rhythm of the *cursus* that governs the Roman priestly
prayers.[113]

The content of these prayers is a most important theological
source. They interpret the common faith of the assembly. Some of
them are even sacramental. They harmoniously unite adoration and
petition. Above all it is they, perhaps more than the doxologies,
that give the liturgy its proper character of trinitarian worship.

All the early Roman formularies and most of the Eastern ones
strictly observe the directive of the third Council of Carthage in 397:

---

[109]To be treated in a subsequent volume.

[110]SRC, instruction of September 3, 1958, n. 22b, 93, 94; *Directoire pour la
pastorale de la messe . . .*, n. 59-67.—In the East, unfortunately it is only the
conclusion (*ekphonese*) of the priestly prayers that is said aloud, the main part
being said quietly by the celebrant during the diaconal litany or during the
chants. But this is obviously a corruption.

[111]Cf. R. Guardini, *The Spirit of the Liturgy* (London: Sheed and Ward, 1930)
pp. 37-46, 56-69; J. Jungmann, *The Liturgy of the Word*, pp. 66-9.

[112]SRC, *op. cit.*, n. 34, 72, 78.

[113]On the *cursus* of the Roman collects: H. Leclercq, "Cursus" in DACL 3 (1913)
col. 3193-205, with the oldest bibliography; one could scarcely omit adding here
L. Laurand, "Le cursus dans le sacramentaire léonien" in QLP 4 (1914) 215-18,
taken up again and further developed in L. Laurand, *Manuel des études grecques
et latines*, 2nd ed. by A. Lauras, vol. 4 (Picard 1949) pp. 270-96: *Ce qu'on sait
et ce qu'on ignore du cursus.*

Ut nemo in precibus vel Patrem pro Filio vel Filium pro Patre nominet, et cum altari adsistitur semper ad Patrem dirigatur oratio.[114] The prayer is addressed to the Father, to whom all liturgy is ultimately directed. The order of processions in the Trinity is always scrupulously observed, even when various parts of the liturgy would suggest otherwise, for example when the Holy Spirit is invoked in the epiclesis. In keeping with the order which Christ gave us, it is always through him that we pray, and this mention of the divine mediator generally serves as conclusion and final doxology of the prayer.[115] However, in reaction to Arianism, some early liturgies, for example that of Spain, sometimes directed the priestly prayers to Christ himself, a usage likewise accepted during the Middle Ages by the Roman rite and still retained in some of its prayers.[116]

II OTHER PRIESTLY FORMULAS

Since the other types of priestly formulas will be explained in the study of the rites of which they form part, we shall limit ourselves here to enumerating them briefly.

1 Indicative formulas

We meet indicative priestly formulas both in the sacraments and in some sacramentals. The baptismal formula used at Antioch at the end of the fourth century is a case in point: "N.N. is baptized in the name of the Father, and of the Son, and of the Holy Spirit."[117] Still earlier, at the time of the *Apostolic Tradition* of Hippolytus, the anointings at Rome were accompanied in the same way: *Ungueo te oleo sancto in nomine Iesu Christi.*[118] The consecration of baptismal water also includes indicative passages, where the celebrant addresses

---

[114]can. 23; Bruns, vol. 1, p. 126.—See J. Lebreton, "La prière dans l'Église primitive" in RechSR 14 (1924) 7-13, 20-32.

[115]This is among the points which have been most studied since the birth of the liturgical movement. Cf. L. Beauduin, *Mélanges liturgiques* . . . (Louvain: Mont César, 1954) pp. 44-73 (=QLP 3, 1912-13, pp. 201-9, 271-80; 4, 1913-14, pp. 350-61); G. Lefebvre, *Liturgia*, 2nd ed. (Lophem-lez-Bruges, 1922) pp. 22-39; A. Coelho, *Cours de liturgie romaine* . . ., pp. 148-63; J. Jungmann, *The Place of Christ in Liturgical Prayer* (London: Chapman, 1965); C. Vagaggini, *Theological Dimensions of the Liturgy*, pp. 107-39.

[116]These points are treated of together by J. Jungmann, *op. cit.*—Pius XII, allocution to the Assisi Congress in *The Assisi Papers* (Collegeville, Minnesota: Liturgical Press, 1957), p. 235, warned against new forms of old errors: "Thus the divinity of Christ cannot remain at the edge of liturgical thought." See also J. Lebreton, *art. cit.*, pp. 97-133.

[117]A. Wenger in *Jean Chrysostome, Huit catéchèses baptismales* (Ed. du Cerf, 1957; sc 50) pp. 96-7, provides the references.

[118]n. 21; B. Botte ed. (LQF 39) p. 50, cf. 53.

not a person but the water: *Unde benedico te creatura aquae*—a procedure found also in the consecration of an altar and elsewhere.

2 *Blessings*

The celebrant frequently exercises his priestly function through *blessings*. The blessings of *things* are generally in the form of prayers conforming to all the characteristics already described above.[119] The blessing of *persons*, both at Mass and in the office, appears more frequently under the form of a wish directed to the entire assembly or to a minister as he exercises his function; but it can also be a prayer, like the Roman *Oratio super populum*. The Visigothic and Gallican Mass contain a special kind of episcopal blessing before the communion, which was kept on in the Middle Ages and remains even today in some churches.[120]

3 *Exorcisms*

Some blessings are preceded by an exorcism over the objects to be blessed. The prebaptismal liturgy, moreover, gives an important place to the exorcism spoken over persons. The exorcism is an adjuration addressed to Satan, with the authority which the Church has received from Christ for that purpose. Its use in the liturgy shows both the hold which the devil had even over things and places as a result of man's sin, and the victorious struggle entered upon by Christ and continued by the Church so that all may return to God.[121]

4 *Private prayers*

At certain moments of the liturgy, especially during Mass, the celebrant turns to private prayer. This is distinguished from the properly priestly prayer by its style, its place, and by the fact that it is said in a low voice to accompany actions which originally did not have any formula.[122] In the East, these prayers, which arose almost by chance, could even occur as a dialogue between concelebrants or between celebrant and deacon.

5 Problems in the expression of liturgical prayer

Among the problems posed by the expression of liturgical prayer in the various cultures or civilizations which the Church meets throughout the world and in the course of the centuries, only two

[119]To be treated in a subsequent volume.
[120]To be treated in a subsequent volume.
[121]C. Vagaggini, *op. cit.*, vol. 1, pp. 201-42.
[122]To be treated in a subsequent volume.

will be dealt with here, namely that of language and that of music. These are selected because of the importance which the Church herself attaches to them and because they are the object of special rulings.

I LANGUAGE IN THE LITURGY

BIBLIOGRAPHY

P. M. Gy, "The Vernacular in the Mass since the Council" in P. Murray ed., *Studies in Pastoral Liturgy* 3 (Dublin: Gill, 1967) pp. 11-28.
A. G. Martimort, "Essai historique sur les traductions liturgiques" in LMD 86 (1966) 75-105 (where reference will be found to all the scientific treatises which deal with the question of liturgical languages).
C. Mohrmann, *Liturgical Latin—Its Origin and Character* (London: Burns and Oates, 1959).

The Church has been faced with the problem of languages from its very foundation, even on the day of Pentecost itself (Ac 2:7-11). This was true not only in respect of the liturgy: there was first the preaching of the gospel and then the transmission of the sacred books to be taken care of. Then there was the presence of different linguistic groups in the same community, beginning with Jerusalem (Ac 6:1). Later the problem was rather that of communication between churches. To find a concrete solution to these problems, the Church seeks both to deepen the Christian life of diverse peoples—which can only be brought about through the medium of their languages—and to consolidate her own unity, local and universal, which requires understanding and communication between different cultural groups.

East and West, because of their different linguistic situations, have provided different solutions to the problem—thus the diversity of present discipline. But we must also take account of the resistance to change stemming from attachment to usages of the past: liturgical fidelity to certain languages constitutes part of the cultural patrimony and individual character of the national groups which have preserved these languages.

1 *The languages of the Eastern liturgies*

The part of the Roman Empire which had come under Hellenic control retained Greek as its everyday language. But several of the peoples of this territory had their own spoken and written language, a literature, and a civilization which rivalled that of Hellenism; hence these languages, especially the Semitic ones, did not die out. The languages which had neither script nor literature benefited from the multilingual character of their environs and, thanks in great part to Christianity, were able to develop on their own.

From her very origin, the Church celebrated the liturgy in Greek

in the great cities of the East, but, since the liturgical gathering had
to be common to all the baptized, she had to provide more and more
for the needs of non-Greek-speaking Christians. This was done by
interpreters who translated during the ceremony,[123] and later by
celebrations that were themselves polyglot. The church in Jerusalem
and the Syrian monasteries were noted for their practice of alternating
languages in the readings and chant.[124] It was principally the monks
who translated the Bible and liturgical texts, and created poetic
compositions in the local languages, such as Armenian, Georgian,
and Ge'ez (the language of ancient Ethiopia). In Egypt translations
into Coptic dialects were begun even before the birth of monasticism.

While in the imperial part of Asia local languages existed side by
side with the Greek, the church which grew up beyond the Euphrates
used only Syriac. Broken off from unity by the Nestorian schism,
it has nevertheless witnessed an extraordinary missionary development, which has produced lasting results in India and has extended
into Tibet, China, and beyond. But it has not created a native
hierarchy. As a result, the liturgy is always celebrated in Syriac, but
with a translation of the readings and sometimes of the chants.

The Byzantine church, on the other hand, accepted the languages
of the countries to which it brought Christianity; this is true especially
of the Slav languages. It is the Byzantine rite which in our day most
readily permits the translation of the liturgy into modern languages.
In the tenth century the Melkites of Syria and Egypt, side by side
with the Greek, adopted Arabic, a language which has also partially
entered into the liturgy of the Syrians, Copts, and Maronites.

2 Discipline governing liturgical language in the West

(i) *Up to the sixteenth century*—The first important church to use
the Latin language was that of Africa. Since the native peoples were
only superficially assimilated into the Roman culture, the collapse
of this culture in these regions resulted also in the disappearance of
Latin;[125] this case is unique in the West.

The Roman church retained the Greek language up to the third
century; the liturgy was not definitively latinized until the second half
of the fourth century. But in the seventh century, when Greek-
speaking Christians were once again very numerous, the liturgy

---

[123]See M. J. Lagrange, *Revue biblique* 34 (1925) 494.

[124]See the classical texts in Egeria, *Peregrinatio*, 47, 3-4, H. Pétré ed. (sc 21)
pp. 260-63, and in St Jerome, *Letter* 108, n. 29, Labourt ed. (Coll. *Budé*), vol. 5,
p. 198, to which must also be added the facts related by O. Hendriks, "Les
premiers monastères internationaux syriens" in *Orient syrien* 3 (1958) 165-84.

[125]C. Courtois, *Les Vandales et l'Afrique* (Paris, 1955) pp. 126-30.

became bilingual in the readings and in certain rites of catechumens; at the same time, chants in Greek were mingling with the Latin ones. The present papal Mass retains a vestige of this in its double reading of the epistle and gospel.

The languages spoken in Gaul and Spain before the Roman conquest have left scarcely any trace. Similarly the tribes who invaded the Western Empire were latinized very quickly; this applies also to the Goths, though in Constantinople they celebrated the liturgy in their own language. Latin remained for centuries the only language of culture in the West, except in Ireland, a country little influenced by Roman civilization; the native language was preserved and developed, though it never gained any real place in the liturgy. The only occasion when there was any question of translating the Latin liturgy was at the time of the evangelization of Moravia by Saints Cyril and Methodius. Objections were raised, in the attempt to justify theologically the de facto situation with respect to the use of Latin.[126] However there still exist today churches of the Roman rite celebrating the liturgy in a Slav translation.

(ii) *From the sixteenth to the twentieth century*—The situation has changed since the sixteenth century in that the national languages of the West are no longer simply the popular dialects that they were in the Middle Ages. Since Protestants upheld the use of these languages in the liturgy for theological reasons that were unacceptable, the Council of Trent had to deal with the problem—session 22, chapter 8 and canon 9.[127] The principal concern of the Council was to dissociate the whole question from any doctrinal considerations in order to keep it solely on the level of discipline.

However the Council did not judge it opportune to introduce modern languages into the liturgy. The Counter-Reformation, in consequence, severely excluded them, not only on the disciplinary level—the Roman Congregations refused to become more tractable, even in favor of the missions—but also on the level of principle, opposing them with impassioned arguments reiterated throughout the eighteenth and nineteenth centuries.

(iii) *The Second Vatican Council and afterwards*—Now, in the middle of the twentieth century, the pastoral problems caused by the dechristianization of the masses and by the second world war have given rise to a reconsideration of the discipline of the Latin church in respect of liturgical language. Already under the pontificate of Pius

---

[126]P. Duthilleul, *L'évangélisation des Slaves: Cyrille et Méthode* (Tournai: Desclée, 1963; *Bibliothèque de théologie*).

[127]Denz. 1749 and 1759; H. Schmidt, *Liturgie en langue vulgaire, le problème de la langue liturgique chez les premiers Réformateurs et au Concile de Trente* (Rome: Univ. grégorienne, 1950).

XII, the Holy See, at the request of national episcopal conferences, quite freely granted the use of bilingual rituals in which certain formulas were translated.[128] Permission was also given to repeat the readings in the vernacular after they had been read in Latin, and to celebrate the "sung Mass with hymns of the people in the vernacular."[129]

(a) The Second Vatican Council wished to re-examine the question in depth, in order to provide a comprehensive solution. Taking account of each of the elements that had been called into question in the course of a long debate, it proposed as a general principle that "though existing special exemptions are to remain in force, the use of the Latin language is to be preserved in the Latin rites; but since the use of the mother tongue is frequently of great advantage to the people in the Mass, the administration of sacraments and other parts of the liturgy, the limits of its employment may be extended."[130] Whatever concessions be made to the language of the country, "nevertheless steps must be taken to ensure that the faithful are able to say or to sing together, also in Latin, those parts of the ordinary of the Mass which are rightfully theirs."[131] *A fortiori* clerics should in principle "according to the ancient tradition of the Latin rite . . . use the Latin language in the divine office."[132]

The conciliar Constitution enumerated certain cases where the vernacular was entirely justified. But it did not thereby close the door to an extension of such cases "if an even more extended use of the mother tongue within the Mass appears desirable in some part of the world."[133]

The Council wished to entrust the responsibility for matters of liturgical language to the national episcopal conferences, which can act in any of three ways. When it is question of deciding, according to local conditions, in which areas it intends to make the concessions proposed by the Constitution, the national conference may draw up decrees, which are then to be approved, that is, confirmed, by the Holy See.[134] But if there be question of extending the use of the

---

[128]P. Gerlier, "Les rituels bilingues . . .," in LMD 47-48 (1956) 83-97.

[129]See A. G. Martimort, in LMD 44 (1955) 161-63.—On the whole question, see H. Schmidt, *Introductio in liturgiam occidentalem* (Rome: Herder, 1960) pp. 209-27.

[130]CSL 36, §§1–2; cf. MD 60.

[131]CSL 54.—Cf. SRC, instruction of September 26, 1964, n. 57.

[132]CSL 101.

[133]CSL 54, cf. 40.

[134]CSL 36, §3.—But where it is question of the private recitation of the office, i.e. without the participation of the people, it is a matter for the local ordinary or competent superior: CSL 101, §§1-2.

vernacular to rites for which the Council has not expressly provided, the episcopal conference is to seek special permission from the Holy See within the framework of the procedure envisaged by the Council for liturgical adaptation.[135] In these two cases it is the national conference which should draw up and approve for its entire territory the official translation, from which no one will be permitted to depart, even where there is question of the office of nuns or of similar communities.[136]

(b) At the request of numerous episcopal conferences, the Holy See effectively extended the faculties granted by the conciliar Constitution. The general discipline as it exists at present is described in the two instructions of the Congregation of Rites dated September 26, 1964[137] and May 4, 1967,[138] to which must be added, for religious, the instruction of November 23, 1965.[139]

II LITURGICAL MUSIC

BIBLIOGRAPHY

R. Aigrain, *La musique religieuse* (Bloud et Gay, 1929; *Bibliothèque catholique des sciences religieuses*).

S. Corbin, *L'Église à la conquête de sa musique* (Gallimard, 1960).

P. Huot-Pleuroux, *Histoire de la musique religieuse* (Presses universitaires de France, 1957).

1 *Historical note on the evolution of music in the liturgy*

The different rites of both West and East, while they "display in their liturgical ceremonies and formulas of prayer the marvellous abundance of the Church, they also, in their various liturgical chants, preserve treasures which must be guarded and defended to prevent not only their complete disappearance, but also any partial loss or distortion."[140]

(a) "Among the oldest and most outstanding monuments of sacred music the *liturgical chants of the different Eastern rites* hold a highly important place. Some of the melodies of these chants . . . had a great influence on the composition of the musical works of the Western church itself."[141] Familiarity with them today is greatly facilitated by recordings, transcriptions, the publication of early

---

[135]CSL 54.

[136]CSL 36, §4; 101, §2; SRC, *op. cit.*, n. 40 (but cf. also n. 88).

[137]AAS 56 (1964) 877-900.

[138]AAS 59 (1967) 442-8.

[139]AAS 57 (1965) 1010-13.

[140]Pius XII, encyclical *Musicae sacrae*, December 25, 1955, in *The Pope Speaks: Addresses and Publications of the Holy Father* 3 (1956) 17.—Cf. CSL 112, 114.

[141]*ibid.*, 17.

melodies and of historical studies in line with scientific requirements.[142]

(b) We know little about the music of the *early Gallican* liturgy. Not only had this liturgy disappeared before the invention of musical notation, but we have not even a non-notated antiphonary which would clearly be of Gallican origin.[143]

(c) As regards the *Spanish* liturgy, side by side with the modern Mozarabic tradition, we do have a magnificent work of the tenth century—the Leonine antiphonary—as well as various fragments, revealing a musical notation which unfortunately has not as yet been deciphered.[144]

(d) The *old Roman* chant, i.e. that which remained proper to the papal and basilican liturgy up to the thirteenth century, has in recent years been the object of noteworthy studies, though certain aspects of its history are still sharply controverted.[145]

(e) The *Ambrosian* church still uses its traditional chant, restored, in accordance with the early manuscripts, by Dom Gregorio Sunyol at the instigation of Cardinal Schuster. The analyses to which it has been subjected in recent years, as well as underlining its relationship with Gregorian chant, show that his editions could be emended.[146]

(f) *Gregorian* chant was diffused throughout the entire Latin West by the Carolingian liturgical reform. It was attributed to St

[142]It is chiefly the Byzantine music that has benefited from an important development in monumental works and studies, principally under the direction of E. Wellesz, whose most accessible work is *A History of Byzantine Music and Hymnography*, 2nd ed. (Oxford: Clarendon, 1961). The same author has written a more general introduction to the music of the Eastern rites: *Aufgaben und Probleme auf dem Gebiete der byzantinischen und orientalischen Kirchenmusik* (Münster: Aschendorff, 1923; LQF 18).

[143]In fact the fragments of the antiphonary of the office published by G. Morin, RB 22 (1905) 329-56, are, in the very sure judgment of A. Wilmart, DACL 6, col. 1091, later and rather of insular origin.—But see A. Gastoué, *Le chant gallican* (Grenoble: Libr. Saint-Grégoire, 1939).

[144]Volume 8, 1954, of *Archivos Leoneses* is devoted entirely to the Leonine antiphonary; see especially the article by L. Brou, "Le joyau des antiphonaires latins," pp. 7-114. Other manuscripts in L. Brou, *Hispania sacra* 5 (1952) 35-65, 341-66. See in addition C. Rojo and G. Prado, *El canto mozárabe . . .* (Barcelona: Diputación provincial, 1929).

[145]R. Andoyer, "Le chant romain antégrégorien," in *Revue du chant grégorien* 20 (1912) 71-5, 107-14; M. Huglo, "Le chant vieux-romain, liste des manuscrits et témoins indirects" in SE 6 (1954) 96-123; S. Van Dijk, "The Urban and Papal Rites in Seventh and Eighth Century Rome" in SE 12 (1961) 411-86; for a bibliography, cf. J. Hourlier, in *Études grégoriennes* 3 (1959) 189-92.

[146]The fundamental work is that of M. Huglo, L. Agustoni, E. Cardine and E. Moneta-Caglio, *Fonti e paleografia del canto ambrosiano* (Milan, 1956; *Archivio ambrosiano* 7).

Gregory the Great, an attribution that is doubtful. At any rate it is not on its origins that the Church judges it: in liturgical law Gregorian chant is called "the sacred song of the Roman church," i.e. that part of the modern Roman liturgy which "is to be found for liturgical use in the various books approved by the Holy See," whether it be question of the earliest collection "piously and faithfully copied from ancient and venerable tradition," or of texts "composed in recent times on the pattern of ancient tradition."[147] In liturgical actions, all else being equal, it is to be preferred to the other types of sacred music, and it is the only type allowed for the Latin chants of the celebrant and ministers, as well as for the replies in Latin made by the people to the celebrant.[148] It has been an object of concern of Popes Pius X, Pius XI, and Pius XII; its melodies have been restored under the influence of the paleographical studies of the Abbey of Solesmes.[149] The Roman church recommends it because of the ease it offers for the participation of the faithful, because of the way in which its melodies help to an understanding of the text, because of its moderation and placid character, and finally because of its universality.[150]

(g) The late Middle Ages and the Renaissance gave such a quality to conventionally notated music as to allow its use in the liturgy; furthermore this period produced a number of masterpieces, thanks above all to the genius of the "Roman school" and notably that of Pier Luigi da Palestrina (d. 1594). The papal choir has perpetuated this music, which the documents of the Holy See call *sacred polyphony*. It is performed without instrumental accompaniment.[151]

(h) Side by side with these historic forms, clearly defined and fixed in their traditions, the Church readily encourages *modern music*, including the use of instruments.[152] The adoption of living language for certain liturgical chants will also demand a great effort of musical creativity which will have to be both of an irreproachable

[147]SRC, instruction of September 3, 1958, in *The Pope Speaks* . . . , 5 (1959) 225f.—See the commentary by F. Picard, in Martimort-Picard, *Liturgie et musique* (Ed. du Cerf, 1959) pp. 30-1.

[148]SRC, *op. cit.,* in *The Pope Speaks* . . . , *ibid.*, 228.

[149]Even though the typical Vatican edition is not in fact the work of Solesmes nor does it exactly represent the result of these studies. For recent bibliography on Gregorian chant cf. J. Smits van Waesberghe, "L'état actuel des recherches scientifiques dans le domaine du chant grégorien" in *Actes du IIIᵉ Congrès international de musique sacrée*, (Paris, 1957) pp. 206-17; U. Bomm, "Gregorianischer Gesang" in ALW 7 (1962) 470-511.

[150]Pius XII, *Musicae sacrae, loc. cit.,* 15-17; cf. MD 191.

[151]SRC, instruction . . ., *loc. cit.,* 226, 228, and comments by F. Picard, *op. cit.,* pp. 31-3, 57-9, 114-16.—Cf. CSL 116; Pius XII, *Musicae sacrae, loc. cit.,* 9-10.

[152]CSL 116 and 120.

L

quality and conducive to the participation of the people.[153] However, since the present repertory of sacred music contains many works composed at times of liturgical decline, and since contemporary creations cannot yet benefit from the judgment made possible by the passage of time, precautions need to be taken and precise rules made before they are admitted into the liturgy.[154] In countries of non-Western culture (Asia, Africa, etc.), creative efforts of native genius comprise part of the work entailed in establishing the Church.[155]

2 *Laws governing liturgical music*

BIBLIOGRAPHY

SRC, *Instructio de musica in sacra liturgia*, March 5, 1967, in AAS 59 (1967) 300-320.
Commentaries:
EL 81 (1967) 193-298: studies by C. Braga, H. Hucke, J. Gelineau *et al.*
H. Hucke, "The Roman Instruction on Music in the Liturgy" in *Concilium* 2, n. 4 (1968) 57-65.
E. Lengeling, "Zur neuen Instruktion über die 'Kirkenmusik innerhalb der Liturgie' " in *Bibel und Liturgie* 40 (1967) 184-98.
A. Milner, "The Instruction on Sacred Music" in *Worship* 41 (1967) 322-33.
H. Rennings, "Die Instruktion über Gesang und Musik im Gottesdienst vom Jahre 1967" in *Liturgisches Jahrbuch* 17 (1967) 161-6.

The Church has frequently intervened in the sphere of liturgical music, to suppress abuses and restore sound traditions, but above all to define its laws.[156] Modern legislation, contained in the encyclical *Musicae sacrae* of Pius XII (December 25, 1955) and in the instruction of the Congregation of Rites dated September 3, 1958,[157] was reiterated in part in the Constitution *De sacra liturgia* of the Second Vatican Council and in the instruction of March 5, 1967. The supreme law of liturgical music is that it be perfectly subordinate to divine worship and its purpose, and, as far as the music itself is concerned, to the text of which it is the vehicle.[158] Hence the exclusion

---

[153]CSL 121; SRC, instruction of March 5, 1967, n. 54, 60.

[154]We have already noted the important place given to the song of the people in the more recent papal documents.

[155]CSL 119; cf. *Musicae sacrae, loc. cit.,* 20-1; SRC, instruction of September 3, 1958, n. 112.

[156]A. Hanin, *La législation ecclésiastique en matière de musique religieuse* (Tournai: Desclée, 1933); F. Romita, *Ius musicae liturgicae* (Rome: Edizioni liturgiche, 1947); A. Pons, *Droit ecclésiastique et musique sacrée* (Saint-Maurice: Oeuvre Saint-Augustin, 1959-1960), 3 vols.—Unfortunately none of these studies satisfies the requirements of historical science.

[157]The official text of these documents is in AAS 48 (1956) 5-25, and 50 (1958) 630-63.

[158]CSL 112, 116.

of music "which, because of its heavy and bombastic style, might obscure the sacred words of the liturgy by a kind of exaggeration, interfere with the conduct of the liturgical service, or, finally, lower the skill and competence of the singers to the disadvantage of sacred worship."[159] Another important law is the necessity of giving to the people the part which belongs to them in the celebration and of avoiding a situation where the faithful become "silent spectators."[160]

The bishops have been commissioned to see that these laws be observed, to judge new works, and, in a word, to give concrete directives. For this purpose they are to be assisted by a liturgical commission and by a commission for sacred music.[161]

---

[159]*Musicae sacrae, loc. cit.,* 18; cf. 15.

[160]CSL 114; cf. 48;—Pius XI, *Divini cultus,* December 20, 1928, n. 9; in A. Bugnini, *Documenta pontificia ad instaurationem liturgicam spectantia* (Rome: Edizioni liturgiche, 1953) p. 65.

[161]CSL 46; cf. SRC, instruction of March 5, 1967, n. 68, 69.

CHAPTER SEVEN

Sacred Signs

BIBLIOGRAPHY

A. Baumstark, *Liturgie comparée*, 3rd ed. (Chevetogne, 1953) pp. 144-67: "L'action liturgique." Engl. tr., *Comparative Liturgy* (revised by B. Botte; Westminster, Maryland: Newman Press; London: Mowbray, 1958).

I. H. Dalmais, *Introduction to the Liturgy* (London: Chapman; Baltimore: Helicon, 1961) pp. 8-12, 119-24.

J. Daniélou, *Primitive Christian Symbols* (London: Burns and Oates, 1964).

M. Eliade, *Images and Symbols* (New York: Sheed and Ward, 1961).

R. Guardini, *Sacred Signs* (St. Louis: Pio Decimo Press, 1956).

H. Musurillo, *Symbolism and the Christian Imagination* (Baltimore: Helicon, 1962).

C. Vagaggini, *Theological Dimensions of the Liturgy* 1 (Collegeville, Minnesota: Liturgical Press, 1959) pp. 19-34.

The liturgy is not only a dialogue, an exchange of words between God and his people: God acts and the people commit themselves to him. That is why the liturgy constantly appeals to other signs, signs more material than the word, more concrete and thought-inspiring, so to speak. It prescribes bodily postures, it involves gestures and actions, it makes use of things, it gets places furnished, has objects made and then consecrates them.[1]

Some of these liturgical signs are sacraments in the precise theological sense of the word (i.e. instituted by Christ, they produce the effects of supernatural grace which they signify),[2] in fidelity to the mission the Church has received from the Lord himself. By an extension of the signs that are sacraments, and always in a similar ("analogous") perspective, the Church has created other signs—sacramentals.[3] But more profoundly, the continual and almost spontaneous use of signs in the prayer of the Church stems from the New Testament vision of man and the created world—in its turn a direct continuation of the Old Testament concept. In this respect, however, it must always be borne in mind that the epoch of the Old

---

[1] The constitution *De sacra liturgia* of the Second Vatican Council stresses signs on various occasions: CSL 21, 24, 33, 34.

[2] CSL 59, cf. 62.—A. M. Roguet, in LMD 77, 133-6.

[3] CSL 60.—A. M. Roguet, *op. cit.*, 136-8.

Testament types has been abolished by the fact of their realization in Christ.

INTERPRETING SACRED SIGNS: THE LAWS OF SYMBOLISM

BIBLIOGRAPHY

E. Masure, *Le passage du visible à l'invisible: le signe; psychologie, histoire, mystère* (Paris: Bloud et Gay, 1953).

R. Pernoud, M. Carrouges, D. Sinor, A. Varagnac *et al.*, "Valeur permanente du symbolisme" in LMD 22 (1950).

M. Righetti, *Manuale di storia liturgica* 1, 3rd ed. (Milan: Ancora, 1964) pp. 64-74.

A. M. Roguet, *Les Sacrements* (Tournai: Desclée, 1945; *Somme théologique, Éditions de la Revue des Jeunes*) pp. 269-346.

F. Van Der Meer, " 'Sacramentum' chez saint Augustin" in LMD 13 (1948) 50-64.

Whether they be sacramental in the strict sense of the term or non-sacramental, whether they have been fixed by Christ himself or by the Church, the liturgical signs follow certain laws, knowledge of which is indispensable for their correct interpretation.

(1) They have been intended as signs: they are not directly or merely utilitarian acts which would only have become symbolic when they had lost their utilitarian significance.[4]

(2) Their signification cannot be determined arbitrarily by imagination or even by the poetic genius of commentators with a view to religious edification, however successful it may be. Such an *allegorical interpretation* of the liturgy normally betrays the commentator's ignorance of the true origin of the signs. This approach was in evidence as early as the end of the patristic era—it had already found its way into some of the commentaries of St Ambrose and was further developed by Theodore of Mopsuestia. The Carolingian epoch imposed it on the entire Middle Ages. The novels of Huysmans have restored it to favor and one cannot be quite sure that it is entirely absent in all modern expositions.

(3) Because liturgical signs are expressive of relationships which are supernatural realities, the relationship between the sign and the thing signified extends beyond the category of mere rational affinity: to a certain extent one can say that the signification has been fixed by the free choice of Christ or the Church. This signification is very

---

[4]This was the error of Claude de Vert (d. 1708) in his *Explication simple, littérale et historique des cérémonies de l'Église* (1706-1713), 4 vols.—But there are in the liturgy some purely utilitarian gestures and actions which have not of themselves any symbolic value, e.g. the prothesis or the ablutions in the Mass. Cf. H. Rabotin, in R. Aigrain, *Liturgia* (Paris: Bloud et Gay, 1935) pp. 378-80; A. Baumstark, *op. cit.*, pp. 144-9.

often expressed or suggested by the word which accompanies the gesture or act. If this is not so, then, in the case of a sign fixed by Christ, it is necessary to determine the intention of Christ as known and authentically interpreted by the tradition of the Church; in the case of a sign fixed by the Church, it is necessary to study as far as possible the *history of the rite*, its origin and development. Knowledge of its origin will usually discover its signification, all the more necessary since unfortunately gestures have often become distorted— either by attenuation or complication.

(4) These signs are not arbitrary or conventional. They have been chosen for their *natural aptitude* as signs, an aptitude vouched for by sociology, depth psychology, and by religious and profane history.[5] We must be able to interpret the hidden word which God has written into things from the first moment of creation and which he has imparted to the innermost recesses of the human soul. This word is all the more intelligible when the signs are basic, primeval, and unadorned, and that even in the era of industrial civilization and scientific mentality.[6]

(5) Above all, many of them are *biblical signs:* their explanation is to be had in the teaching of our Lord contained in Sacred Scripture.[7] It is as biblical signs that the sacramental signs have been chosen by Christ and as such they signify the grace they contain. In its prayer-gestures and in its actions, the liturgy takes up again the gestures and actions of those who have gone before us in the faith since the time of Abraham. It reproduces the images which the Bible has used to express the economy of salvation.

(6) Of course these signs continually run the risk of becoming degraded through human routine and inattention, and through the loss of a true Christian spirit resulting from the influence of an idealistic or rationalistic mentality. These ever-possible abuses do not prevent the Church from affirming the utility and suitability of ritual signs.[8]

[5] Various aspects of this problem are treated in LMD 22. There is hardly any fully satisfactory synthesis in this extremely complex sphere.—The comparison between liturgy and the practices of ancient cities or of pagan religions has been one of the fundamental preoccupations of F. Dölger, especially in the six volumes of *Antike und Christentum* (Münster, 1929-1950).

[6] Cf. the valuable analysis by V. Ayel, "Mentalité technique et ouverture à la liturgie" in LMD 40 (1954) 57-85.

[7] CSL 24.

[8] To the references to CSL given above in footnote 1, add: Council of Trent, sess 22, ch. 5 and can. 7; Denz. 1746 and 1757.—See H. Schmidt, "Grandeur et misère du rite" in LMD 35 (1953) 110-29.

1 Postures, gestures and actions

BIBLIOGRAPHY

F. Cabrol, *Liturgical Prayer—its History and Spirit* (Westminster, Maryland: Newman Press, 1950) pp. 80-87: ch. 8, "Attitudes during Prayer and Liturgical Gestures."

L. Eisenhofer and J. Lechner, *The Liturgy of the Roman Rite* (New York: Herder and Herder; Edinburgh: Nelson, 1961) pp. 85-96: ch. 3, "The Actions of the Liturgy."

L. Gougaud, *Dévotions et pratiques ascétiques du moyen âge* (Desclée de Brouwer, 1925; Coll. *Pax* 21) pp. 1-42.

H. Lubienska de Lenval, *The Whole Man at Worship* (New York: Desclée; London: Chapman, 1961).

M. Righetti, *Manuale di storia liturgica* 1, 3rd ed., pp. 362-415.

I LITURGY AND THE HUMAN BODY

The liturgy is an object of wonder, even a cause of uneasiness for anyone with an idealistic mentality: far from being simply mental prayer, it finds its expression in the spoken word and in bodily postures and gestures. These postures and gestures are not left to the whim of the individual, but are fixed by established laws. In this the liturgy follows revelation and Sacred Scripture, which teach us not to dissociate body and soul, but to discern the unity which is man, created and saved by God. "In man," writes Dom Capelle, "the material and the spiritual are not juxtaposed, but united, and this union is not a composition of two distinct things, but the internal correlation of two elements of one and the same being. This union makes up a real and substantial unity; that is why a purely spiritual cult not only would not be human and as such would have to be rejected, but in fact impossible."[9]

The body, destined for glorious resurrection, has by baptism already become here below the temple of the Holy Spirit and is nourished by the Eucharist. Already at the beginning of the third century, Tertullian emphasized that the sacraments are wrought on the body to sanctify the soul.[10] Moreover there is no authentic sentiment which cannot express itself spontaneously in posture or gesture; conversely, postures, gestures, or actions demand such an involvement of the whole man that they express, intensify, or even provoke the interior attitude. On this point modern psychology and pedagogy thoroughly confirm the traditional teaching of the theolo-

[9]B. Capelle, *Travaux liturgiques de doctrine et d'histoire* 1 (Louvain: Abbaye du Mont César, 1955) p. 40.—Cf. R. Guardini, *L'esprit de la liturgie* (Plon, 1930) pp. 179-89. Engl. tr., *The Spirit of the Liturgy* (London: Sheed and Ward, 1930) pp. 70-84.

[10]Tertullian, *De resurrectione* 8, 3; CC 2, p. 931.

gians.[11] Finally, these signs are required by the communitarian character of the liturgy: unanimity of hearts is expressed at least as much by bodily postures as by song; and bodily postures are at any rate an easier manifestation of this unanimity. The understanding of the spoken word, especially that of the celebrant, is enhanced by gesture.[12] Christ himself made use of gestures to work miracles where a single word would have sufficed: he could, notes St Augustine, have cured the man born blind without using spittle and mud.

II LITURGICAL POSTURES

During the liturgical celebrations of the early centuries it was the deacons' function to indicate bodily postures to the people. They did this by means of *invitations* or *proclamations*, a good number of which are still in use: the *Flectamus genua, Levate, Humiliate capita vestra Deo, Procedamus in pace,* and *Ite missa est* in the Roman rite; the *Humiliate vos ad benedictionem* in the rite of Lyons; the *Pacem habete* and *Offerte vobis pacem* in the Ambrosian rite, and the ὀρθοί, πρόσχωμεν, στῶμεν καλῶς, στῶμεν μετὰ ψόβου of the Byzantines, etc.

The liturgical decline in the West during the Middle Ages resulted in a serious neglect in concern for the postures of the people, while at the same time the rules for the postures of the clergy and monks were becoming infinitely complicated. Thus even today liturgical books, the *Caeremoniale* and *Missale,* legislate solely for the choir, according to the practices current in the sixteenth century. But the liturgical renewal has rightly recalled attention to the postures of the faithful as being a particularly important element of active participation and a means of expressing the spiritual unanimity of the assembly. Thus we have the prescriptions incorporated into the *Ordo Hebdomadae Sanctae* (1955) and the more general rule proposed by the Second Vatican Council for the reform of the liturgical books: their rubrics should take account of the role of the faithful, among other things indicating their postures.[13]

[11]M. D. Chenu, "Anthropologie et liturgie" in LMD 12 (1947) 53-65; H. Lubienska de Lenval, "Symbolisme de l'attitude" in LMD 22 (1950) 121-8.—R. Guardini, *Les signes sacrés,* p. 30 (*Sacred Signs,* p. 12): "*doing* is something elementary in which the whole man is involved with his creative forces, a living experience, realization, contemplation."

[12]*Directoire pour la pastorale de la messe à l'usage des diocèses de France,* 2nd ed. (1960) n. 125-7, 131;—J. Travers, *Valeur sociale de la liturgie* (Paris: Ed. du Cerf, 1946; *Lex orandi* 5).

[13]CSL 30-31.—Cf. SRC, instruction of September 3, 1958, n. 22b: *Adstantium vero participatio plenior evadit, si internae attentioni accedat externa participatio, actibus scilicet externis manifestata, uti corporis positione (genuflectendo, stando, sedendo)* . . .; and n. 29: . . . [*participationem*] *externam, iuxta varias regionum probatas consuetudines.*

When there is no deacon, the "commentator" gives the necessary directions to the people. One should always bear in mind that it is above all a matter of achieving and expressing an interior attitude. For this reason the purpose of standing, sitting, and kneeling at determined times should be carefully explained to the faithful, so that they can see in these postures another and complementary dimension of Christian prayer.

1 *Standing*

The standing posture is that of the minister who serves at the altar, of the priest who sacrifices, as testified by St John Chrysostom,[14] and in keeping with the tradition of ancient Israel (Si 50:13).

It is also the most basic liturgical posture for the faithful. First, it is, in its wholly natural and obvious sense, a sign of respect: one stands up in the presence of a person one wishes to honor; that is why the assembly should stand during the entry and exit of the bishop or celebrant and during the reading of the gospel; they also stand to reply to the greeting of the celebrant. In the Old Testament the Israelites likewise stood while listening to the Lord speaking to them (Ex 20:21; 38:10; Ne 8:5).

But standing is more than a simple mark of respect. In fact it was the normal posture of Jewish prayer (cf. Mk 11:25; Lk 18:13) and is also the characteristic posture of Christian prayer, as is witnessed by the paintings in the catacombs, the carvings on early sarcophagi, the writings of the first ecclesiastical authors, and by the prescriptions of the Council of Nicaea.[15] And still today the faithful join together in standing during all the solemn prayers of the celebrant.

The Fathers considered this the expression of the holy liberty of the children of God acquired at baptism. Christ has raised us up again and by his grace has freed us from sin and death: we are no longer slaves, no longer in disgrace; we approach God respectfully but also confidently, since we share in the dignity of sonship. Standing is also the attitude of those awaiting the blessings of the Parousia: only those will remain standing in the presence of the Son of man who have nothing to fear from his justice (Ml 3:2). It was certainly standing and ready to leave in haste that the Hebrews in Egypt ate the Pasch (Ex 12:11). Finally, it is the posture of thanks-

---

[14]St John Chrysostom, "In epist. ad Hebraeos," *Homil.* 18, 1, PG 63, col. 135-6.

[15]St Justin, *First Apology* 67, M. Dods *et al.* ed. (ANF 2), p. 65; St Cyprian, *De dominica oratione* 31, Hartel ed. (CSEL 3), vol. 1, p. 289; Council of Nicaea, can. 20, Bruns ed., p. 20; St. Basil, *De Spiritu Sancto* 27, B. Pruche ed. (SC 17), pp. 236-8, B. Jackson ed. (NPF 8), p. 42; St Benedict, *Regula monachorum*, ch. 19, McCann ed., *The Rule of St Benedict* (London: Burns and Oates, 1952); etc.

giving of the elect in heaven (Rv 7:9; 15:2). The eschatological signification completes the others and predominates over them:

> As we stand in prayer on the day on which we commemorate the resurrection, we call to mind the grace which has been given us, and this not only because we are risen with Christ and have a duty to seek the things that are above, but also because that day seems to be in some way an image of the world to come.[16]

That is why, today as in antiquity, the liturgy is prayed standing on Sundays and during Paschaltide. This rule is, however, less strict than formerly, since it is now no longer forbidden to kneel down.[17]

2 *Kneeling*

Prayer on one's knees was in fact considered by the Fathers as specifically penitential: according to St Basil, to kneel down "is to show in action that sin has cast us to the ground."[18] It is a sign of mourning, of humility, and of repentance, and so is incompatible with paschal joy, but characteristic of times of fasting. Still today, on days of fasting, we kneel down for certain prayers, notably the *preces feriales* of the office; it is above all on ember days and in Lent that we hear the invitation of the deacon "*Flectamus genua.*"

However, to pray on one's knees is not exclusively a sign of penance. It is equally the posture of individual prayer: one kneels down to meditate a reading in silence, as did the monks of Egypt. Before his martyrdom, St Stephen fell on his knees (Ac 7:60), and we find again the same posture adopted for prayer on the most ordinary occasions by St Peter (Ac 9:40), by St Paul (Ac 20:36), and by the Christians who came out to take leave of St Paul at the time of his departure (Ac 21:5); the same Paul tells us that he prays "kneeling before the Father" (Ep 3:14).

The practice in Western piety of kneeling at certain times in adoration of the Eucharist, e.g. during the consecration and to receive holy communion, is of relatively recent origin.

3 *Sitting*

Sitting is the posture of the teacher while instructing and of the leader while presiding: that is why the bishop has a throne (*cathedra*),

---

[16]St Basil, *De Spiritu Sancto* 27, Pruche ed. (SC 17), pp. 236-7.

[17]But such rubrics still remain here and there.—The prohibition against kneeling down on Sundays and during Paschaltide is mentioned as traditional by Tertullian, *De oratione* 23, CC 1, pp. 271-2; *De corona* 3, 4, CC 2, p. 1043; see also the texts mentioned above in footnote 15.

[18]St Basil, *op. cit.*, p. 238.

from which he presides and from which he speaks. His priests are seated around him on benches.

But the people are also invited to be seated at certain moments of the liturgical celebration. Although formerly the places of worship did not have seats for the faithful, some bishops had them sit down on the floor for the readings and homily, an indulgence which was not allowed in other places. However, the practice of sitting down was already known to the apostolic communities (Ac 20:9; 1 Co 14:30). It is in fact not only the posture of the teacher, but also of the listener: the child Jesus was sitting among the doctors (Lk 2:46); Mary, sitting at the feet of the Lord, listened to his words (Lk 10:39). This is why the new rubrics specify for the readings of the paschal vigil: *Celebrans et ministri, clerus et populus, sedentes auscultant.* By and large the faithful are seated while listening to each of the readings (except the gospel), the meditation chants (gradual, etc.) and the homily.

4 *Bowing*

The invitation to bow one's head always precedes certain prayers of blessing: the *oratio super populum* of the Roman Lent, the episcopal blessing before holy communion in some churches (formerly the general practice in Spain and Gaul). The formularies themselves allude to this posture. But bowing has frequently been replaced by genuflection, e.g. as prescribed for the faithful at the blessing of the bishop or priest. The monastic liturgy has retained the practice of bowing deeply for many prayers. The celebrant of the Roman Mass says certain prayers of intense supplication while bowed to a greater or less extent, according to the rubrics (e.g. "*supplices rogamus . . .*").

5 *Prostrating*

In the current Latin liturgy prostrating oneself for prayer is a rather rare posture, and, because of this, it implies an exceptional solemnity. Thus it is prescribed for the bishop-celebrant during the singing of the litany of the saints (though in a mitigated form, it is true: *procumbit super faldistorium*), and also for those who are to receive from the bishop a definitive consecration: ordinands, virgins, abbots. As is testified by some Frankish *Ordines*, prostrating was also the manner for the celebrant and his ministers to venerate the altar at the beginning of Mass, a practice which has left its traces even up to the present day.[19] The Romantic era gave the prostration melo-

[19]For the celebrant and sacred ministers of the liturgy on Good Friday.—Cf. OR 15, n. 15; OR 17, n. 25; Andrieu OR 3, pp. 99 and 178-9.

dramatic meanings which have always been foreign to the liturgy. Suffice it to recall that its use was more widespread in the early centuries, and that in the Bible it is one of the frequent postures of prayer (Gn 17:3; Dt 9:18; Ne 8:6; Tb 12:16; Jdt 9:1; 10:1-2; 2 M 10:4; Mt 17:6; 26:39; Rv 4:10, etc.).[20]

III LITURGICAL GESTURES

Among the liturgical gestures there are those which are simply utilitarian, such as the washing of one's hands after certain actions. Others accompany quite naturally the spoken word whose meaning they underline, e.g. the gestures pointing out the bread and wine in the course of the Roman canon or the Eastern anaphora. There are also gestures of respect or veneration towards persons and things, and these gestures sometimes find their inspiration in local customs: for example, the practice of covering one's hands with a vestment or veil while carrying some venerable object is copied from the court ceremonial of the late Roman Empire;[21] joined hands are the gesture of the vassal paying homage to his suzerain.[22] All these gestures have endured for a longer or shorter length of time during the course of liturgical history, in proportion to the profundity and naturalness of their *raison d'être*.

Other gestures are of specifically Christian origin, such as the *sign of the cross*. From the beginning of the third century, the tracing of the sign of the cross on the forehead in the course of the rites of initiation appears to have been traditional in Africa and Rome to show membership in Christ and to imprint, as it were, an invisible seal. The Christians crossed themselves quite frequently.[23] The sign

---

[20]We should also mention the prayer towards the East, which had a very important place in the liturgy outside Rome: *Didascalia of the Apostles* 12, H. Connolly ed., pp. 119-20; St Basil, *De Spiritu Sancto* 27, Pruche ed. (sc 17), pp. 233, 236; F. Dölger, *Sol salutis* . . . (Münster: Aschendorff, 1920; lqf 16-17), pp. 98-108, 115-93, 245-58; C. Vogel, "Versus ad orientem" in *Studi medievali* (Spoleto) 3rd series, 1, 2 (1960) 447-69 (cf. lmd 70, 67-99); *id.*, "Sol aequinoctialis, Problèmes et technique de l'orientation dans le culte chrétien" in RevSR 36 (1962) 175-211; *id.*, "L'orientation vers l'Est du célébrant et des fidèles pendant la célébration eucharistique" in *Orient Syrien* 9 (1964) 3-37.—The Roman church neither understood nor accepted it: St Leo, *Sermon* 7, n. 4, J. Leclerq and R. Dolle ed., vol. 1 (sc 22), pp. 142-4; it is probable that the rubrics of the or which prescribe prayer towards the East were all added in Frankish territory: cf. Andrieu or 2, p. 7.

[21]M. Righetti, *op. cit.*, pp. 403-4.

[22]P. Oppenheim, *op. cit.*, pp. 449-50.

[23]Hippolytus, *The Apostolic Tradition*, n. 21 and 42, B. Botte ed. (lqf 39), pp. 54-5, 98-9; Tertullian, *De resurrectione mortuorum* 8, 3, cc 2, p. 931; *De corona*, 3, 4, *ibid.*, p. 1043, etc.—Cf. B. Botte, "Un passage difficile de la Tradition apostolique sur le signe de la croix" in rtam 27 (1960) 5-19.

of the cross was later extended to the organs of sense and became an exorcism.[24] Another form of the sign of the cross is the gesture of blessing in which either the whole hand or some fingers only are extended: this varied according to the practice of the individual churches and from epoch to epoch, and was influenced by allegorical considerations. The Orientals often gave the blessing while holding a cross in the hand. Finally, the large sign of the cross, familiar to the faithful today, seems to have been of rather late development; sometimes it has become almost mechanically attached to formulas which are badly understood (*Benedictus . . ., omni benedictione . . ., in nomine Domini . . .*).[25]

Some gestures are still richer in meaning, because they are of biblical origin and sometimes they are even the gestures of Christ. Some of them, such as the imposition of hands, have a sacramental character, but without thereby being confined to sacramental usage. The kiss of peace seems to have been already a liturgical gesture in the apostolic writings. To breathe on someone or something is ordinarily a gesture of exorcism, but can signify also communication of a sanctifying power.[26] Three gestures, naturally expressive of the prayer which they accompany, merit special mention: *striking one's breast*, as a sign of repentance and humility, like the publican in the parable or the witnesses of the crucifixion;[27]—*raising the eyes to heaven*, which today is only prescribed for the celebrant at certain moments of the Mass, but which was common among the faithful of the early Church,[28] in imitation of Jesus himself;[29]—*raising and extending the hands*, another gesture which today is reserved to the celebrant at Mass and ordination, and is characteristic of the strictly priestly prayers, but which was practised by all Christians in the early centuries, as is witnessed by contemporary writers and iconography. According to Tertullian it represents the gesture of Christ on the cross, reproduced with discretion and re-

[24]Hippolytus, *op. cit.*, n. 20, pp. 44-5.

[25]H. Leclercq, "Croix (signe de la)" in DACL 3 (1914) col. 3139-44; M. Righetti, *op. cit.*, pp. 367-73.

[26]These gestures will be studied further on in the context of the various liturgical actions of which they form part.

[27]Lk 18:13; 23:45;—cf. Jr 31:19; Ezk 21:17 (but in these last two texts the penitent strikes himself on the thigh).—St Augustine complains about the faithful who strike their breast each time they hear the *Confiteor* without giving any thought to the meaning of praise which this word also has in biblical language: *Sermon* 67, 1, PL 38, col. 433.

[28]Tertullian, *Apologeticum* 30, 4, CC 1, p. 141.—See M. Righetti, *op. cit.*, p. 379.

[29]Mk 6:41 (= Mt 14:19; Lk 9:16); Mk 7:34; Jn 11:41; 17:1.

serve;[30] but more probably it is the continuation of a Jewish practice.[31]

The liturgical gestures should be carried out in a way in which they can be seen and understood; they will avoid all theatrics if they spring from a true interior impetus and an effort at identification with the Lord. Stripped of all sentimentalism, they must remain modest and suitable for worship: the individual shows his deference to the act of the Church and of Christ.

IV ACTIONS

The liturgy is not content with gestures alone; it also includes actions. In fact the whole liturgy is one entire action,[32] but at certain moments it prescribes, either for the people or for the celebrant alone, a material action to which it gives a spiritual meaning. Thus the bishop in making chrism exercises the art of the perfumer as is shown e.g. in Ex 30:35; in burying relics in the altar which he is consecrating, the bishop does the work of a mason; the *agape* of the early Christians was a true family meal, given a more solemn character through prayer and the presence of the bishop;[33] the funeral liturgy includes the entire procedure of burial. The charity collections for our needy brothers have an authentic place in the liturgical celebration as already attested by St Paul and St Justin.[34]

2 Sacred things and places

GENERAL BIBLIOGRAPHY

The liturgy's understanding of things and places can be gleaned from the liturgical actions which are described in the second part of the Pontificale Romanum: *the dedication of churches, blessing of bells, consecration of sacred vessels, blessing of cemeteries, etc. The dedication ceremony above all makes the fullest use of material things: water, oil, incense, light, salt, ashes, etc.; it also provides the greatest number of prayers of blessing for these things (a special bibliography for*

[30]*Nos vero non attollimus tantum (manus), sed etiam expandimus et, dominica passione modulata, tum et orantes confitemur Christo . . . Cum modestia et humilitate adorantes magis commendabimus Deo preces nostras, ne ipsis quidem manibus sublimius elatis, sed temperate ac probe elatis, ne vultu quidem in audaciam erecto:* Tertullian, *De oratione* 14 and 17, 1, cc 1, pp. 265 and 266; cf. *Apologeticum* 30, 4, *ibid.*, p. 141; see also *The Odes of Solomon* 27, Labourt-Batiffol ed., p. 28.

[31]Ex 9:29; Ps 28:2; 63:5; 134:2; Is 1:15; Lm 3:41; 1 Tm 2:8.—See M. Righetti, *op. cit.*, pp. 373-7.

[32]See above, ch. 1.

[33]H. Chirat, *L'assemblée chrétienne à l'âge apostolique* (Paris: Ed. du Cerf, 1949; *Lex orandi* 10), pp. 187-8; LMD 18 (1949): "Le repas, le pain et le vin."

[34]H. Chirat, *op. cit.*, pp. 222-43.

the dedication ceremony itself will be given further on). *From the historical point of view, the fundamental work is:*

A. Franz, *Die kirchlichen Benediktionen im Mittelalter* (Freiburg: Herder 1909), 2 vols., especially vol. 1 and section 5 of vol. 2.

I MATERIAL ELEMENTS

BIBLIOGRAPHY

F. Cabrol, *Liturgical Prayer—its History and Spirit* (Westminster, Maryland: Newman Press, 1950) pp. 203-36.
O. Casel, *The Mystery of Christian Worship* (Westminster, Maryland: Newman Press; London: Darton, Longman and Todd, 1962) pp. 9-48.
A. Coelho, *Cours de liturgie romaine* 1 (Lophem-lez-Bruges, 1928) pp. 94-102.
I. H. Dalmais, *Introduction to the Liturgy* (Baltimore: Helicon; London: Chapman, 1961) pp. 119-24: "The Liturgy and Things."
L. Eisenhofer, *Handbuch der katholischen Liturgik* 1 (Freiburg: Herder, 1932) pp. 282-317. Engl. ed., L. Eisenhofer and J. Lechner, *The Liturgy of the Roman Rite* (New York: Herder and Herder; Edinburgh: Nelson, 1961) pp. 96-105.
C. Vagaggini, *Theological Dimensions of the Liturgy* (Collegeville, Minnesota: Liturgical Press, 1959) pp. 178-83.

In this section we are not treating of things which the Church blesses to sanctify their everyday use by Christians,[35] but those which she uses in the liturgy.

Does this use spring from a theology of earthly realities? So it is thought by the authors whose opinion O. Casel has summed up in these remarkable words:

> The Christian too knows that nature groans under sin, along with man; it longs for redemption, which will come to it when it comes to the children of God. But he also knows that nature is a work of God's; because it is, he can love it, see in it the print of God's passing. Yet he stands over it; nature is tool and image of the spiritual. The liturgy, therefore, from the very beginning, from the time when the Lord made bread and wine the elements of the Mass, has given nature its part to play. The Church was not afraid to take over natural symbols which the heathen had used in their worship and, by putting them into proper place, to give them their true value. By doing so she has made them holy, just as through the sacraments and sacred gestures, she made the human body; in fact the Church has given to nature the first-fruits of glory, the gifts of the children of God.[36]

In any case, the acts of Jacob, Moses and the prophets, as well as the legislation of Aaronic worship, had accustomed the Israelites to see certain material elements as symbols of the relations between God and his people and thus as a means of expressing their liturgy:

[35]This will be treated in a subsequent volume.
[36]O. Casel, *The Mystery of Christian Worship* (Westminster, Maryland: Newman Press, 1963) p. 87.

the stone erected in memory of the meeting with God (Gn 28:18) or destined to receive the victims of sacrifice (Ex 20:24; Dt 27:5-7; 1 M 4:44-47); the oil poured out (Gn 28:18) or used for the royal and priestly anointings; the incense whose smoke suggests the rising up of prayer pleasing to God (Ps 141:2); the water of ritual purifications; the ash or dust sprinkled over the head as a sign of penance; the sprig of hyssop used in the purification rites;[37] the salt "of the Covenant with your God" which purifies the offering of the firstfruits (Lv 2:13; Nb 18:19; cf. Mk 9:49), or which makes the waters wholesome (2 K 2:20f).

Christ also made some material elements symbols of the New Covenant, but in this case they are efficacious symbols: bread, wine, water, oil, and balsam are sacramental signs. Following in the wake of the institution by the Lord, the Church makes use of materials to broaden, as it were, the sacramental signs or to extend them: thus she uses water, oil, perfume, and bread for other rites also; and by using material elements in the liturgy she concretizes in a certain manner the images of the Old and New Testaments thus bringing out their pedagogical function: new fire, light, stone, ash, the milk and honey characteristic of the Promised Land . . .[38] Sometimes she has taken up practices of the Old Law, such as the use of incense, though it is true that in this case the heavenly visions of the Apocalypse encouraged the imitation; another example is the sprinkling of the altar in the Old Gallican rite of dedication.[39] But sometimes biblical tradition does not suffice to explain the symbolism entirely, and we ought to admit, as O. Casel suggested above, a legitimate imitation of pagan practices.

Most of the rites in which these material elements are used will be studied in their place.[40] It will suffice here to give some particulars on light, holy water, and incense because of their frequent use in the liturgy.

---

[37]Hyssop is an aromatic plant whose thick fibrous leaves make it suitable for use in sprinklings; Ex 12:22 (cf. Heb 9:19) indicates that a bunch of hyssop is to be used to sprinkle the lintel and doorposts with the blood of the lamb at the passover of the Lord; in Lv 14:4, the hyssop is probably used for the seven sprinklings over those who are to be purified of their leprosy; in Nb 19:18, it is more expressly a matter of sprinklings with lustral water in a case of legal impurity; Psalm 51:9 goes on from this rite to beg for an interior purification, given only by God. Hyssop is prescribed for the lustration of the church, altar, and bells to be consecrated; its usage is mentioned in OR 42, n. 29, OR 41, n. 12, and Ge 3, 76.

[38]To be taken up again in a subsequent volume.

[39]See below, **3**, II.

[40]See above, ch. 2.

Parenzo, the sanctuary, *circa* 533-543

Service photograghique de la Bibliothèque royale de Belgique

1 *Light*

BIBLIOGRAPHY

F. Dölger, *Sol salutis, Gebet und Gesang im christlichen Altertum*, 2nd ed. (Münster: Aschendorff, 1925; LQF 4/5).

F. Dölger, "Lumen Christi . . . " in *Antike und Christentum* 5 (Münster: Aschendorff, 1925) pp. 1-43.

Light has given to the liturgy several elements of symbolism. Naturally an important place is occupied by the light of the sun whose rising and setting recall to anyone who is familiar with the Bible Christ, the sun of justice: thus the Church was able to fight effectively against the infatuation with sun worship at the beginning of the fourth century. But we must mention here above all the role of the lampstand, lamps, branched candlestick, and candles. Already in the Old Testament there burned in the tent in the presence of Yahweh the perpetual flame of pure oil (Ex 27:20; Lv 24:2-4; 1 S 3:3) on the seven branches of the golden candlestick (Ex 25:31-40); in the same way St John, in the Apocalypse, sees "seven flaming lamps" burning before Him who sits on the throne (Rv 4:5), and seven golden lampstands surrounding the Son of man (Rv 1:12f). The lights as used in the synagogue and in Jewish family liturgy are also attested to in the assemblies of the early Christians (Ac 20:8) where they were certainly more than mere utility lighting. As early as the third century the act of lighting the lamps at nightfall inspired magnificent prayers,[41] which later on the *lucernarium* uses and develops; it is probably from the *lucernarium* that the paschal candle derives its origin. The lampstand, simultaneously a sign of joy, a reminder of a sacred presence, and a symbol of the prayer to which it bears witness or to which it invites, appears around the tombs of the martyrs, then in the basilicas, then before altars and images, and much later before the Blessed Sacrament.

The Church at Jerusalem created another of the expressive actions of the paschal liturgy, the *Lumen Christi*. The baptism lamp or candle has likewise an obvious and precise symbolism. The use of torches and candles at burials on the other hand is perhaps the continuation of a Roman custom, to which the Christians gave a new meaning. In the same way the carrying of candles in the procession on February 2 has a lasting meaning only because it illustrates the Canticle of Simeon, *lumen ad revelationem gentium*.

The lampstand likewise was a mark of honor when used in escort— Roman court practice inspired this[42]—but it was so apt that it was

---

[41]Hippolytus, *Apostolic Tradition* 25, Botte ed. (LQF 39) pp. 64-5; the φῶς ἱλαρόν certainly originated in the third century.

[42]P. Batiffol, *Études de liturgie et d'archéologie chrétienne* (Paris: Gabalda et Picard, 1919) pp. 209-13.

M

worth retaining. This honor goes first to the bishop, who according to the ceremonial of the *Ordo Romanus* 1, is to be preceded by seven *"cereostata,"* a practice still in force at Rome and Lyons; from the fact that these candlesticks were put down near the altar after the arrival of the procession, they became part of the adornment of every altar where the bishop of the place celebrated solemn Mass. The two candlesticks carried by the acolytes in the Roman rite are a reduced form of this practice. This honor is given also to the gospel book, which is carried in procession with a similar solemnity.

2 Water

BIBLIOGRAPHY

A. Franz, *op. cit.*, vol. 1, pp. 43-220.
M. Righetti, *Manuale di storia liturgica* 4, 2nd ed. (Milan: Ancora, 1959) pp. 525-32.

Certain current uses of holy water recall the baptismal water of Christian initiation.[43] However, in its origin and according to its most frequent use, it is a water of purification, as in the pagan religions. First sanctified by a prayer of the Church, it is intended to be sprinkled over places to exorcise and purify: the formulas of the *ordo ad faciendam aquam benedictam* in the missal clearly testify to this. Some salt is mixed in with the water, perhaps in imitation of the action of Elisha (2 K 2:20-22); it has been the usage since at least the sixth century.[44] In the ritual of the dedication of a church other ingredients are added. But holy water was always intended for the sprinkling of places: houses, places of worship, fields.[45] The Sunday *Asperges* itself seems to have originated in a ceremonial sprinkling of monastery apartments;[46] its subsequent retention and widespread practice is due to its being considered in later times as a reminder of baptism.[47]

3 Incense

BIBLIOGRAPHY

C. Atchley, *A History of the Use of Incense in Divine Worship* (London: Longmans, 1909; *Alcuin Club* 13).

[43]B. Fischer, "Formes de la commémoration du baptême en Occident" in LMD 58 (1959) 132.

[44]LP 1, pp. 54 and 127, speaking of Pope Alexander: *Hic constituit aquam sparsionis cum sale benedici in habitaculis hominum.*

[45]For the history of the texts for the blessing of water, see A. Chavasse, *Le Sacramentaire gélasien* (Tournai: Desclée, 1958), pp. 50-56. See also F. Cabrol, "Eau" in DACL 4 (1921) col. 1680-90 and of course A. Franz, *loc. cit.*

[46]To be treated in a subsequent volume.

[47]Cf. the texts cited by M. Righetti, *op. cit.*, p. 531.

R. H. Connolly, "The Use of Incense in the Roman Liturgy" in EL 43 (1929) 171-6.

E. Fehrenbach, "Encens" in DACL 5 (1922) col. 2-21.

A. M. Forcadell, "El incienso en la liturgia cristiana" in *Liturgia* 10 (1955) 219-25.

Incense, as we have said, was used in Jewish ritual as a very expressive symbol of prayer (Ps 141:2): in the temple there was before the Holy of Holies an altar of gold on which was burned every morning and evening an aromatic incense as a sacrifice of praise.[48] In the temple of heaven, in the Apocalypse, the same rite continues to be performed, carried out by the angels, but the vision is only symbolic: it is the prayers of the saints that are offered up (Rv 8:3-5). Incidentally the "thurible" in this text ($\lambda\iota\beta\alpha\nu\omega\tau\acute{o}\nu$, *thuribulum*) is not what we would call a censer: it is rather a container permitting the removal of the live charcoal from altar to altar. Another vision of the Apocalypse (5:8) shows us the twenty-four elders, each holding a bowl of burning incense ($\theta\nu\mu\iota\acute{a}\mu\alpha\tau\alpha$): its symbolism is identical to that of Rv 8:3-5. Despite these biblical precedents the Western Church put off for a long time the burning of incense in the liturgy[49] —perhaps because this act had an idolatrous signification in the surrounding paganism. In the East it probably did not have such unpleasant associations. In Jerusalem at the end of the fourth century, in the course of the Sunday vigil censers were brought into the chapel of the Holy Sepulchre when the gospel of the resurrection was about to be read.[50] Pseudo-Dionysius testifies to the use of incense in those regions of Syria where they later saw such a notable development.[51]

At Rome incense and censers were used widely during funeral rites, a practice acknowledged by tradition. Then in the basilicas were found stationary censers, on stands, such as are still used today in the liturgy of Lyons. These served both to perfume the surrounding area and to pay due honor to the holy places.[52] They were also found suspended by chains before relics and icons. Finally, in the authentically Roman *Ordines* of the seventh and eighth centuries, the ceremonial procession of the pope and of the gospel included,

[48]Ex 30:1-10, 34-38; 37:25-29; Nb 4:11; 1 K 6:20-21; Lk 1:8-11.

[49]Tertullian, *Apologeticum* 30, 6, J. Waltzing ed. (Coll. *Budé*) p. 71; St Augustine, *Enarrationes in psalm.* 49, 21, CC 38, p. 591.—The texts of St Ambrose which are quoted in the opposite sense as witnessing the use of incense in the liturgy (*In Luc.* 1, 1; *Liber de Joseph patriarca* 3, 17) seem to have been misunderstood.

[50]Egeria, *Peregrinatio,* H. Pétré ed. (SC 21) p. 196.

[51]Pseudo-Dionysius, *Ecclesiastical Hierarchy* 3, 2 and 4, 2; PG 3, col. 425 and 473.

[52]LP 1, pp. 174, 177, 183, 233, etc.

together with the seven *cereostata*, a *thymiamaterium* carried by a subdeacon. This was a simple pan on which perfumes were burned. The usage was probably borrowed from imperial practice.[53] In the *Ordo* 5, representing the practice in the Rhineland at the middle of the tenth century, the term *thymiamaterium* is replaced by *thuribulum*, already used in the Gelasian Sacramentary and corresponding to the Old Gallican terminology.[54] The same *Ordo* incorporates into the offertory of the Mass a rite of offering of incense already noted by Amalar as a Frankish practice and probably inspired by the ritual, equally Gallican, of the dedication of a church.[55]

II THE OBJECTS USED IN WORSHIP

We shall not describe in detail here all the objects destined for use in the liturgy which throughout the centuries have been the product of the minor arts—gilding, illuminating, vestment making. The Church has passed special legislation for this area, and provides in each case a consecration or blessing. Books and vestments have already been discussed above; here we shall only deal with sacred vessels, crosses, pictures, and bells.

1 The sacred vessels

BIBLIOGRAPHY

F. Eygun, "Les vases sacrés" in R. Aigrain, *Liturgia* (Bloud et Gay, 1935) pp. 261-304.
M. Righetti, *Manuale di storia liturgica* 1, 3rd ed. (Milan: Ancora, 1964) pp. 584-615.

Only two of the sacred vessels are *consecrated*, because they are directly connected with the celebration of Mass: they are the *chalice* and the *paten*.

The cup (ποτήριον, *calix*) is expressly mentioned in the four accounts of the Last Supper, and also in the words of Jesus, as recorded in 1 Co 11:25 and Lc 22:20. It was in fact a biblical sign both of the passion of Christ and of the exercise of the justice of God who rewards and who punishes.[56] This single cup from which, according to the ritual of the paschal meal, all the guests should

---

[53]Andrieu OR 2, p. 80 (OR 1, 41); 82 (n. 46); 88 (n. 59 and 61), etc.

[54]*ibid.*, p. 195.

[55]*ibid.*, p. 218; Amalar, *Liber officialis, Prooemium*, 21, J. M. Hanssens ed., *Amalarii opera liturgica* 2 (Vatican City, 1948; *Studi e testi* 139) p. 18; cf. in the index of vol. 3 the references to *Turibulum* and *Tus*, p. 479.

[56]The chalice of the passion: Mt 20:22; Mk 10:38; Mt 26:39 and 42; Mk 14:36; Lk 22:42; Jn 18:11.—The chalice of the divine reward: Ps 16:5; 23:5.—The chalice of divine vengeance: Is 51:17 (and references indicated in the *Jerusalem Bible*, p. 1227, note j); Ps 11:6 (and references *op. cit.*, p. 795, note d); 75:8.

drink was already in the epistles of St Paul (1 Co 10:16) the symbol of the unity of the Church—it also contains the grace of this unity. That is why the early liturgies had to solve the problem of giving communion to all the faithful under the species of wine, while at the same time keeping intact the principle of having only one chalice on the altar.[57]

The first chalices were of glass; they could be adorned with a painted or gilded base. But even by the time of St Augustine they were being made of precious metals; from that time on, this was the rule, except in times of persecution or great need.[58] It is permitted today that the cup be of a different material from the base, and in this case it is only the cup that need be of gold; it may also be of silver, but then the inside must be gilded.[59]

The paten has not the same importance; consequently only its concave surface need be gilded. In the present Roman Mass the paten holds the bread or breads to be consecrated for the communion of the celebrant or concelebrants. If there be a large number of breads for the faithful, they are placed directly on the corporal or simply offered in ciboria.

The bishop, or a priest who has received the appropriate faculty from him, consecrates the chalice and paten with the oil of chrism, following the formulas of the pontifical. Several of these formulas are of Old Gallican origin, and appear already in the *Missale Francorum*,[60] from which they have passed into the Gelasian Sacramentary.[61] The others appear for the first time in the Romano-Germanic Pontifical.[62]

The other vessels which contain the Eucharist—ciborium, custodia and lunette—receive a simple blessing as indicated in the missal, pontifical, or ritual. They should have a gilt interior. Their history will be recounted later.[63]

2 Crosses and images

The present-day legislation requires that a cross with the image of Christ be placed on the altar or close to it, above it or even on the

[57]M. Andrieu, *Immixtio et consecratio* (Ed. Picard, 1924) pp. 5-19.

[58]St Augustine, *Enarrationes in psalm.* 113, *Serm.* 2. n. 5-6, CC 40, p. 1645 (PL 37, col. 1484).—See LP 3, p. 195, for various references to the word *calix*.

[59]On the present canonical prescriptions, see L. Stercky, *Manuel de liturgie et cérémonial*, 17th ed., vol. 1 (Paris: Gabalda, 1940) pp. 63-5.

[60]In the ritual of dedication: L. C. Mohlberg ed. (Rome: Herder, 1957), n. 62-5, pp. 18-19.

[61]Ge 1, 88, L. C. Mohlberg ed. (*ibid.*, 1960) p. 109.

[62]PRG, 40, 88-95, vol. 1, pp. 155-6.

[63]To be treated in a subsequent volume.

wall,[64] in such a way that it can be seen by the faithful and normally also by the celebrant. At first, in the twelfth century, this was the processional cross, placed facing the altar by the subdeacon on the arrival of the procession.[65] Later it became simply a small cross placed on the altar or preferably a very large cross suspended from the triumphal arch.

The Western Church readily admits sacred images into her places of worship: they receive a blessing and can become the objects of veneration, but they do not have any part in the liturgy. Care, however, should be taken that they do not distract the attention of the faithful from the liturgy itself or from the worship of the Eucharist, and that they do not clutter up the building or spoil it by their shoddiness. But, on the other hand, the systematic exclusion of sacred images would be contrary to tradition and equally reprehensible.[66] In the Byzantine rite icons are actually a requisite in the place of worship and certain liturgical acts are carried out before them.

3 *Bells*

BIBLIOGRAPHY

H. Leclercq, "Cloche, clochette" in DACL 3 (1914) col. 1954-77.
M. Righetti, *op. cit.*, pp. 481-5.

In the early centuries various means more or less primitive were used to call the faithful to liturgical functions. Some Eastern churches have remained faithful to the wooden *simantron* or *sidêroun*, suspended wooden boards which are struck with a mallet. The use of bells (*signum, nola, clocca, campana*) became widespread towards the end of the fifth or beginning of the sixth century. The Gelasian Sacramentary reformed under Pepin (the eighth-century Gelasian) introduced into the ceremony of the dedication of a church a rite *ad signum ecclesiae benedicendum*[67] which remained in use up to 1961: the bell was washed with water blessed for that purpose; during the washing Psalms 146-150 were sung and afterwards the bishop said the prayer *Deus qui per Moysen*; after this the antiphon *Vox Domini super aquas* and Psalm 29 were sung; the bell was

---

[64]SRC, n. 1270, ad 2.

[65]To be treated in a subsequent volume.

[66]Second Council of Nicaea (786), Denz. 600-603, 605; Council of Trent, sess. 25, *ibid.*, 1823; Second Vatican Council, CSL 111 and 125.

[67]Sacramentary of Angoulême, P. Cagin ed., pp. 143-5, n. XLI-XLIII (=2042-9); Sacramentary of Gellone, cf. P. de Puniet, in EL 51 (1937) 116, n. 354; Sacramentary Coll. Phillips (Berlin) MS 1667, cf. P. de Puniet, *ibid.*

anointed with chrism[68] seven times on the outside and four times on
the inside, after which the bishop said the prayer *Omnipotens . . .
qui ante arcam foederis*; censers with incense and myrrh were placed
under the bells and the ceremony concluded with the prayer *Omnipotens . . . dominator Christe*. This whole rite, to which only little
was added in the Middle Ages,[69] is characteristic of the Old Gallican
liturgy, ever anxious to retain a link with the Old Testament. From
this it can be seen that the bell had something more than the simple
function of calling together the faithful: it is a kind of sacramental
on which the prayer of the Church confers, as it were, the power to
expel demons and ward off bad weather. Finally the bell took on the
function of inviting the absent faithful to unite themselves by their
prayer with the liturgy—hence this ringing of the bell during the
actual liturgical celebration; it also served to call them to brief
private prayer, e.g. the ringing of the *Ave Maria* or Angelus.

At present there are two distinct ceremonies: the one, simpler
than that in the earlier pontifical and reserved to the bishop, is a
consecration; the other, still more reduced, is a simple blessing and
is found in the ritual. This second form is not permitted for the bells
of churches which have been consecrated. But the instruction of
September 3, 1958 of the Congregation of Rites introduced yet
another, and welcome, distinction: only true bells may be consecrated or blessed, as distinct from carillons, which are entirely
excluded from all liturgical use.[70]

III SACRED PLACES

In the words of canon 1154 of the 1917 code, "sacred places are
those which are destined for divine worship or the burial of the
faithful, by a consecration or blessing prescribed for this purpose
by approved liturgical books." This definition omits baptisteries,
since the code presupposes that they are already inside a place of
worship (cf. can. 773-775), while the liturgical books take account
of the traditional existence of distinct baptisteries. Furthermore, the
present discipline demanding a special rite of blessing or consecra-

[68]It is not known why Durandus of Mende introduced the use of the oil of the
catechumens for the seven anointings: Andrieu PR 3, p. 535, and even less how the
oil of the sick was substituted for it in the Roman pontifical.

[69]There was added a preparatory psalmody consisting of the antiphon *Deus in
sancto* with some verses of Psalm 77, together with the gospel account of Martha
and Mary (this last was introduced by Durandus, probably under the influence
of local practices).

[70]SRC, instruction of September 3, 1958, n. 86-92.—See Martimort-Picard,
Liturgie et musique (Paris: Ed. du Cerf, 1959) pp. 172-6.

tion contrasts with the original usage by which places, as well as things, were consecrated by their very use.

1 The church and the altar

BIBLIOGRAPHY

J. Braun, *Der christliche Altar* (Münster, 1932) 2 vols.
F. Debuyst, *Modern Architecture and Christian Celebration* (London: Lutterworth Press, 1968; *Ecumenical Studies in Worship* 18).
P. Hammond, *Liturgy and Architecture* (New York, 1961; London, 1960).
LMD 63 (1960): "Le lieu de la célébration"; and especially LMD 70 (1962): "La dédicace des églises."
A. Raes, *Introductio in liturgiam orientalem* (Rome: Istituto Orientale, 1947) pp. 30-40: "De divisione interna ecclesiae ut loci cultus liturgici" (bibliography included).
M. Righetti, *op. cit.*, pp. 416-553.
J. Wagner, "Liturgical Art and the Care of Souls" in *The Assisi Papers* (Collegeville, Minnesota: Liturgical Press, 1957) pp. 57-73.

The Christian places of worship are far removed not only from the concept of the pagan temples but also from that of the Jewish temple. The temple at Jerusalem was the dwelling place of the Lord as was the tent of the covenant in the period of the wanderings of Israel; in addition it sheltered the ark where God made himself known over the cherubim, and from the time of its dedication by Solomon it was filled with the cloud as a sign of the glorious presence of Yahweh.[71] But in the New Covenant the temple is no longer something made by man: from now on it is the sacred humanity of Jesus that is the temple of God.[72] Christians, identified with Christ by baptism, are also temples of the Holy Spirit; the Trinity dwells in each of the faithful.[73] The whole Church is also as it were a temple built with living stones, the dwelling place of God.[74]

The buildings of stone or brick used or constructed by Christians are not thereby temples. They are houses where the praying assembly gathers: *domus ecclesiae*, οἶκοι ἐκκλησίας.[75] Modern law distinguishes *church* and *oratory*, the differentiating factor being the

[71] K 8:10-13, and the many references given at this passage in the *Jerusalem Bible*, p. 429.—See Y. Congar, *Le mystère du Temple* (Paris: Ed. du Cerf, 1958; *Lectio divina* 22) pp. 21-129 Engl. tr., *The Mystery of the Temple* (Westminster, Maryland: Newman Press, 1962); "Le Temple du Seigneur" in *Evangile* 32 (1958); "Le Temple Nouveau" in *Evangile* 34 (1959); X. Léon-Dufour, *Dictionary of Biblical Theology* (New York: Desclée, 1967) pp. 68-9, 521-5.

[72] Jn 2:19; Col. 2:9.—Y. Congar, *op. cit.*, pp. 145-80; "Le Temple Nouveau," *op. cit.*, 57-79.

[73] Rm 8:9-11; 1 Co 3:16-17; 6:19-20; 2 Co 6:16.—Y. Congar, *op. cit.*, pp. 181-8.

[74] Ep 2:19-22; 1 P 2:5.—Y. Congar, *op. cit.*, pp. 188-205, 207-39.

[75] On these expressions and on the first church buildings, see A. Raes, *op. cit.*, p. 19; M. Righetti, *op. cit.*, pp. 416-23.

community for which each is intended. A church is "the sacred building dedicated to divine worship and intended to be used for this publicly and by all the faithful" (can. 1161). The oratory is *per se* limited to a restricted group, even if in fact it be open to the public (cf. can. 1188).

This intended purpose dictates the entire style of construction of the building.[76] The changing fortunes of the liturgy as well as its diversity can profoundly modify the plan and appointments of churches. The styles which one can distinguish are not explained in terms of archeological classification alone; they are the expression of mentalities varying according to place and era. We must learn to appreciate them, otherwise we run the risk of underrating the great richness and the legitimate value of these mentalities.[77] The people of the classical epoch who rejected the art of the Middle Ages were no more justified than those who at the end of the nineteenth century found themselves strangers to baroque art. In fact the baroque church represents an important attempt at liturgical restoration resulting from the Counter-Reformation. The buildings of the fourteenth and fifteenth centuries, on the other hand, corresponded to the exercise of a very decadent liturgy overrun with superfluities, deformed by allegorical commentaries, and forgetful of the presence of the people.

It is the churches of the early centuries that appear most perfectly adapted to liturgical celebration. They were so planned as to divide the assembly into two clearly distinguishable groups: the altar separated the people on one side from the clergy on the other. The faithful, gathered together, should be able to see and hear from all sides, an effect obtained either by a rectangular hall or radial ground-plan, or by a cruciform shape with the altar situated at the point of intersection of the nave and transepts. The altar being the true center of the building is the focus of attention from all sides; its central position is sometimes stressed by a canopy or later by means of such architectural features as a cupola or skylight, etc. But the altar is not the sole center of the liturgical celebration: also of importance are the chair from which the bishop presides over the prayer before or apart from Mass, and the ambo or dais[78] from which the scriptural texts are read and the deacons make their announcements to the people. In Western churches the bishop's chair was

---

[76]CSL 124 and 128; SRC, instruction of September 26, 1964, n. 90-99; instruction of May 25, 1967, n. 24.

[77]On this point see CSL 122-3.

[78]A. Raes, *op. cit.*, pp. 32-3, 37.—St Cyprian, *Epist.*, 38 and 39, Bayard ed. (Coll. *Budé*), vol. 1, pp. 96 and 99.

situated at the center of a shallow apse and was higher than the altar so that he could see the whole assembly before him and be heard by all.[79] The ambos situated on either side enabled readers to look out upon the congregation and to be heard by all. The gospel ambo was more ornate and at a slightly higher level. On either side of the bishop's chair was a semi-circular bench intended for the priests; the deacons and other ministers remained standing.

The Eastern churches have sometimes presented an original solution to the various problems of the planning of the place of worship. Thus for example the Nestorians constructed two separate daises (βήματα), one for the altar and the eucharistic celebration, the other in the middle of the nave for the bishop's chair, the readers, and in general for the liturgy of the word, after which the celebrant and his ministers went in procession from one dais to the other.[80]

The Western arrangement, with the bishop's chair and priests' bench in the apse behind the altar, was retained up to the fourteenth century, even where the celebrant used to celebrate the Eucharist with his back to the people, i.e. outside Italy. Due to various factors the celebrant and bishop abandoned the apse for movable chairs situated at the side, from which they no longer overlooked the assembly,[81] while the altar, moved back against the wall of the apse, became surmounted with pictorial and sculptural decoration to an ever greater extent. The presence of numerous clergy, monks, canons, and members of the mendicant orders in the choirstalls separated the people ever further from the altar, while various considerations combined to enclose the altar itself behind walls, rood-screens, or—in the East—iconostases.[82] Moreover, the faithful preferred to the high altar, which had become so isolated, the side altars and chapels, which increased in number throughout all parts of the church especially from the fourteenth century onwards.[83]

[79]Cf. the texts of St Augustine collected by W. Roetzer, *Des heiligen Augustinus Schriften als liturgie-geschichtliche Quelle* (Munich: Max Hueber, 1930) pp. 79-80.—The *Caer. ep.*, bk 1, ch. 13, n. 1, still presupposes the same arrangement.

[80]A. Raes, *op. cit.*, p. 32; J. Dauvillier, "L'ambon ou bêmâ dans les textes de l'Église chaldéenne et de l'Église syrienne au moyen âge" in *Cahiers archéologiques* 6 (1952) 11-30.

[81]On this development, cf. Andrieu OR 2, pp. 144-5; P. Salmon, *Étude sur les insignes du pontife dans le rite romain* (Rome: Officium libri catholici, 1955) pp. 23, 29-32, 36-7, 48-9, 68-71; M. Durliat, LMD 70 (1962) 100-104.

[82]For the situation in the East, cf. A. Raes, *op. cit.*, pp. 36-9.—In some Eastern rites there are also curtains which are drawn to hide the altar at certain moments: A. Raes, *op. cit.*, pp. 35, 38-9.

[83]Thus the side chapels in Notre Dame in Paris and in many other churches are a later addition. The early texts require that there be only one altar: M. Righetti, *op. cit.*, pp. 504-5.

Traditionally the place of worship was adorned primarily in order to provide a festive setting for the assembly and the liturgical celebration: drapes, lamps, and precious materials have always been used for this purpose.[84] Decorative art (frescoes, mosaics, sculptures, stained-glass) contributes to this festive atmosphere, but in addition is a continuation of the liturgical signs themselves, notably underlining the heavenly and eschatological aspect of the liturgy. For this reason its themes cannot be left to mere chance: in the East they are often fixed down to the last detail. Where this is not so, they should at least be in harmony with the liturgical celebration and in no way distract attention from it.

The veneration of relics and pictures, pilgrimages, the growth in eucharistic devotion which has resulted in giving a more important place to reservation of the Eucharist,[85] have all contributed to an increase in private visits to churches for individual prayer, so that we can say of the church buildings what the books of the Old Testament said of the temple (Hab 2:20; 1 K 8:27-43; 9:3; 2 Ch 6:20-39; 7:12-16). This practice is of no small importance in our days when the faithful have the greatest difficulty in achieving recollection in prayer and the sense of the presence of God.[86] For this reason modern church architecture should take account of the two-fold function, namely community use by the assembly and individual use for private prayer.

The sacred character of the church building demands at all times respect, veneration, and silence, and excludes everything which would cause one to forget that it is a house of prayer.[87]

The altar is the most venerable part of the church; its consecration constitutes the principal part of the ceremony of dedication. It is the object of various marks of respect in the celebration of the liturgy and merits the reverence of the faithful.[88] In fact the Church attaches important symbolic value to the altar, both by the traditional prescriptions governing its structure and by the actions performed during its consecration. Even when the celebration of the Eucharist

---

[84]Egeria, *Peregrinatio* 25, H. Pétré ed., pp. 202-5; LP 1, pp. cxli-cliv.

[85] To be treated in a subsequent volume.

[86] Protestants today also emphasize the role of the church building, although they do not believe in the permanence of the real presence in the Eucharist: R. Paquier, *Traité de liturgie* (Neuchâtel: Delachaux et Niestlé, 1954) p. 47.

[87] Si 4:17; 5:1.—The legislation on this point is contained in CIC, can. 1178 and in SRC, instruction of September 3, 1958, n. 55, 70-77.

[88]G. Chevrot, "La dévotion à l'autel" in LMD 2 (1945) 84-92 and especially L. Gougaud, *Dévotions et pratiques ascétiques du moyen âge* (Paris: Desclée de Brouwer, 1925; Coll. *Pax* 21) pp. 50-64.

is authorized outside a church building,[89] a consecrated altar must be used[90] (in this case a portable altar, chiefly distinguished from a fixed altar by its dimensions, reduced to the minimum, and by the lesser solemnity of its consecration).[91]

Essentially the altar is a table of consecrated stone, with a cavity which its consecrator seals after having placed in it relics of martyrs. It is a real table (*mensa, τράπεζα*), since on it is celebrated the Eucharist, which was instituted by Christ during a meal and under the signs of a meal (bread and wine), and which terminates in holy communion. Thus the first Christian altars were movable wooden tables.[92] But to want simply to return to this primitive form would be an example of the "archeologism" justly condemned by Pius XII,[93] since the Latin church has subsequently required that the table be of stone, so that it will be understood that it is also an altar and that the Eucharist is a sacrifice.

Stone has in fact a double symbolism in the Bible, where it is a type of Christ. First there is the theme of the stone itself, the rock from which Moses caused the water to flow, "and that rock was Christ" (1 Co 10:4), the foundation or cornerstone of the whole building.[94]

Then there is the theme of the altar of stone, the first intimation of which is found in Genesis (28:18) and which is more exactly indicated in the legislation of Deuteronomy as the altar for the offering of holocausts.[95] In the New Law Christ is the unique altar just as he is the unique temple.[96] Just as Christ its prototype, the Christian altar

---

[89]CIC, can. 485, 822, 1164, 1194-6.

[90]In the East, however, it is counted sufficient to have an *antimensium*, a decorated piece of cloth, blessed by the patriarch, and into which relics are sewn; bishops of the Latin rite can under certain circumstances allow their priests the use of an *antimensium*: Paul VI, *Pastorale munus* (November 30, 1963), n. 9; RR, tit. 9, cap. 9, n. 21; NRC, n. 525; PR, part 2.

[91] Since the reform of 1961, the pontifical distinguishes two formularies of blessing: the one solemn, intended for altars of normal size, but of which only the table is blessed (*altare portatile*) and which are thus not irrevocably fixed to their base (cf. CIC, can. 1197); the other simple, intended for those "tables" or altar-stones of reduced size which are used for celebrating Mass outside the church building or which are placed in a false altar in a church—a practice which is to be discouraged.

[92]M. Righetti, *op. cit.*, pp. 490-94.

[93]MD 62.

[94]Ac 4:11; Ps 118:22; Mt 21:42; 1 P 2:4-7; Is 28:16; Ep 2:20; 1 Co 3:14; X. Léon-Dufour, *Dictionary of Biblical Theology* (New York: Desclée, 1967) pp. 510-12.

[95]Dt 27:5-7; 1 M 4:44-46, 47.—Cf. Ex 20:25; X. Léon-Dufour, *op. cit.*, pp. 9-10.

[96]Pseudo-Dionysius, *Ecclesiastical Hierarchy* 4, 12.—Cf. O. Rousseau, "Le Christ et l'autel" in LMD 29 (1952) 32-9.

carries as it were the stigmata—five engraved crosses—and receives an anointing.

The link between the bodies of the martyrs and the altar at which is celebrated the eucharistic sacrifice could have been suggested by the Apocalypse (6:9-11). At any rate this link was sought after in face of enormous architectural difficulties by the builders of the Roman cemeterial basilicas of the fourth to sixth centuries. Subsequently the practice of putting secondary relics (*brandea, sanctuaria*) under almost every altar became widespread. Finally, both in East and West, the transferring and insertion of relics became one of the most essential and most solemn rites of the dedication of churches and altars.[97]

Most of the Eastern rites, as well as that of Lyons, always require that one can pass right around the altar, especially for the incensation.[98] The Roman pontifical still presupposes this, although since the Middle Ages the altar has been frequently built against the wall or reredos.[99]

The altar should always be covered with three blessed altar-cloths and outside Mass with a special altar-cover. The chanting of Psalm 22 as an accompaniment to the stripping of the altars on Holy Thursday gives an allegoric sense to an action that was formerly performed daily, since the altar-cloths were only placed on the altar for the duration of the eucharistic celebration.[100]

2 The baptistery

BIBLIOGRAPHY

Actes du Ve Congrès international d'archéologie chrétienne (Aix-en-Provence, 1954; Vatican City, 1957; *Studi di antichità cristiana* 22). See especially the article by A. Grabar, pp. 187ff.

L. de Bruyne, "La décoration des baptistères paléochrétiens" in *Miscellanea liturgica in honorem L. Cuniberti Mohlberg* 1 (Rome: Ed. liturgiche, 1948) pp. 189-220.

J. G. Davies, *The Architectural Setting of Baptism* (London: Barrie and Rockliff, 1962).

As early as the third century there appeared buildings constructed and planned for exclusive use as baptisteries. Their decoration was inspired by the biblical typology of Christian initiation, such as we find already in Tertullian and Hippolytus. The practice of baptism

[97]Andrieu OR 4, pp. 361-8, 373-84.
[98]A. Raes, *op. cit.*, p. 35.
[99]On this development and its consequences, cf. M. Righetti, *op. cit.*, pp. 506-12.
[100]M. Righetti, *op. cit.*, pp. 532-5.—The question of the cross and candlesticks has been treated above. The question of the reservation of the Eucharist will be treated in a subsequent volume.

by immersion required a supply of running water, and often a heating system. The baptistery had to be distinct from the church building, and furthermore, since baptism was reserved to the bishop, there was only one baptistery in each large town.

Its architecture, inspired by the design of ancient bathrooms, was radial in form, and for allegoric reasons often octagonal in shape.[101] That the baptistery was the object of a special veneration is shown by the magnificent works of art which it inspired (in Italy right up to the Renaissance) and also by liturgical rites in connection with it, especially in Rome where every evening during Easter week the newly-baptized went in procession to the baptistery.[102]

The decline in adult baptisms, and especially the discontinuation of baptism by immersion, have reduced the baptistery to a specially marked-off space inside parish churches, near the entrance. It should be enclosed by railings, neatly kept, and, if possible, adorned with an image of the baptism of Christ. Within this area the place of honor is occupied by a basin or font in which the baptismal water is kept; this should be made from solid material and artistically decorated.[103] It is a good practice to have here also a worthily constructed cabinet for the reservation of the oils. Finally there must be a sacrarium with a drain to allow the used water to run off. For pastoral reasons, the consecration of the baptismal water during the paschal vigil no longer takes place in the baptistery. The law also makes provision for baptisms to be held in other places. But all in all the baptistery, today as formerly, should be a sacred place venerated by the faithful, and a reminder of their initiation through baptism.[104]

3 *The cemetery*

Although Christians did not immediately have separate cemeteries and although they adopted from local funeral customs elements that were not incompatible with their faith and their hope, the early Christian influence can be very easily recognized, not so much by their exclusive practice of burial as by their inscriptions and iconography. From the beginning of the third century, the Christian community at Rome had its own cemeteries, of which only the underground parts remain today. Their appearance was radically altered after the era of the persecutions, resulting from the wish of

[101]F. Dölger, "Zur symbolik des altchristlichen Taufhauses" in *Antike und Christentum* 4 (1934) 153-87.

[102]To be treated in a subsequent volume.

[103]RR, tit. 2, ch. 1, n. 46.

[104]PRG and the pontifical of Durandus of Mende had a formulary of blessing for the baptistery: PRG, LII-LIII, vol. 1, pp. 190-92; Andrieu PR 3, p. 533; for the most part it was taken from Ge 1, 94, *Orationes et preces in dedicatione fontis.*

many Christians to be buried close to the martyrs. In the Middle Ages graves were normally situated in the grounds around the church building, though many sought the honor of being buried within the church itself. The graveyard, which as it were unites in brotherhood the bodies of all who are awaiting the resurrection, should be a witness of this expectation and so avoid all pomposity, vanity, and wealth, and especially all that would savor of paganism (can. 1211).

It is the constant wish of the Church that the Christian place of burial be a defined area dominated by a cross and solemnly blessed by the bishop,[105] and in which are buried only the bodies of the baptized who have died in the peace of the Lord (can. 1205-1206). When this is not possible, each grave is blessed individually at the time of the funeral.

The formula in the pontifical for blessing a cemetery is an abbreviation of the rite put together from earlier elements by Durandus of Mende at the end of the thirteenth century;[106] three of its prayers go back to the Romano-Germanic Pontifical.[107]

IV REQUIREMENTS FOR THE LITURGICAL USE OF THINGS AND PLACES

Objects and places destined for use in the liturgy nearly always receive a blessing and sometimes even a consecration, which definitively sets them apart from all profane use and invites respect and veneration. According to the norms of canon law,[108] consecration and blessing can be lost either by a substantial alteration in the place or object, or especially by a serious profanation.

In the use of things, one must be on guard against the all too frequent tendency to false economy which results in attenuating a sign and destroying its symbolism, e.g. an ablution reduced to a few drops of water, an anointing which is no more than a touching with a damp finger, an incensation whose smoke is scarcely visible and whose aroma cannot be perceived, etc. One should be particularly careful about the authenticity of things: our Lord is not honored by false imitations which reduce the symbolism even more and which have an ugly effect.[109]

---

[105]Or with a shorter formula, if done by a delegated priest: RR, tit. 9, ch. 9, n. 22.

[106]Andrieu PR 3, pp. 504-10.

[107]PRG, n. LIV 1, pp. 192-3, and incorporated into PR at the end of the eleventh century.—The pontifical of Appamée gives a much richer form of the rite, PR 1, pp. 286-8, from which Durandus drew his inspiration.

[108]Can. 1170, 1172, 1200, 1305.

[109]Cf. CSL 21; see A.M. Roguet, "Plaidoyer pour la vérité des choses" in LMD 20 (1949) 117-26.

Places and objects intended for worship should be beautiful in appearance; but this is possible only if they are perfectly adapted to their intended purpose. For this reason the Church has frequently made detailed rules which *sacred art* should follow.[110] No matter how noble, sacred art is not autonomous but only the servant of divine worship. It cannot be more than a reflection or expression of faith. It should share in the pastoral solicitude of the Church not to disturb or hurt the feelings of the simple faithful. But it should nonetheless make use of all technical resources; it should express liturgical values in the language of its time and culture, for the Church is on guard against anachronisms and the importation of forms of Western art into countries which have their own culture. Sacred art requires both sincerity and the elimination of individualism. Sometimes it is expressed especially in magnificence, sometimes in simplicity.

3 The dedication of churches

BIBLIOGRAPHY

Andrieu OR 4, pp. 311-413.

S. Benz, "Zur Geschichte der römischen Kirchweihe nach den Texten des 7. bis 9. Jahrhunderts" in *Enkainia, gesammelte Arbeiten zum achthundert-jähringen Weihegedächtnis der Abteikirche Maria Laach* . . . (Düsseldorf: Patmosverlag, 1956) pp. 62-109.

A. Chavasse, *Le Sacramentaire gélasien* (Tournai: Desclée, 1958) pp. 36-56.

L. Duchesne, *Origines du culte chrétien*, 5thed. (De Boccard, 1920) pp. 420-39. Engl. tr., *Christian Worship—its Origin and Evolution* (London: SPCK, 1931) pp. 399-418.

For the Byzantine rite: LMD 70 (1962) 131-40.

For the Coptic rite: R. Coquin, in *Orient Syrien* 9 (1964) 149-88.

The peace granted to the Church by Constantine immediately made it possible for Christians to restore their places of worship and to build new ones, frequently with the support of imperial grants. Their inauguration, as recorded by Eusebius,[111] was the occasion of magnificent festivities in which the bishops of the region took part and which attracted large crowds of people. But it was only with the passing of time that there evolved a ritual of dedication. In this

---

[110]Principal sources for the present legislation on sacred art: CIC, can. 1164, 1279-80; MD 189, 195-6; instruction of the Holy Office of June 30, 1952; Pius XII, encyclical *Musicae sacrae*, n. 18-26 (in *Musique et liturgie*, 50-51, 1956, 6-8); CSL 122-9.

[111]*Hist. eccl.* 10, 2-4, G. Bardy ed., vol. 3 (SC 55) pp. 79-104; *The Ecclesiastical History*, J. Oulton ed., vol. 2 (Harvard University Press, 1942) pp. 395ff (chapter 4 gives an account of the dedication of the church at Tyre and of the long sermon given by Eusebius, in which he describes the building and gives its symbolism).

Procession of the relics at a dedication
Ivory, sixth century
Trier, reliquary of the cathedral

Archives photographiques de l'Abbaye de Maria-Laach

process of evolution, each local church had its own original feature to contribute, then reciprocal influences caused these practices to become closely intermingled. The dedication ceremony as contained in the modern Roman pontifical is an exceptionally lavish collection of actions, chants, and prayers originating in Rome, Gaul, Byzantium, Spain, and even Ireland. In the Middle Ages it had become overloaded with complications and useless repetitions; the removal of these sufficed to uncover again the striking biblical and symbolic richness of the early rites.

I THE EARLY FORMATION OF THE ROMAN RITE OF DEDICATION

1 *The Mass as the essential act of the dedication*

There can be no rite of dedication without the Mass, which not only constitutes the essential element of this ceremony, but which was also in former times frequently the only act of dedication. For a long time most of the urban churches of Rome were not dedicated to any one saint; still in the time of St Gregory the Great, churches were inaugurated without relics: they were consecrated by the celebration of the Eucharist itself,[112] as can be gathered from certain Mass-formulas for the dedication in the Gelasian Sacramentary.[113]

2 *The placing of relics beneath the altar*

From the third quarter of the fourth century there appeared outside Rome a new element which immediately aroused the enthusiasm of popular devotion. Though not the originator, St Ambrose has given us the most striking example of it: for the dedication of the basilica later called Sant' Ambrogio Maggiore, he exhumed the bodies of the martyrs Gervasius and Protasius; they were brought to the basilica of Fausta where there took place an all-night vigil; the people begged Ambrose to prolong the feast for several days, and finally the remains of the saints were brought to the new church and buried beneath the altar.[114]

In Rome up to the middle of the seventh century, there was a strong bias against disturbing the tombs of the martyrs, and so, as we have already remarked, basilicas were erected over them and so

---

[112]Vigilius, *Letter to Profuturus of Braga* (538), n. 4, PL 84, col. 832; St Gregory, *Dialog.* 3, 30, PL 77, col. 288. Le 132 (*mense aprili*, 34, preface) presupposes the existence of a basilica dedicated to St Peter in which there were none of his relics.

[113]A Chavasse, *op. cit.*, pp. 37-8; Ge 1, 89-90, Mohlberg ed., n. 703,705, 712, 713.

[114]St Ambrose, "Letter 22 to his sister Marcellina," PL 16, col. 1019-26; details confirmed by St Augustine, especially in *De civitate Dei* 22, 8. On this and other translations of relics, cf. H. Delehaye, *Les origines du culte des martyrs*, 2nd ed. (Brussels, 1933; *Subsidia hagiographica* 20) pp. 75-80; Andrieu OR 4, pp. 367-8.

designed that the altar would be in immediate contact with their remains. But in the sixth century the use of secondary relics, or *brandea*, became widespread, a practice which permitted the setting-up of fictitious tombs of the saints in non-cemeterial churches, the altar being as it were a mausoleum beneath which the *brandea* were placed.[115] From the time of St Gregory onwards this practice seems to have been a fixed part of many dedication ceremonies.[116]

3 *Sprinkling with exorcized water*

Popes Vigilius and Gregory the Great testify to a sprinkling with exorcized water as a third element in the rite of dedication; but in fact this was only practised when a pagan temple was converted into a church.[117]

The Gregorian Sacramentary provides four prayers for the dedication.[118] The substantially Roman *Ordo* 42 describes in more detail the procession with the relics and their burial;[119] however, this *ordo* has not reached us in its original form, but has been influenced by some elements of the Old Gallican liturgy.[120]

II THE OLD GALLICAN RITUAL AND ITS ACCRETIONS

At Rome the burial of the relics became, together with the Mass, the characteristic ceremony of the dedication—the anointing of the altar with chrism was only added later to conclude the ceremony, and only one prayer was said during the clothing of the altar. In Gaul, on the other hand, it was the consecration of the altar which predominated—this ceremony was to undergo considerable development; the procession and burial of the relics were simply added as a conclusion.

1 *Consecration of the altar*

A. Chavasse has shown that the oldest Gallican *ordo* of the dedication ceremony is that preserved in the Sacramentary of Angoulême.[121] According to this *ordo*, the bishop together with his

---

[115]Andrieu, *op. cit.,* pp. 361-76.

[116]*ibid.,* pp. 361, 368.

[117] Vigilius, *loc. cit.*; St Gregory, *Registrum* 1, 2, ep. 56, Ewald ed., vol. 2, p. 331.

[118] H 194-6.

[119] Andrieu OR 4, pp. 397-402.

[120] It is thus that the sprinkling of the church, which is in fact misplaced (n.17), did not appear in the version of OR 42 which was used by the editor of OR 43. —Similarly the interruption of the procession by the rites carried out inside the church by the bishop alone, n. 3-6, could only have been later and seems to be an imitation of Old Gallican usage.

[121]Ed. Cagin, f° 140 v and ff, n. 2020; A. Chavasse, *op. cit.,* p. 42.

clergy enters the empty church to the chant of a litany. He blesses a mixture of water and wine with which he sprinkles the building and then the altar; after this he says a prayer of blessing over the altar, anoints it in five places and anoints the walls in several places with chrism. He then blesses the altar linen and the sacred vessels. When the altar has been prepared and the lights lit, the relics are brought in by a great procession;[122] they are placed on the altar and the bishop celebrates Mass. The various priestly prayer formularies which go to make up this rite are found in the *Missale Francorum*, which, for the consecration of the altar, adds rites inspired by Ex 29:12-18 and by Lv 8:11. We still use practically all of these, especially the offering of incense.[123]

2 *Subsidiary rites and psalmody*

The *Ordo* 41, dating from the time of Pepin the Short, shows that this set of rites developed in two ways. First through numerous rites borrowed from diverse sources: the bishop knocks at the door before entering, and inside traces the alphabet on the ground (two rites probably of Irish origin);[124] at the mixing of the water and wine (Byzantine origin), salt and ashes are added; the sprinklings and anointings are more numerous and complicated; a priest continually goes around the altar incensing it (likewise of Byzantine origin). But what is most noteworthy is that the entire ceremony is already accompanied by an almost continuous psalmody whose refrains emphasize the meaning of the actions,[125] and which is one of the gems of the dedication ceremony in the Roman pontifical. The Old Gelasian Sacramentary seems to be the one adapted to the ceremonial of the *Ordo* 41.[126]

III THE MERGING OF THE TWO RITUALS AND FURTHER DEVELOPMENTS

The later Gelasian sacramentaries have enriched the formulary of

---

[122]A similar description is given by Gregory of Tours, *In gloria confessorum* 20, W. Arndt and B. Krusch ed. (MGH) vol. 2, pp. 759-60.

[123]*Ponis super cornua altaris digito tuo vinum cum aqua mixtum, et aspergis altare septem vicibus, relicum autem fundes ad basem et offeres incensum super altare, odorem suavissimum Domino: Missale Francorum*, L. C. Mohlberg ed., n. 57-8.

[124]Andrieu OR 4, pp. 319-20.

[125]Psalms 24 and 51 were already to be found in the Byzantine ritual: *ibid.*, pp. 316-17.

[126]Ge 1, 88-93; Mohlberg, n. 689-729. To the formula of the *Missale Francorum* it adds a further two: *Deus qui loca, Deus sanctificationum;* Andrieu OR 4, p. 335, judges them to be Gallican, while L. Duchesne, *op. cit.*, pp. 435-6 and A. Chavasse, *op. cit.*, pp. 45-9, regard them as Roman.

the Old Gelasian with a certain number of prayers, some of which have come down in usage to the present day.[127] One of these, the Sacramentary of the Phillips' collection, adds to it the ritual of the Gregorian. A similar effort at combining formularies can be seen in the *Ordo* 43 of the collection of Saint-Amand.[128] About 825 the Sacramentary of Drogo (Metz) mentions for the first time the triple lustration of the exterior walls of the church as well as the triple dialogue between the bishop who knocks at the closed door and a cleric inside the church. The general plan of the ceremony is noticeably that of the modern Roman pontifical: after the bishop has entered the church and performed the aspersions, the burial of the relics takes place and finally the consecration of the altar.[129]

A new phase is marked by the Romano-Germanic Pontifical about 950: for the ceremony of dedication the author has assembled an extensive collection of prayers and didactic texts,[130] many of which have passed into the modern pontifical, either through the Roman pontifical of the twelfth century[131] or through that of Durandus of Mende.[132]

It is from the Romano-Germanic Pontifical and through Durandus that we have received fragments of the Spanish liturgy, especially two beautiful chants.[133] But this time Durandus is not so inspired as usual: he increased what was already excessive, giving us seven preparatory psalms, the singing of the *Veni Creator* and the *Veni Sancte*, as well as numerous prayers.

IV THE PRESENT RITE (April 13, 1961)

BIBLIOGRAPHY

P. Jounel, *Dédicace d'une église* (Tournai: Desclée, 1962).
A. G. Martimort, "Le nouveau rite de la dédicace des églises" in LMD 70, 6-31.

---

[127]These are the formulas *Singulare illud* (on which see R. Coquin, in LMD 78, 161-75), *Domine sancte Pater omnipotens aeterne Deus clemens et propitius* (used up to 1961), and *Fac nos Domine sanctorum.*

[128]Andrieu OR 4, pp. 411-13.

[129]J. B. Pelt, "Études sur la cathédrale de Metz" in *La liturgie*, vol. 1 (Metz, 1937) pp. 92-4.

[130]PRG, n. XXXIII-XLV, vol. 1, pp. 82-178.

[131]Andrieu PR 1, pp. 176-95.

[132]Andrieu PR 3, pp. 455-78.

[133]Prayers for the blessing of the salt, *Liber ordinum*, M. Férotin ed., col. 13;— of the water, *ibid.*, col. 14; —of the incense, *ibid.*, col. 177; the formula *Sanctificare*, a mixture of two formulas taken from *ibid.*, col. 29-30 and 21 (suppressed in the 1961 revision); the antiphon *Unxit te Deus* and the responsory *Induit te* (the latter was unfortunately removed in 1961): *Antifonario de León*, fº 267 recto et verso. Durandus also introduced the chant of the *Dirigatur*, which was to be repeated four times.

In its recent revision, the rite of the dedication has preserved all its important elements, but the repetitions have been eliminated and the whole structure simplified. Thus the bishop performs only one aspersion outside the church, after which there takes place before the closed door the dialogue with a deacon who is inside. The bishop, clergy, and faithful then enter to the singing of the litanies. The bishop sprinkles the church and the altar, then traces the alphabet and sings the first preface. The relics are solemnly brought in; the bishop anoints with chrism the walls and the altar, on which incense is then burned. Finally the bishop sings the second preface and the ceremony concludes with the Mass, which is the crowning of the entire rite. Throughout the whole ceremony each action is accompanied by the singing of antiphonal psalms in a form that encourages clergy and people to an active participation.

The simplified ceremony of the dedication of a church as we find it in today's Roman pontifical is the most beautiful of all the liturgical actions. It presents symbolism of great richness: the pouring of chrism, the burning of incense, the processions and ablutions. In it are evoked all the biblical themes of the encounter with God and his dwelling among men.

The Theology of Liturgical Celebration

A. G. Martimort

CHAPTER EIGHT

The Twofold Movement of the Liturgy: Worship of God and Sanctification of Man

BIBLIOGRAPHY

M. Festugière, *Qu'est-ce que la liturgie?* (Maredsous, 1914) pp. 37-65.

J. M. Hanssens, "De natura liturgiae ad mentem sancti Thomae" in *Periodica de re morali, canonica, liturgica . . .* 24 (1935) 127*-65*.

P. Oppenheim, *Notiones liturgiae fundamentales* (Turin: Marietti, 1941; *Institutiones systematico-historicae in sacram liturgiam* 6) pp. 81-107.

C. Vagaggini, *Theological Dimensions of the Liturgy* 1 (Collegeville, Minnesota: Liturgical Press, 1959) pp. 68-87.

The preceding analysis of the structure of liturgical celebration brings out first of all that the liturgy is "the privileged encounter between God and man; under the veil of signs, God comes toward man, and man goes toward God."[1] Liturgy implies, then, a twofold action—men towards God to offer him the prayer of adoration and thanksgiving, and God towards men to pour forth his gifts on them. This is vividly demonstrated in the prayer of the Roman canon:

> Almighty God, we pray that your angel may take this sacrifice to your altar in heaven. Then, as we receive from this altar the sacred body and blood of your Son, let us be filled with every grace and blessing.[2]

[1]C. Vagaggini, *op. cit.*, p. 68.—Cf. *ibid.*, pp. 16-18; B. Capelle, SL 11 (1933) 9.

[2]The prayer *Supplices te rogamus;* B. Botte and C. Mohrmann, *Ordinaire de la messe . . .* (Paris: Ed. du Cerf, 1953; *Études liturgiques* 2) p. 83 (and footnotes, *ibid.*).—Cf. also the prayer *Suscipiat: ad laudem et gloriam nominis sui, ad utilitatem quoque nostram totiusque Ecclesiae suae sanctae;* the prayer over the gifts, for the tenth Sunday after Pentecost: *Tibi Domine sacrificia dicata reddantur, quae sic ad honorem nominis tui deferenda tribuisti, ut eadem remedia fieri nostra praestares.*—SCL 7: "Christ indeed always associates the Church with himself in the truly great work of giving perfect praise to God and making men holy. The Church is his dearly beloved Bride who calls to her Lord, and through him offers worship to the eternal Father. Rightly, then, the liturgy is considered as an exercise of the priestly office of Jesus Christ. In the liturgy the sanctification of man is manifested by signs perceptible to the senses, and is effected in a way which is proper to each of the signs; in the liturgy full public worship is performed by the mystical Body of Jesus Christ, that is, by the head and his members."—Cf. CSL 10.

1 Liturgy, worship of God

The ascending motion towards God of the prayer of adoration and praise is what first attracts our attention. Within the liturgy it elicits from the faithful a renewed conversion and a detachment from what is worldly. The liturgy amazes many people by its disinterestedness, its latitude and contemplative leisure, and its theocentric emphasis. For all those who have had the joy of participating fully in it and of really appreciating it, the liturgy has been a marvellous school of divine service of the Lord, of the experience of God.[3]

I PRAISE AND THANKSGIVING

The Church has inherited its understanding of God from the Old Testament. But the revelation of the Father brought by Christ and the fulfilment in him of all the biblical figures make the prayer of the Church both a continuation of and a break with Jewish prayer.

1 *Prayer of praise and thanksgiving in Old Testament forms*

The Church, we have seen,[4] gives the psalms and biblical canticles a special place in the liturgy. Even when she does not use them word for word, she is inspired by them. From biblical prayer the Church seeks to recapture a description of God's perfections, affirming his holiness, his transcendence, his eternity and power. The manifestations (theophanies) of the Old Testament permit union with the song of the angels, especially as in Is 6:3.

From the contemplation of the perfections of God, Jewish prayer evolves into thanksgiving for his "*mirabilia*," the wonders of creation and his merciful interventions for his people. The discovery of sin and spiritual misery accentuates still more this conviction of a loving, merciful and healing God. The Church makes all these forms her own, but gives them a richer meaning because the *mirabilia* of the God of the New Testament go beyond those of the Old Testament by continuing them and bringing them to completion.

2 *Praise and thanksgiving according to the New Testament*

Since Christ has revealed to us the secrets of God's ways, the liturgy is filled, as we have stated above,[5] with trinitarian doxologies, often borrowed from the epistles of St Paul. The prayers of the

[3]This point, very often developed in books on the liturgy, has been particularly emphasized by Guardini, *The Spirit of the Liturgy* (London: Sheed and Ward, 1930) pp. 96-106.

[4]See above, ch. 6.

[5]See above, ch. 6.

celebrant, addressed to the Father, put all their stress on the mediation of Jesus, Son of God, and invoke the Holy Spirit.[6] The most important acts of the liturgy, the consecratory prayers, are prayers of thanksgiving, prefaces or anaphoras, fashioned according to the Jewish prayer of blessing.

Although the prayer of the celebrant is usually addressed to the Fatheɪ, the Church in her prayer also accords divine worship to Jesus. She applies to him the title ot Lord (*Kyrios*), which in the Septuagint was proper to God. In this way, the Church, when praying the psalms, thinks of Christ.

The prayer of thanksgiving is more characteristic of Christian than it is of Old Testament prayer. In the book of Revelation it is the song of the heavenly liturgical assembly;[7] St Paul wants it to be the lasting attitude of the faithful.[8] It is the awareness of the mystery of redemption, the cry of recognition to the Christ who has washed us in his blood, the praise of the eternal designs of God who has called us, who has accepted us with an unmerited love. The liturgical community, by the mere fact of its coming together, is a manifestation of salvation in Christ.[9]

3 *Sacrifice of praise*

BIBLIOGRAPHY

J. Juglar, *Le sacrifice de louange* (Paris: Ed. du Cerf, 1953; *Lex orandi* 15).

The liturgy reaches its climax in the eucharistic celebration which is the sacrifice of adoration and thanksgiving—"sacrifice of praise"— at the same time that it is an efficacious memorial of the redemptive act. Since Christ offered the unique sacrifice of the cross, the rites in which the Old Testament people of God expressed their adoration and praise have been abolished: "You who wanted no sacrifice or oblation, prepared a body for me. You took no pleasure in holocausts or sacrifices for sin; then I said, just as I was commanded in the scroll of the book, 'God, here I am! I am coming to obey your will ' "(Heb 10:5-7). It is the clearest break between New Testament and Old Testament worship: reality surpasses the figures which preceded. In order to recognize the sovereignty of God, the Church

---

[6]On this aspect, see L. Beauduin, "Essai de manuel fondamental de liturgie," ch. 1: "Le terme du culte, la sainte Trinité" in *Mélanges liturgiques recueillis* . . . *à l'occasion de ses quatre-vingts ans* (Louvain: Mont César, 1954) pp. 45-73.

[7]Rv 4:8-11; 5:8-14; 7:9-12; 11:15-18; 14:1-7; 15:2-4; 19:1-10.

[8]2 Co 2:14; 4:15; Ep 5:19-20; Ph 4:6; Col 3:16-17; 1 Th 5-18.—Cf. J. Juglar, *Le sacrifice de louange* (Paris: Ed. du Cerf, 1953) pp. 281-7: "La tonalité eucharistique de la piété chrétienne primitive."

[9]This point is emphasized in CSL 6.

has no other sacrifice of first-fruits or holocausts than Christ. It is a perfect praise, "a fragrant offering and a sacrifice to God" (Ep 5:2). It is the only sufficient expiation, the plea of him "who is living forever to intercede for all who come to God through him" (Heb 7:25).

II LITURGY AND THE HUMAN CONCEPT OF WORSHIP

BIBLIOGRAPHY

J. Lécuyer, "Réflexions sur la théologie du culte selon saint Thomas" in *Revue Thomiste* 55 (1955) 339-62.

O. Lottin, *Morale fondamentale* (Tournai: Desclée, 1954; *Bibliothèque de théologie*) pp. 350-63 and 434-5 with the bibliography indicated p. 363 and 435.

1 *Analysis of the notion of worship*

Theologians hold that worship and the virtue of religion are necessary even to men who have not the benefit of divine revelation. St Paul, in Rom 1:19-22, judges the pagans culpable:

For what can be known about God is perfectly plain to them since God himself has made it plain. Ever since God created the world his everlasting power and deity—however invisible—have been there for the mind to see in the things he has made. That is why such people are without excuse: they knew God and yet refused to honor him as God or to thank him; instead, they made nonsense out of logic and their empty minds were darkened.

For this reason, in moral theology worship is often treated in the framework of Aristotelian ethics and according to the Latin moralists, especially Cicero. Likewise, treatises on the history of religions have an importance which the Christian should not underestimate, despite the errors of method and the prejudices which have sometimes weakened this discipline. Missionaries think that worship practised by pagans can, in spite of its ambiguities, be a providential preparation for Christian worship, and that the latter should satisfy their religious instinct, by purifying and elevating it.[10]

In these perspectives worship is the ensemble of acts by which man wishes to express his relationship with God. Worship proceeds from a natural disposition: religion; it is composed of distinct and precise acts which have as their sole end to manifest this religion.[11] Two attitudes can be distinguished, although they are closely

[10] G. van Bekkum, "Le renouveau liturgique au service des missions" in LMD 47-8 (1956) 157-64.

[11] St Thomas often repeats the word *exibere* with regard to acts of worship; J. M. Hanssens, *op. cit.*, p. 145*: *quoniam igitur verbum* exhibere *apud s. Thomam idem valet quod affere, offere, praestare, impendere, tribuere et ea praeterea agere cum aliqua ostentatione, seu cum manifesta intentione aliquid iis actionibus demonstrandi, sine dubio affirmare possumus actum divini cultus proprium esse in aliqua testificatione seu protestatione positum.*

related: honor rendered to God in recognition of his goodness, and submission (*obsequium, servitus*):

> Faced with the majesty of God, he (man) conceives necessarily a feeling of admiration, fear, respect and submission before this formidable Being who transcends him and overwhelms him; and this spontaneous movement is already an act of adoration.
>
> Then, when he reflects on this sentiment which has sprung up in his soul, he consents to it with full freedom and makes it his response to that debt of dependence which he has recognized toward him who is first principle and last end of all things.[12]

Going beyond the rudimentary notion of this initial awareness, man desires to know God and to praise him; in this truly consists the glory of God, *clara notitia cum laude*, which is the aim of worship.[13] Through this very fact, man discovers his nothingness, his misery and even his sin, for humility always accompanies true knowledge of God.[14] These sentiments are expressed in prayer, gestures of adoration, and offering.

The scholastic distinction between interior and exterior worship is of little practical importance: the exterior manifestations of worship are meaningful only if they proceed from an attitude of the soul, but yet it is of the nature of worship to express itself. This is proved by the history of religions, verified by the analysis of philosophers and theologians.[15]

Nevertheless, it must be granted that without the help of revelation worship cannot be preserved from corrupting influences which continuously threaten it. Man is tempted to seek religious emotion for its own sake instead of seeking God. He risks the danger of remaining at the spontaneous and subjective stage of his feelings, balking at the intellectual effort required in order to know God and at the demands of holiness which its discovery implies. Above all, he risks losing the sense of the divine transcendence.[16]

2 *Insufficiencies of natural worship*

Revelation has not only rectified and purified the cultic demands imposed on man, it has placed him in a new cultic world.

---

[12]C. Vagaggini, *op. cit.*, p. 71.—A very penetrating analysis of the sentiment of man towards God, from a Lutheran viewpoint, is found in R. Otto, *The Idea of the Holy* (London: Penguin, 1959).

[13]This point is developed by J. Lécuyer, *op. cit.*, pp. 340-41.

[14]A. G. Martimort, "Le sens du sacré" in LMD 25 (1951) 48-9 (and the references given there).

[15]St Thomas, *Summa theol.*, II-II, q. 81, a. 7; MD 23ff.

[16]I. H. Dalmais, *Introduction to the Liturgy* (Baltimore: Helicon, 1961) pp. 17-21.

The primary, essential innovation is that God has spoken the language of men: the unknowable makes himself known; he has permitted Abraham and Moses to see his glory, has spoken through the prophets and has intervened in the midst of a people chosen for himself. "Wisdom has appeared on the earth and has spoken to men" (Ba 3:38). After having spoken through the prophets, God spoke through his son: "No one has ever seen God; it is the only Son, who is nearest to the Father's heart, who has made him known" (Jn 1:18). The coming of Christ makes the brightness of God shine before our eyes: *per incarnati Verbi mysterium nova mentis nostrae oculis lux tuae claritatis infulsit.*[17] This brings with it a complete transformation of the notion of worship which Jesus explains to the Samaritan woman: "We worship what we do know . . . But the hour will come—in fact it is here already—when true worshipers will worship the Father in spirit and truth" (Jn 4:22-23).

On the other hand, although the Lord reigns supreme and the Christian must always approach him with respect and with a sense of his unworthiness and sin, through Jesus Christ the love of God for men has been manifested, inviting them to intimacy and union.

For the Christian, worship and the virtue of religion cannot be disassociated from faith and love. Theologians experience some difficulty in placing religion in the hierarchy of the virtues.[18] For this reason also, Christian worship cannot be conceived without the dialogue between God and his people, and because of the important and unique place which the word of God occupies in the liturgy, Christian worship cannot be compared to any other.[19]

There is another, more radical and fundamental difference. If the passion of Christ has abolished the worship of the Old Testament and of other ancient religions, it is because it is a sacrifice, an act of worship. This sacrifice is acceptable to God in itself; it is unique and could only be renewed sacramentally; it is efficacious independent of the faith and devotion of those who will unite themselves to it. Yet it is destined for the salvation of men, for it contains a spiritual grace, rendering them capable of taking part in this worship which he began. It establishes the Church, a new and worshiping society, destined to continue the priesthood of Christ.[20]

---

[17]Roman missal, Christmas Preface.

[18]It does not pertain to us to enter into the details of the controversy and still less to take part in it. A bibliography on the subject and the *status quaestionis* will be found in O. Lottin, *op. cit.*, to which can be added C. Vagaggini, *op. cit.*, pp. 70-73.

[19]I. H. Dalmais, *op. cit.*, pp. 35-7.

[20]CSL 5.

Worship in the Church cannot be equiparated with the duty which falls on every society to have a public worship. The Church is *essentially* a worshiping society, founded by an act of worship, the sacrifice of Christ. It is through its worship that the Church receives new members, that the degrees of her hierarchy are manifested, that she becomes aware of her inner nature, of the presence and action of her head, and that she discerns the end towards which she travels.

The purpose of liturgy is not only to give worship to God, but also to give the grace of God to men. Liturgy is more than worship.[21] In the liturgy the signs, the exterior acts, are not only the manifestation of interior attitudes and the means of fulfilling their social nature: they contain the sanctification of men, they are sacraments or sacramentals. Even before men praise God or are capable of praising him, God prepares them with his gifts.

2 Liturgy, sanctification of man

As we have seen above, a certain confusion concerning the very definition of liturgy was prominent among authors before Pius XII's encyclical *Mediator Dei*. Some wanted to limit it to rites and rules instituted by the Church to the exclusion of all that is of divine origin in the Mass and sacraments.[22] Understandably these authors had found difficulty in attributing a sanctifying end to the liturgy or had only admitted it as an accessory, insofar as the liturgy was edifying and led to virtue.[23] This opinion, which is no longer acceptable since *Mediator Dei* and especially since Vatican II, was contrary to tradition and is only explained by prejudiced viewpoints, for the Mass and the sacraments are the essentials of the liturgy. However, in recognizing this fundamental fact, other authors, fearful of a too narrow definition of worship, tried to explain that the sacraments are part of liturgy because they are "indirectly" orientated to the glory of God.[24] But historians of the liturgy have emphasized, following the magisterium, that the sanctification of men, the gift coming from the grace of the redemption, is essential to Christian worship to the point that it is the preliminary condition for the fulfilment of the service of God in praise and thanksgiving.

---

[21]It is *"un élargissement de la notion du culte:"* B. Capelle, "Que faut-it entendre par participation active?" in sl 11 (1933) 9.

[22]See above, ch. 1.

[23]C. Callewaert, *De sacra liturgia universim,* 4th ed. (Bruges: Beyaert, 1944) pp. 42-9; A. Coelho, *Cours de liturgie romaine* (Lophem-lez-Bruges, 1928) pp. 214-28.

[24]It seems that this is the position of J. M. Hanssens, *op. cit.,* pp. 155*-9*.

_I SANCTIFICATION OF MAN: AN ESSENTIAL END OF LITURGY

It is a fact that all sacramental acts, including penance, have always figured in liturgical books, and have never been treated other than as actions of the Church at prayer.[25] It is also a fact, upon which we have already insisted, that the Word of God occupies an important place in the celebration. These two facts would suffice to show that in the liturgy the gift of God to man is not accessory, but essential— service of God, it is also service of man.

1 *The sanctification of man by the Word of God in the liturgy*

BIBLIOGRAPHY

A. Bea, "The Pastoral Value of the Word of God in the Sacred Liturgy" in *The Assisi Papers* (Collegeville, Minnesota: Liturgical Press, 1957) pp. 74-90.
G. Garrone, "Mes paroles sont esprit et vie" in *Parole de Dieu et liturgie* (Paris: Ed. du Cerf, 1958; *Lex orandi* 25) pp. 363-80.

"The word of God is something alive and active: it cuts like any double-edged sword but more finely: it can slip through the place where the soul is divided from the spirit, or joints from the marrow; it can judge the secret emotions and thoughts" (Heb 4:12). "Although Sacred Scripture cannot be called a sacrament in the technical sense of the word, as some have sometimes desired, it cannot merely be referred to as a sacramental, as if it produced its effects only *ex opere operantis Ecclesiae*, in virtue of the dignity and the powerful intercession of the Church. Inherent in the very words of Sacred Scripture, read and explained with the required dispositions, is a light and a strength which surpass the light and strength of purely human words and give them an authority with a singular and unique power."[26]

2 *The sanctifying role of the sacraments and sacramentals*

The primary aim of the sacraments is to give the grace of God to men, to make the redemption beneficial to them and to lead them to salvation. They are *propter homines*, and their effect is produced by the rites themselves, the gestures and words. Therefore these gestures and words are directly and essentially liturgical in essence, independent of the framework of the celebration in which the Church inserts them.

Moreover, the sacramental word is often a prayer of the celebrant. As regards the sacrament of holy orders, the fact is clear since the

---

[25]Cf. CSL 6: "... Christ ... sent the apostles ... that they might exercise the work of salvation which they were proclaiming, by means of sacrifice and sacraments, around which the entire liturgical life revolves." See especially CSL 7, quoted above, note 2.

[26]A. Bea, *op. cit.*, p. 82.—Cf. CSL 33, 7.

constitution *Sacramentum ordinis*. Penance was formerly administered in the same way. It is also verified in the anointing of the sick,
although this may be less apparent; as for the Eucharist, although the
form is indicative, it is part of a continuous prayer of thanksgiving.

The entire sacramental plan is fundamentally bound to the
liturgy. On the one hand, the sacraments draw their present efficacy
from the passion of Christ which is the sacrifice of the New Law.
On the other hand, it is one of the effects of the sacraments to
provide the liturgy with its participants and ministers. The sacraments of baptism, confirmation and orders imprint a character,
which, according to the doctrine of St Thomas, delegates one to
divine worship and is a participation in the priesthood of Christ.[27]
Through baptism the faithful take an active part in the liturgy; by
their ordination the bishop and his priests preside over the liturgy.

A good many of the sacramentals instituted by the Church have
as an end, in imitation of the sacraments, the sanctification of men,
based on the *opus operantis Ecclesiae*—a notion which will be
treated in the following chapter. They are also, of necessity, liturgical
acts, and their administration is always a prayer in the name of the
assembly, if not a prayer in the midst of the assembly.

3 *Eucharistic sacrifice, gift of God to men*

It is the Eucharist which manifests most concretely the twofold
movement of the liturgy. Sacrifice offered to God, supreme act of the
worship of adoration, it is *par excellence* the gift of God to man.
We have received the victim presented to the Father from the
Father himself (*de tuis donis ac datis*) through transubstantiation.
After we have offered him to God, he is given to us as food; although
communion is not essential to sacrifice, it is required for its fulness
(at least on the part of the celebrant). Thus, the act of worship most
disinterested and most theocentric, the sacrifice of praise, is at the
same time the act by which we receive from God the very source of
all grace.[28]

4 *Objective and subjective sanctification*

Sanctification offered by the liturgy is an objective reality, independent of the person performing the ceremony. It is salvation
acquired by Christ, given *ex opere operato* or *ex opere operantis
Ecclesiae*, depending on whether it is a sacrament or not:

> It is an unquestionable fact that the work of our redemption is continued
> and that its fruits are imparted to us, during the celebration of the liturgy,

[27]*Summa theol.*, III, q. 63, a. 2 and 3.
[28]See the beautiful passages in A. Bea, *op. cit.*, pp. 86-7.—Cf. CSL 47-8.

notably in the august sacrifice of the altar. Christ acts each day to save us, in the sacraments and in his holy sacrifice. By means of them he is constantly atoning for the sins of mankind, constantly consecrating it to God. Sacraments and sacrifice do, then, possess that "objective" power to make us really and personally sharers in the divine life of Jesus Christ. Not from any ability of our own, but by the power of God, are they endowed with the capacity to unite the piety of members with that of the Head, and to make this, in a sense, the action of the whole community.[29]

Insisting on this aspect, we should not forget that the faithful, who are to receive this grace, ought to be prepared for it, to approach it with the right dispositions and afterwards to correspond with it, for liturgy is not a magical action.[30] For the interior, "subjective"[31] effort, liturgy brings its help. It excites, illuminates and develops faith; its prayer expresses the love of God while its communitarian life is a school of fraternal love. Liturgy achieves this by continuously putting before the eyes of the faithful the mysteries of Christ and the example of the saints. These elements have often been analysed from the beginnings of the liturgical movement.[32]

II THE CLOSE LINK BETWEEN WORSHIP AND SANCTIFICATION

These two movements which can and ought to be distinguished in the liturgy—of men towards God and God towards men—are closely linked, not only in the very celebration, but in the nature of things. St Thomas even attributed to every act of religion this two-fold action: theocentric and sanctifying—worship is for the good of man.[33] But these two ends are subordinated. Sanctification is in view of worship; salvation in Christ, fruit of his worship towards the Father, has its end in the heavenly liturgy where God is all in all.[34] It is the priesthood of Christ, of which the liturgy is the exercise, which explains the unity of this twofold action and the ultimate relation of all rites to the adoration and glorification of God.

[29]MD 28; cf. 26-7.
[30]CSL 10-11; MD 28-36.—Cf. A. Lécuyer, *op. cit.*, pp. 360-61.
[31]The use here of the words "objective" and "subjective" does not correspond in the same way to the controversy on "subjective" or "objective" piety. Cf. L. Bouyer, *Liturgical Piety* (Notre Dame University Press, 1955) pp. 17-18; C. Vagaggini, *op. cit.*, pp. 102-6: "The Liturgy and the Law of Objectivity."
[32]As St Thomas had already done in his theology of worship; this can be seen in the texts assembled by J. Lécuyer, *op. cit.*, p. 348.—Cf. L. Beauduin, *Liturgy, the Life of the Church* (Collegeville, Minnesota: Liturgical Press, 1926); C. Callewaert, *op. cit.*, pp. 48-52; R. Guardini, *op. cit.*, 130-49; A. Coelho, *op. cit.*, pp. 214-28; P. Oppenheim, *op. cit.*, pp. 100-07; B. Capelle, *Travaux liturgiques* 1 (Louvain: Mont César, 1955) pp. 68-100.
[33]J. Lécuyer, *op. cit.*, pp. 343f.
[34]CSL 8 and 48.

CHAPTER NINE

Liturgy and the Mystery of Salvation

I. H. Dalmais

BIBLIOGRAPHY

L. Beauduin, *Mélanges recueillis parmi les oeuvres de Dom Lambert Beauduin à l'occasion de ses quatre-vingts ans* ... (Louvain: Mont César, 1954) pp. 73-81.

L. Bouyer, *The Paschal Mystery* (Chicago, 1950; London: Allen and Unwin, 1951).

L. Bouyer, *Liturgical Piety* (Notre Dame University Press, 1950); published in England as *Liturgy and Life* (London: Sheed and Ward, 1958).

O. Casel, "La notion de 'jour de fête' " in LMD 1 (1945) 23-36.

O. Casel, "Pâques, la fête des fêtes" in LMD 9 (1947) 55-9.

O. Casel, *The Mystery of Christian Worship* (Westminster, Maryland: Newman Press; London: Darton, Longman and Todd, 1962).

"Dom Casel (1886–1948), La doctrine du mystère chrétien" in LMD 14 (special number) 1948.

J. D. Crichton, *The Church's Worship—Considerations on the Liturgical Constitution of the Second Vatican Council* (London: Chapman; New York: Sheed and Ward, 1964) pp. 23-60.

I. H. Dalmais, *Introduction to the Liturgy* (London: Chapman; Baltimore: Helicon, 1961) pp. 56-95.

I. H. Dalmais, "The Christian Liturgy and the Mystery of Salvation" in *True Worship*, L. Sheppard ed. (Baltimore: Helicon; London: Darton, Longman and Todd, 1963) pp. 1-13.

"L'économie du salut et le cycle liturgique" in LMD 30 (1952) 3-103 (congress of the Centre de pastoral liturgique at Vanves, 1950).

L. McMahon, "Towards a Theology of the Liturgy: Dom Odo Casel and the 'Mysterientheorie'" in *Studia Liturgica* 3 (1964) 129-54.

H. Oster, *Le grand dessein de Dieu dans la pastorale et la prédication* (Paris: Ed. du Cerf, 1955; *L'esprit liturgique* 10).

R. Paquier, *Traité de liturgique* (Neuchâtel: Delachaux et Niestlé, 1954) pp. 15-53.

P. de Puniet, "Actualité des mystères de la vie du Christ dans la liturgie" in SL 13 (1935) pp. 9-25.

A. M. Roguet, "Commentaire de la Constitution conciliaire sur la liturgie" in LMD 77 (1964) 20, 30.

C. Vagaggini, *Theological Dimensions of the Liturgy* 1 (Collegeville, Minnesota: Liturgical Press, 1959) pp. 3-67.

1 Theological foundations

The specific nature of Christian worship is determined by the nature of the assembly which performs it. The Church of Christ does not belong to the same order as human societies; it is the manifestation among men of the mystery of the Savior-God (1 Tim 3:16). It is the community engaged in the definitive alliance by which God was pleased to link himself with a people, whom he had gratuitously chosen to be the beneficiary and the witness among the nations of his plan of salvation. The secret of this plan, its "mystery"—to use the word which Christian tradition has received from St Paul—is "the hidden plan he so kindly made in Christ from the beginning to act upon when the times had run their course to the end: that he would bring everything together under Christ, as head, everything in the heavens and everything on earth" (Eph 1:9-10).

The liturgy of the Church then has as its function not only to offer to God the worship which is due him, but to render present and active among men his mystery of salvation.[1]

I THE LITURGY OF THE NEW COVENANT IN THE SPIRIT

The Church is conscious of being the Israel of the last times and of fulfilling the promise of a new and definitive covenant announced by the prophets. She must therefore exercise the spiritual worship which is characteristic of this Covenant.[2]

(1) Insofar as it is an expression of the Covenant between God and his people, this worship is entirely sustained by the Word of God which assembles this people, gives it his commands, and reveals to it his secret plan for it. Since the inspired expression of this word is found in the Scriptures, the Christian liturgy will be a biblical liturgy.[3]

(2) Insofar as it is an expression of the final Covenant, the Christian liturgy possesses an eschatological character. It reaches out in expectation toward the coming of the kingdom. Under the veil of sacramental signs, i.e. signs which effect what they signify, it already presents the pledge of these final realities, which will mean full communion between God and man, when he will be all in all (1 Co 15:28).[4]

(3) Insofar as this final Covenant is characterized by the outpouring of the Spirit, the Christian liturgy constitutes "spiritual worship," not because it would refuse to make use of material realities, but because it places them entirely under the influence of

---

[1]CSL 5-6;—cf. J. Daniélou, *Essai sur le mystère de l'histoire* (Paris: Seuil, 1953) pp. 147-273.

[2]Cf. J. Juglar, *Le sacrifice de louange* (Paris: Ed. du Cerf, 1953; *Lex orandi* 15) pp. 115-53.

[3]CSL 5-6, 7, 24, 33.

[4]CSL 8.

o

the Spirit, and at his service. As a result, these material realities—
language, gestures, or any of the elements which can find place in
worship—while retaining their own natural meaning, take on a
higher meaning which makes them efficacious signs of the grace
communicated by the Spirit of Christ for the sanctification of the
faithful, and signs too of the filial prayer which the Spirit generates
in their hearts (Rom 8:26-7).[5]

(4) Insofar as this covenant is the messianic Covenant characterized by the sovereign intervention of Christ in whom and by whom
the presence of God in the midst of his people (Emmanuel) is realized,
the Christian liturgy is, in all respects, "christic." Christ is the unique
and definitive high priest of the new Covenant who has offered
himself in sacrifice and "by virtue of that one single offering has
achieved the eternal perfection of all whom he is sanctifying" (Heb
10:14). The whole liturgy of the Church will be only a vicarious and
ministerial liturgy, which unites the assembly of the faithful to the
worship which Christ continues to render to his Father in this Church
which is his Body.[6]

II THE WORSHIP OF THE MYSTICAL BODY OF CHRIST

The Church is not only the people of God. The economy of
salvation inaugurated by Christ includes, with the gift of the Spirit,
such an intimacy between the leader (Christ) and the people that the
best analogy for it which we can provide is that of the body and its
members animated by the same unique vital principle, subject to the
influence of one head which rules it completely. St Paul, who has
made extensive use of this analogy, closely joins to it in the captivity
epistles the analogy of the spiritual temple substituted for the
material sanctuary in which all the sacrificial worship of Israel had
been concentrated.

By reason of this intimacy we surmount the paradox of a liturgy
whose celebrant would no longer be visibly present among the men
who are called upon to associate themselves with him. There is
actually only one liturgy in heaven and on earth and it is the same
priest who carries it out. This liturgy is offered by him in the glory
of the Father, with whom he remains to intercede for us forever
(Heb 7: 25); it is offered on earth through the ministers whom he has
chosen among men to represent him and to preside in his name and
with his authority over the visible celebrations of the Church.

Thus, according to the Second Vatican Council:

[5]CSL 7.
[6]*ibid.*

Rightly, then, the liturgy is considered as an exercise of the priestly office of Jesus Christ. In the liturgy the sanctification of man is manifested by signs perceptible to the senses, and is effected in a way which is proper to each of these signs; in the liturgy full public worship is performed by the mystical Body of Jesus Christ, that is, by the head and his members.[7]

The Church is the people of God designated to be the witness in the midst of humanity to the plan of salvation and the mediator of divine grace. She is a priestly community, because of her intimate union with Christ the priest, who communicates to her his Spirit. Consequently the Church must express this double character in her liturgy. Her worship will be that of a community organized to manifest the fulfilment in Christ of God's design of reconciling the world to himself in order to call it to the communion of his holiness. But her liturgy will also be the worship of the spouse of Christ who exercises a maternal role toward humanity and inaugurates in her liturgy the dialogue of love for which man has been created. In the power of the Spirit and through Christ who lives in her, she begets sons of God and makes them grow by her sacraments until they are formed to the perfect image of Christ, firstborn of a multitude of brethren (Rom 8:29).

2 The liturgy as act of the Church

Every liturgical celebration is a sacred action of the community. But the Christian liturgy has a unique quality of taking hold of those who participate in it to the most intimate depths of their being, in order to regenerate them and to introduce them, as by a new creation, into the divine world of which they are made citizens. Hence the Christian liturgy cannot know passive assistants. From the moment the liturgical function begins, all those who take part in it are "in act," are offering official service to God. In the liturgical action the participants exercise in its fullness the virtuality communicated to man by baptism: to be members of the kingdom of God.[8]

The liturgy brings about the awareness of the Church as a social body, in that which constitutes it here on earth: to be the dispenser of the mystery of salvation among men. This is the characteristic proper to the liturgy. It is not primarily a teaching, although it is, as Pius XI said, the *didascalia* of the Church and the most important organ of her ordinary magisterium; it cannot be penetrated by speculation but by experience. Neither the texts nor the rites (still less the rubrics which explain them) constitute the liturgy. These elements become liturgy only when they are aptly performed by

[7]CSL 7;—cf. MD 19-20.
[8]CSL 11 and especially 14.

qualified ministers for the purpose for which they have been instituted: the communication of the mystery of salvation.[9]

I AN ACTION WHICH CONSTITUTES THE CHURCH

It is by means of liturgical celebrations, and above all by those which constitute the sacramental rites properly speaking, that the Church begets her children in the faith, that she nourishes and strengthens them through the whole course of their earthly pilgrimage. Faith is inseparable from the sacraments of faith. The history of the liturgy shows how the Church has endeavored to emphasize by meaningful rites the diverse aspects under which this life in the faith can be seen in its various stages, which are analogous to those of natural life.

It is obviously in the eucharistic celebration, center and summit of all the Christian liturgy, that this function of the liturgy is realized most perfectly. This sacrament is the efficacious sign of the divine and human reality which constitutes the Church. Distinct individuals, separated and opposed by all the seeds of division which they bear in them by reason of their sinful condition, but by the washing of regeneration transferred into the kingdom which the resurrection of the Lord has inaugurated, become in the eucharistic celebration through communion in the Body and Blood of Christ, who integrates them into his redemptive sacrifice, a single being, an organic unity, multiform but coherent. One source of life, one unique influence emanating from him who is simultaneously the head and the fullness—or the fulfilment—one same vital breath, the Spirit, who works differently in the individual members and prepares in them, by the ministry of all, the harmonious growth of the whole to the full stature of the perfect man, until the day when the one total Christ will present himself to the Father in the final, definitive Pasch (cf. Eph 4:11-16).[10]

These signs, which directly or indirectly build up the ecclesial Body, can be traced through the entire sacramental economy: the reintegration of members by penance; the transmission of the hierarchic power and the perpetuation of the apostolic tradition in the sacrament of orders; marriage which incorporates and elevates the divine injunction given to the species: "Increase and multiply." In spiritually adapting a Christian to his special condition of illness, the anointing of the sick signals the new function which is assigned to him in the Church and which makes him a privileged witness of

[9]CSL 26.
[10]CSL 2.

the redemptive mystery. One could thus undertake a study of all the Christian rites under the aspect of the building up of the Church.

II AN ACTION WHICH EXPRESSES THE CHURCH

Most of the secondary rites offer a wealth of profound views on the inner reality of the Church, a reality not immediately perceptible in itself, by which she realizes the plan of salvation in the world. This revelation of inner reality through exterior rites is a consequence of the economy of the incarnation freely chosen by God. Because the Church is herself parable and sacrament of the kingdom, her liturgy will express in mystery the ultimate realities of this kingdom. And this expression will not be accidental or superfluous: it constitutes the true splendor of the divine-human reality which is the Church. She expresses, by the sole fact of her existence and according to the modalities of this existence, what she is and what she brings about. But these realities are too rich to find adequate expression in a particular rite, marked with the imprint of a given culture.[11]

It is important to make use of all the liturgical creations of the West and of the East in order to form an exact idea of what the Church, in the consciousness which she has formed up to now, intends to express in her liturgy. A certain trait which is emphasized in one rite appears elsewhere only vaguely. Could we discern it in the second instance, had we not met it elsewhere more clearly delineated? And, on the other hand, only this comparison, or synoptic view, will permit us to recognize the essential constants and the secondary developments which are the results of the needs or of the particular tastes of individual communities. However deficient or awkward they may be, they are expressions of a reality of which we must retain both the divine aspect, which is immutable and perfect, and the human aspect, which is changeable and dependent on the conditions of the milieu in which the Church must live.[12] Quite often, an insufficient, clumsy or forced sign attracts our attention to an aspect which the classic lines of the great liturgies concealed in the balance of the whole. The Roman liturgy, for example, by reason of its restraint, frequently risks hiding some nuance—which it has nevertheless indicated to some degree—from a cursory study.

III THE LITURGY, PRIVILEGED PLACE OF THE PRESENCE OF CHRIST

At the heart of the ecclesial economy of the new Covenant, there is but one unique priest, Christ. The liturgy, which is the expression of

[11]Cf. CSL 37-8.   [12]CSL 21.

the priestly character of this economy, will consequently be a privileged place of the presence of Christ in his Church: a presence which is immediate in the sacramental celebrations properly speaking and mediate in the signs which the Church, animated by the Spirit of Christ and instructed by his word, proposes to the faithful. Classical theology translates the first mode of presence by the expression *ex opere operato,* the second by *ex opere operantis Ecclesiae.* In the first case, the salvific power of Christ is exercised, provided only that the will of those who take part in the celebration does not positively place an obstacle to it and provided that the forms recognized by the Church be respected, according to the importance which she attributes to them. In the second case, the efficacy of the celebration is directly assured by the faith and charity of the Church.

1 *The sacramental presence of Christ and its degrees*

This active intervention of Christ is itself exercised in various degrees.[13] In the eucharistic celebration it goes so far as totally to withdraw the elements of the bread and wine from their natural mode of existence in order to make them the sign of the Body and Blood of Christ, substantially present under their "species." In baptism and confirmation, it communicates to the elements of water and oil the power of introducing the subject into the paschal mystery of regeneration and into the new life according to the Spirit. In the other sacramental rites, this active power (*virtus*) of Christ is exercised through diverse signs, gestures whose significance is specified by the spoken word, and which can vary from one liturgy to another and in the course of their development.

2 *The presence of Christ in his word*

Another mode of Christ's presence in the liturgical assembly is realized by the reading of the Scriptures. The gospel holds an incomparable place among these readings and Christian tradition has set it on a plane analogous to that of the Eucharistic presence. Hence the exceptional honors rendered to the book of the gospels: candles, incense, kisses. But Christ, who as subsistent word has fulfilled in himself all the Scriptures, makes himself heard and recognized also in the other texts of the Old and the New Testaments, inasmuch as they have been recognized as a privileged expression of the Word of God.

[13]CSL 7.

3 *The presence of Christ in his ministers*

By the apostolic institution, Christ designated for himself "authorized representatives," *locum-tenentes* (lieutenants), associated in a special manner in his messianic mission in virtue of the royal and prophetic priesthood. Even more than in the other acts of their ministry, in the liturgical functions they are called upon to act *in persona Christi*. In properly sacramental acts, their role becomes even purely instrumental, although it is clearly understood that this instrument is a person whose freely posited intention is a decisive element for the validity of the sacramental act.[14] But it is important to add that, in various degrees and according to the mandate which has been given to them under the responsibility of the bishop, guardian of the apostolic hierarchy, all ministers contribute to realizing this presence of Christ in the midst of the assembly.

4 *The presence of Christ in the assembly*

The assembly itself, in the liturgical act, constitutes a particular mode of the presence of Christ whose Body it is. Under the responsibility of the celebrant who represents Christ the head, this whole Body expresses itself and acts. That is why in psalmody and in prayer it can make its own the expressions which, in the proper sense, pertain only to Christ.[15] Just as the ordained ministers most represent Christ in the liturgical celebrations, so by means of these celebrations the mystery of the Church as Body of Christ makes itself most perceptible, anticipating by signs and sacraments that community of life with him which will be fully manifested only at the parousia.

5 *Conclusion*

In the liturgy therefore the act of Christ and the act of the Church must not be separated from one another. From Christ, the Church receives all her active power for the accomplishment of the mystery of salvation. But besides the clearly determined cases to which classical theology has reserved the name of sacrament—acts in which this power is exercised directly through the rites performed by the competent ministers—the Church, spouse of Christ, sovereignly organizes her liturgy and assures its efficacy under the motion of the Spirit whom she has received as dowry and pledge of her heritage.

---

[14]St Thomas, *Summa theol.*, III, q. 64, a. 8 and A. M. Roguet's note 108 in the edition of the *Revue des Jeunes* (Paris: Desclée, 1945) p. 247.

[15]Cf. B. Fischer, "Le Christ dans les psaumes" in LMD 27 (1951) 86-113.

3 The "mystery" of worship

BIBLIOGRAPHY

Th. Filthaut, *La Théologie des mystères, exposé de la controverse* (Tournai: Desclée, 1954).
J. Gaillard, "La théologie des mystères" in *Revue Thomiste* 57 (1957) 510-51.
B. Neunheuser, "The Mystery Presence" in *The Downside Review* 76 (1958) 266-74.
B. Neunheuser, "Mystery Presence" in *Worship* 34 (1960) 120-27.
I. Oñatibia, *La presencia de la obre redentora en el misterio del culto* (Vitoria: Ed. del Seminario diocesano, 1954).
E. Schillebeeckx, *De sacramentele Heilseconomie* 1 (Anvers: 't Groeit, 1952; Dutch text with summary in French).
E. Schillebeeckx, *Christ the Sacrament of the Encounter with God* (New York and London: Sheed and Ward, 1963).

Christian language traditionally uses the word "mystery" to designate the Eucharistic celebration in the expression "the sacred mysteries." At the present time, there is a tendency to extend the term to express a fundamental quality of the Christian liturgy: the active presence in it of the "mystery of salvation." This latter expression must be understood in a very precise sense. A theology of liturgical celebration has been worked on for a half century, at the instigation of a Benedictine monk of the Abbey of Maria Laach in the Rhineland, Odo Casel. This "doctrine of the mysteries" (*Mysterienlehre*) has been the object of many and varied discussions. It seems indispensable to present it here, summarily, in order to avoid all ambiguity.

All the recent developments which aim especially at the founding of a theology of the liturgy, which had remained until now in the embryonic state, originate in the incontestable fact, much neglected by modern theologians, that the Christian liturgy in its totality participates—in various degrees—in this sacramentalism which is inherent in the whole life of the pilgrim Church in her temporal condition.

This situation is a paradoxical one. On the one hand, with the glorification of the risen Lord, who has brought human nature with him into the kingdom of God, and with the gift of the Spirit, who brings to the Church the pledge of this kingdom, a radically new order has been inaugurated: the eschatological order. This is the order of the "last things," the communication to men of the divine life so that God may be all in all.

But on the other hand, historical duration continues its course apparently unchanged, calling for the mediation of institutions and sensible signs, which alone correspond to the present condition of humanity. The time of the Church will consequently be characterized by the active presence of the paschal mystery in signs.

This means that the whole life of the Church is sacramental, if one understands by "sacrament" a sign which has a divine power. The density of such signs however can be quite diverse. The liturgical signs have for their immediate object to refer us to those ultimate realities which constitute the mystery of the Church. We must emphasize this intimate union of sign and reality signified, grasped in a single glance.[16]

In all cases, in varying degrees, there will be in the liturgical celebration and in each of the elements which compose it, both presence and prophecy: presence of the mystery of God communicated to men in Jesus Christ at the end of a long economy of preparation, active presence of the paschal mystery which reconciles men with God in the ecclesial community; prophecy of the kingdom which is inaugurated in sacramental signs and will manifest itself in the parousia of Christ at the end of history.

I THE MYSTERY OF WORSHIP IN CHRISTIAN TRADITION

It was St Paul who brought the term "mystery" into Christian language. He did so, it is more and more universally recognized today, not in reference to the uses of this word in the Hellenic world,[17] but, as the translators of the Septuagint had done before him, to designate the secret of God communicated to men by a gratuitous revelation.

From the First Epistle to the Corinthians (2:1-12), it serves to designate an aspect of the divine wisdom, and the three terms *sophia, apocalypsis,* and *mysterion* appear closely linked.[18] It is that economy of salvation which has been declared definitively in Jesus Christ and has revealed its ultimate meaning in the glorification of the risen Lord.

The captivity epistles will amply develop this theme. *Mystery* there becomes one of the names of Christ inasmuch as we have in him knowledge of the mystery of God the Father (Col 2:2-3). It is to him that grace has been given

> to explain how the mystery is to be dispensed. Through all the ages, this has been kept hidden in God, the creator of everything. Why? So that the Sovereignties and Powers should learn only now, through the Church, how comprehensive God's wisdom really is, exactly according to the plan which he had had from all eternity in Christ Jesus our Lord. This is why we are bold enough to approach God in complete confidence, through our faith in him (Ep 3:9-12).

[16]See A. M. Roguet, *op. cit.,* 314-24.
[17]Cf. L. Bouyer, "Le salut dans les religions à mystères" in RevSR 27 (1953) 1-16.
[18]See L. Bouyer, *Liturgical Piety,* pp. 93-5.

In the Epistle to the Colossians, it is the theme of reconciliation which is put to the fore. The mystery, says Paul to the Gentile converts, "is Christ among you, your hope of glory" (1:26), for Christ

is the Beginning,
he was first to be born from the dead,
so that he should be first in every way;
because God wanted all perfection
to be found in him
and all things to be reconciled through him and for him,
everything in heaven and everything on earth,
when he made peace
by his death on the cross (1:18-20).

In the Epistle to the Ephesians, we meet rather the theme of the recapitulation. Christ is the re-assembler of humanity divided by the sin of Adam. The "mystery" manifested in Christ is

the hidden plan he (God) so kindly made in Christ from the beginning
to act upon when the times had run their course to the end:
that he would bring everything together under Christ, as head,
everything in the heavens and everything on earth (1:9-10).

This "mystery" is now perceptible to the angels and men in the Church whose head is Christ, this Church "which is his body, the fulness of him who fills the whole creation" (Ep 1:23).

This teaching of St Paul, confirmed and completed by that of St John, will bear fruit in tradition. On the whole, the Fathers remain faithful to it and use the term "mystery" in the sense in which the Apostle has used it. For a long time therefore they will not think of applying it to worship. The concern not to create ambiguity with the mystery cults of Greece or of the hellenized Orient imposed this precaution. Nevertheless the Alexandrian school, and particularly Clement of Alexandria, will be able to take the word, following Plato, to designate a teaching communicated by symbols. But for them, these "mysteries" are the texts of Scripture and not the acts of worship. It seems, however, that it is in large measure thanks to them that the mystery vocabulary will be introduced into the liturgy in the fourth century. In any case it appears in the writings of St Cyril of Jerusalem who played a large part in the liturgical and theological development of the East. His works show for the first time with absolute clarity the idea that "mystery" designates the salutary content, accessible to faith alone, both of the events of the life of Christ and of the rites of the Church.[19] This idea will be found

[19]On Christian and pagan mysteries: L. Richard, *Le mystère de la Rédemption* (Desclée, 1959) pp. 87-93. On the use of the word *mysterion* in the Fathers, see the studies of K. Prumm, ZKT 61 (1937) 391-425 (Origen); 63 (1939) 207-25)

again both in the Cappadocian Fathers and in St John Chrysostom. It is to be noted that its appearance accompanies the development of a reverential fear which penetrates the liturgical celebrations more and more. Pseudo-Denis will carry this tendency to the extreme, but with him the tradition of Platonism clearly prevails over the biblical conception of mystery.

In the West, while St Hilary and St Ambrose remain closely dependent on Greek patristic thought, we find a deepening of the doctrine of the liturgical mystery in St Augustine. For him, "there is *sacrament* when, in the celebration, the commemoration of a past deed is made in such a way that it proposes to our understanding the sign of a sacred reality which one must receive in a holy way."[20] In this sense, "Easter is a *sacramentum* because this celebration of the saving event—the death and resurrection of Christ—represents for us the passage from death to life, the sacred reality which the sign shows to our intelligence but which we must really receive in our life by faith, hope, and charity."[21] Christmas, on the other hand, involves only the mysterious symbol of the light which Christ comes to spread (*habet mysterium lucis ejus*).[22]

A decisive step will be taken by St Leo.[23] For him, in the liturgical celebration the power of the mystery remains, even though the event commemorated is definitely past in its historical circumstances. Each feast commemorates and renews the unique mystery of salvation under a particular aspect.[24]

The Roman liturgical books will perpetuate this conception, but the development of theology will not exploit it as much as might have been desirable. On the contrary, the weakening of the liturgical sense in the last centuries of the Middle Ages and the hardening of scholasticism gradually led to its neglect. This concept is nevertheless at the basis of all true theology of the liturgy. It alone permits us to indicate clearly the place of the liturgy at the center of theological reflection on the communication to the world, by the Word of God made flesh in Christ, of the great secret which gives creation its

(Hippolytus), 350-59 (Athanasius); J. C. M. Fruytier, *Het woord "musterion" in de Catechesen van Cyrillus van Jerusalem* (Nijmegen, 1950); G. Fittkau, *Der Begriff des Mysteriums bei Johannes Chrysostomus* (Bonn: P. Hanstein, 1953).— A review of these last two works by J. Daniélou, RechSR 42 (1954) 602-10.

[20]*Ep.* 55 *ad Januarium* 1; PL 33, col. 205.

[21]*ibid.* Cf. J. Gaillard, "Noël, memoria ou mystère" in LMD 59 (1959) 40.

[22]*Sermo* 190 (*In die Natali* 7), PL 38, col. 1007.

[23]J. Gaillard, *art. cit.*, pp. 44-52.

[24]Cf. *Sermo* 74, 2, PL 54, col. 398, cited by O. Casel in *The Mystery of Christian Worship*, B. Neunheuser ed. (Westminster, Maryland: Newman Press, 1962) p. 28.

meaning and reveals to it its vocation. The "liturgical mystery" is the actualization of the "mystery of salvation" by means of signs invested in various degrees with a power of sanctification which they have received from Christ or from the Church.

II THE "MYSTERIENLEHRE" OF DOM CASEL

Renewed awareness of the mystery character of the liturgy is largely attributable to the thought and work of Dom Casel, but it is not necessarily limited to him. A brief exposition of his theory and of the controversies which it has aroused will make it possible to distinguish the points definitively established, those which have been proved weak, and those which are still an object of discussion.

1 *The theory of "mystery"*

Dom Casel[25] never presented a synthetic exposition of the whole of his teaching. By reason of his philological formation and his own turn of mind, he was unsympathetic to over-systematized expositions. He never recognized his theories in the formulations proposed by others in the course of the debates. It is without a doubt his book *The Mystery of Christian Worship*[26] which furnishes the most complete view of the whole of his thought. But it is important to complement it by some works published in the *Jahrbuch für Liturgiewissenschaft*.[27] In the present exposition, the effort will be made to let him speak for himself as much as possible.

(1) The divine mystery is first of all "*God considered in himself*, as the infinitely distant, holy, unapproachable, to whom no man may draw near and live ... And this all-holy one reveals his mystery, comes down to his creatures and reveals himself to them; yet once again, *in mysterio*, that is to say, in a revelation by grace, to those whom he has chosen, the humble, the pure of heart, not the proud and the self-important" (p. 5).

---

[25]On Dom Odo Casel (1886-1948) see the biographical sketch written by Dom B. Neunheuser, LMD 14 (1948) 11-14. For complete bibliography see *Archiv für Liturgiewissenschaft* 10 (1967) 7-77.

[26]*Das christliche Kultmysterium*, 1st ed. (1932); 4th ed. (1960), enlarged by various texts chosen by B. Neunheuser; Engl. tr., *The Mystery of Christian Worship* (Westminster, Maryland: Newman Press; London: Darton, Longman and Todd, 1962). The references given hereafter correspond to this translation.

[27]In particular: "Das Mysteriengedächtnis der Messliturgie im Lichte der Tradition" in JLW 6 (1926) 113-204; "Mysteriengegenwart" in JLW 8 (1928) 145-224; "Art und Sinn der ältesten christlichen Osterfeier" in JLW 14 (1938) 1-78, French tr., *La fête de Pâques dans l'Église des Pères* (Paris: Ed. du Cerf, 1964; *Lex Orandi* 37); "Glaube, Gnosis und Mysterium" in JLW 15 (1941) 155-305.

(2) "For St Paul μυστήριον is the marvellous *revelation of God in Christ* . . . The *Logos*, his Son, has become man, and in a way which escapes our grasping, has shown the wholeness of his Father's love on the Cross . . . *Christ is the mystery in person*, because he shows the invisible godhead in the flesh" (p. 6).

(3) "Since Christ is no longer visible among us, in St Leo the Great's words, 'What was visible in the Lord has passed over into the mysteries' (*Serm.* 74, 2). We meet his person, his saving deeds, the working of his grace in the *mysteries of his worship*. St Ambrose writes: 'I find you in your mysteries' (*Apol. Proph. David* 5, 8)" (p. 7). "The content of the *mystery of Christ* is, therefore, the person of the God-man and his saving deed for the Church; the Church, in turn, enters the mystery through this deed" (p. 12). "The Christian thing, therefore, in its full and primitive meaning of God's good word, or Christ's, is not as it were a philosophy of life with religious background music, nor a moral or theological training; it is a *mysterium* as St Paul means the word, a revelation made by God to man through acts of God-manhood, full of life and power; it is mankind's way to God made possible by this revelation and the grace of it communicating the solemn entry of the redeemed Church into the presence of the everlasting Father" (pp. 12-13). "How is it possible to do this great work where God and man are fellow-actors (each according to his own proper fashion; God as the master craftsman, man receiving what God does, yet sharing in the workmanship)? For this purpose the Lord has given us the *mysteries of worship*: the sacred actions which *we* perform, but which, at the same time, the Lord performs upon us by his priests' service in the Church. Through these actions it becomes possible for us to share most intensively and concretely in a kind of immediate contact, yet most spiritually too, in God's saving acts" (pp. 14-15).

(4) If Dom Casel had kept to this presentation of the liturgical mystery, deeply rooted in the mystery of salvation as St Paul had taught it, he would have remained in the firmest line of patristic tradition and would have been immune to all serious objections. The encyclical *Mediator Dei* of Pius xii (1947) in fact reiterated the essentials of this doctrine.[28] But for Dom Casel, the liturgical mystery, insofar as it is concerned with the *mystery of worship*, is organically linked with a reference to the mystery cults of the ancient hellenized Mediterranean world.[29] Besides prayer and sacrifice, the old Covenant knew no other form of worship than commemoration.

---

[28]See especially the passages quoted by Dom J. Gaillard, "La théologie des mystères" in *Revue Thomiste* 57 (1957) 520-22.

[29]Cf. *The Mystery of Christian Worship*, pp. 50-62.

There is from this point of view an abyss between the Pasch of Israel and the Pasch of Christ: the former was not a "mystery" in the proper sense of the word,

> because it was related first of all to human events, and a human deliverance. It was the Pasch of Christ, his bloody death, which saved the world from its sins and fed it with food of everlasting life, god-life. On the eve of the earth's pasch, the savior made of this pasch a complete mystery (p. 31).
>
> But God, in his providence, had seen to the growth of certain religious forms which, while not approaching closely to Christian reality, could offer words and forms to express this new, unheard-of thing in a way open to men's understanding . . . The fundamental idea (of the pagan mystery cults) was participation in the lives of the gods (p. 32).

Dom Casel certainly does not claim that the pagan mysteries have had a direct influence on the organization of Christian worship. He affirms, on the contrary, that the identity of terminology denotes a basic analogy, not on the plane of the realities referred to but on that of the modes of expression.[30] In fact, however, the newness of the Christian mystery requires forms of worship which have nothing in common with those of the official religions, whether pagan or Jewish. The traditional exterior forms of sacrifices are abolished and, moreover, according to the Christians,

> here was *the only true sacrifice:* the mystical Christ sacrificing with and for his Church, filling her with his Spirit. This is where the official ritual language of the Jews and pagans gave up; this mystical common work of Christ and the Church could, if at all, and then only to a limited degree, find expression in the language of the mysteries, purified of everything merely natural, and made resplendent. In any case we observe that even quite early expressions from the mysteries are used for the Christian mystery . . . From the peace of Constantine, the Church's triumph over paganism, the language of the ancient mysteries was used even more unhesitatingly to express the unfathomable content of what she herself possessed, as far as this was possible at all; indeed many ancient forms and customs were taken over to enrich and adorn Christian simplicity (p. 33-4).

But the studies which have multiplied in these last decades have, on the contrary, given us a clearer consciousness of the independence of the Christian tradition even with regard to vocabulary, at least until a rather late epoch.

(5) Still more delicate and more disputed is the question of the mode of presence of the mystery of salvation in the liturgical mysteries. Dom Casel always affirmed the presence not only of the effect, that is, of the grace conferred, but of the redemptive work itself: "The mystery (of worship) is not the particular application of the graces which derive from the past salvific action of Christ; it presents the reality of the salvific work in a sacramental manner; and

---

[30]*ibid.,* p. 16, note 2.

from this reality the effect flows."[31] He bases the necessity of this reactualization on the fact, in his opinion indisputable in tradition, that we share in the mystery of salvation only by a mystical and real participation in the life and death of Christ. Such a participation, however, demands a life and death of Christ in the very act of the sacrament which renders us participants in it. One has the impression sometimes that this reactualization is extended even to the historical aspect of the saving act.[32] But elsewhere he resolutely rejects this interpretation.[33] And in his last work he specifies: "The mystery of worship has, insofar as it is an image . . . the power to distil out the historical event the essential of the saving act, which is precisely its eternal meaning of salvation, to present it and actualize it in the symbol."[34] But the fear of seeing the realism of the presence of the mystery attenuated, and the incapacity which he seems to have had of entering into more conceptual modes of thought, prevented him from doing justice to interpretations like those of G. Söhngen.[35] His disciples have thought it possible, without being unfaithful to his thought, to propose explanations more nuanced and more conformed to the perspectives of classical theology.[36]

2 The present state of the doctrine of mysteries

The most original and powerful effort at the present time appears to be that of E. Schillebeeckx.[37] Following the lead of L. Monden,[38] he undertakes to extend the explicit teaching of St Thomas on the virtual permanence of the redemptive acts in the glorified Christ.[39] According to an apposite expression of Cardinal Journet, "the motion of the divinity conferred on this transitory and localized act an instrumental influence affecting the whole course of time and the whole extent of space."[40] Consequently, its effect will be realized at the time when the divine will, eternally actual, determines that it

[31]JLW 13 (1935) 123.

[32]JLW 8 (1929) 158, 163, 171, 186; 15 (1941) 262.

[33]JLW 8 (1929) 170, 191; 13 (1935) 157, 170; 15 (1941) 251, 263.

[34]JLW 15 (1941) 212, translated in T. Filthaut, *op. cit.,* p. 26.

[35]The principal works of G. Söhngen: *Symbol und Wirklichkeit im Kultmysterium* (Bonn, 1937), and especially *Der Wesenbau des Mysteriums* (Bonn, 1938). The essential of his thought will be found in: "Le rôle agissant des mystères du Christ dans la liturgie d'après les théologiens contemporains" in QLP 24 (1939) 79-107, and in the work cited by T. Filthaut.

[36]Principally Dom V. Warnach and Dom B. Neunheuser.

[37]See works mentioned in the last bibliography.

[38]L. Monden, *Het Messoffer als Mysterie* (Roermond-Maaseik, 1948).

[39]For example, III, q. 22, a. 5, ad 2.

[40]Charles Journet, *L'Église du Verbe Incarné* 2 (1951) p. 180.

should be realized.[41] But it is above all by the sacraments and by the other mysteries of worship instituted by the Church that the mystery of salvation is, by Christ's will, communicated to us.

It is, however, certain, according to St Thomas, that the beatific vision makes one participate in eternity and gives to him who enjoys it the power to dominate the flow of time.[42] But the soul of Christ enjoyed here below the beatific vision:[43]

> The Savior was at the same time both *viator* and *comprehensor*. There was, therefore, in his acts, besides the time-bounded external element and the interior element, insofar as it was the product of the human soul, a permanent content, namely the act of vision and the act of charity deriving from the vision. This unchangeable act of beatific charity, by which Christ has willed and merited our salvation, was the soul of the redemptive sacrifice and of all the other mysteries accomplished in the flesh of the Savior. This act was expressed, it was signified, without being repeated, but as a permanent act, in all the actions of Christ during his mortal life, in the passion as well as in the resurrection and ascension, where it no longer admitted of meritorious value but continued to cooperate instrumentally with the divine will to our salvation. This is the permanent element which explains the actuality of the content of the liturgical mysteries: this same act of unchangeable immolation, which was signified in the historical acts of our salvation and is now still expressed under another form in the heavenly liturgy which the glorious Christ celebrates, is signified also in the mysteries of the liturgy of the earthly Church. It is the *mysterion* of the saving acts. While the historical act is represented in a symbolic image, its transcendent content, which is the act of beatific charity, can be really met since it is an eternal act.[44]

This doctrine seems to sum up well the best of the theories proposed by the pioneers of a renewal of sacramental theology: Père de la Taille, Dom Vonier, Canon Masure.[45] But it likewise saves what appears to have been the basic intuition of Dom Casel: that the fulness of the saving *mysterion* is actualized in the various mysteries of Christian worship. As Dom J. Gaillard says:

> It is the total act, the entire redemptive work, which has saved us. Of this work only the element most intimate to the Savior, the act of beatific charity, remains forever actual. But the total work continues to save us *virtute divina* according to the explicit teaching of St Thomas recalled above. So that, in the liturgical mysteries, we have at the same time the actual presence of the

---

[41]J. Gaillard, *art. cit.,* p. 539 on III, q. 48, a. 6, ad 1; q. 50, a. 6; *In IV Sent.,* dist. 43, q. 1, a. 2, qla. 1, ad 1.

[42]I, q. 10, a. 3, ad 1; a. 5, ad 1; *Contra Gent.,* III, 61.

[43]III, q. 9, a. 2; q. 10.

[44]J. Gaillard, *op. cit.,* 540-41, on Schillebeeckx, 168-74; Monden, pp. 117-20.

[45]M. de la Taille, *Mysterium Fidei* (Paris: Beauchesne, 1921); Engl. tr., *The Mystery of Faith* (London: Sheed and Ward, 1941), 2 vols; A. Vonier, *A Key to the Doctrine of the Eucharist* (London: Burns Oates and Washbourne, 1925); E. Masure, "Le sacrament clé de la doctrine eucharistique" in *Année théologique* (1943) 1-10.

transcendent element and the virtual presence of the total act (passion, resurrection . . .), always active, although it is definitively past in its transitory elements. Thus through the mysteries we meet the saving historical act not only in itself, with regard to its permanent element, but also *in virtute divina*, with regard to that part of the act which has passed with time. The liturgical mysteries are truly the celebration and the manifestation of the historical saving act, although they have as *actual* content only the *mysterion*, i.e. the permanent element and the instrumental power.[46]

Another point on which the theology of St Thomas has permitted Fr Schillebeeckx to advance the doctrine of the mysteries is the use of the Thomistic theory of sacramental character. "It is *in* the cultic activity-sign of the Church," he declares, "that Christ accomplishes his mystery of salvation. The sacramental character, as *participation in the priesthood of Christ* (St Thomas), is the real foundation of this unity (of the various liturgical mysteries) and hence occupies a key position in Catholic sacramentalism. It is thanks to the *character sacramentalis* that the symbolic worship of the Church becomes a *mysterion*; through this *mysterion*, the sacraments are the very acts of Christ in and by the Church."[47]

It does not seem possible to extend further the analysis of the liturgical mysteries according to the lines of classical speculative theology. Such a study is, however, extremely enriching in that it permits one to understand the profound unity which exists between the mystery of salvation, in the manner in which it was accomplished in the mystery of Christ, and the liturgical acts of the Church. These latter deserve to be called mysteries, not because they present analogies of form with the mystery cults of non-Christian religions, but because they assure the active presence in the Church of the mystery of salvation.

But it seems very important to complete this speculative study by a consideration of the liturgical realities carried out according to the phenomenological method.

4 The liturgy as paschal mystery

BIBLIOGRAPHY

L. Bouyer, *Liturgical Piety*, pp. 115-271.
J. Hild, *Dimanche et vie pascale* (Tournhout: Brepols, 1949).
Le Jour du Seigneur, congress of the C.P.L., Lyons 1947, (Robert Laffont, 1948).
P. Murray, "Christ in our Midst" in *Studies in Pastoral Liturgy* 3 (Dublin: Gill, 1967 pp. 163-180).

Dom Casel defines the mystery of worship as: "a sacred act of

---

[46]J. Gaillard, *art. cit.,* p. 541.
[47]*op. cit.*, p. 670, cited by J. Gaillard, *art. cit.,* p. 545.

P

worship in which a redemptive work of the past is rendered present under a determined rite; the worshipping community in accomplishing this sacred rite participates in the redemptive act evoked, and this acquires its own salvation."[48] This definition seems suitable to include all the acts of the Christian liturgy by connecting them to the paschal mystery as to the source from which they derive their meaning and value.

It is in fact the law constitutive of the Christian liturgy, more than any other activity of the Church, that it is accomplished by signs whose efficacy in the order of salvation emanates from the salvific acts accomplished by Christ during his earthly life.[49] It is in this sense that the Christian liturgy belongs entirely to the sacramental order, beginning with the sacraments in the strict sense of the word, and extending to the celebrations which, by the sanctification of time or of things, manifest throughout the whole of creation the reflection of the paschal mystery and the announcement of the renovation in the parousia of the Lord. According to an expression of O. Cullmann taken up by Fr Schillebeeckx, "the future is realized in the present on the basis of the past."

This paradoxical situation is the result of the new dimension introduced into temporal duration by the resurrection of Christ. Whereas the rhythm of the cosmic cycles and the events of history continue their course apparently unchanged, a new order has been introduced, perceptible only in faith: by his death Christ has triumphed over "the powers," the "rulers of this world"; by his resurrection, he is the Lord, head and master of creation. From now on, as the book of Revelation discloses, it is he who directs the course of events.[50] But even more radical than the substitution of the Lord for the prince of this world is the ontological transformation which makes humanity, and through it all creation, pass from the era of development, of evolution, to that of recapitulation, of involution. It is this transformation which characterizes properly, or better, which constitutes, the "time of the Church."[51] The Lord is both present and absent: so intimately present that he acts directly by the sacraments which instrumentally prolong his holy humanity,[52] and nevertheless absent, sitting at the right hand of the Father

---

[48]*The Mystery of Christian Worship*, p. 54.

[49]CSL 5-6.

[50]Cf. L. Bouyer, "Les deux économies du gouvernement divin: Satan et le Christ" in *Initiation théologique* 2 (Paris: Ed. du Cerf, 1952) pp. 503-57.

[51]Cf. I. H. Dalmais, "Le temps de l'Église" in *L'Église et les Églises* (Chevetogne, 1954) 87-103.

[52]III, q. 62, a. 5; cf. CSL 7.

whence he will return to judge the living and the dead. This time of the Church is already *eschatological time*, since there is nothing more radical, new to await, because the work of creation is achieved and the revelation sealed; it is still *historical time* nevertheless, during which the manifold work of creation is progressively recapitulated and the revelation recalled.

That is why the center of Christian worship is the celebration of the *Pasch of the Lord*,[53] which brings together the two great celebrations of the Old Covenant. The Mosaic law placed at the spring equinox the solemn commemoration of the liberating passage of God in the midst of his people at the time of the exodus from Egypt. This commemoration had taken up the rituals of first-fruits from the traditional rites of shepherds and farmers, to give them a new meaning inside a historical religion and a historical revelation. At the autumn equinox, which was less associated with historical remembrances, the feast of the new year was celebrated, which seems to have been at first a feast of the Covenant and culminated with the day of atonement. Christ has integrated into the Pasch of the New Covenant the memorial of this Covenant, which was sealed by his blood, when, by his death, he entered the definitive and perfect sanctuary, as the Epistle to the Hebrews teaches.

Hence for the first Christian centuries, Easter is *the feast*, not merely the feast *par excellence*, the feast of feasts as the martyrology calls it today, but the only feast, beside which no other could exist.[54] What is characteristic of the feast, says Dom Casel, "is that the divine life descends effectively somehow into the midst of those who take part in the religious solemnity. This is not a simple remembrance, it involves also a presence. God has appeared among those who serve him in the celebration . . . He is not merely there; he has come to act, to help, to overcome in suffering, just as in his first epiphany he suffered, struggled, conquered. But his disciples, in worship, act with him because he is among them."[55] So Easter is the feast because it reveals Jesus as Lord. Now, the proper expression of the religious feast is worship. If Easter is *the* Christian feast, all Christian worship will be paschal and will have no other object than to open out the multiple virtualities of the paschal mystery and to make it really and efficaciously present as long as the Church is engaged in the duration of history and of the world.

Feast, memorial, passage, and presence—the Christian Pasch can be all this because it is a *"mystery."* The "paschal mystery" is the

[53]CSL 5-6, 106-7.

[54]CSL 102, 106, 109, etc.

[55]"Le mystère de la Fête" in LMD 1 (1945) 25.

liturgical expression of the ' mystery of salvation" in all its dimensions. In it the Pauline and Hellenistic conceptions of "mystery"
meet and in it also the different aspects of the "liturgical mystery"
find their unity. The "mystery of salvation," however, embraces the
whole life of Christ, and through his life, the whole history of the
people of God:

> The birth of Christ and the whole saving design, then, are one great sacrament,
> since in the visible man the divine majesty worked inwardly for our consecra-
> tion what took place in a secret invisible fashion through its power. Therefore,
> the incarnation is rightly called a mystery or a sacrament.[56]

The liturgical mystery therefore should evoke the manifestation of
the Word Incarnate, from his apparition on earth to his glorious
return into heaven. But since, as St Paul says, this *mystery of Christ*
is only the highest manifestation and accomplishment of a *mystery
of salvation* which comprehends the whole of human history, from
the creation to the final consummation, a liturgy adequate to the
mystery of salvation will also have to represent this whole development in its rites: this is the role of the *temporal* cycle.[57]

It will also have to take into account the different moments and
acts which the participation of man in the mystery of salvation
includes. After he has been born to the divine life in Christ by
baptism, man must let himself be molded by the saving acts of
Christ until his entry into the kingdom of the Father or the day
when, according to the ancient formula of the Latin liturgy of the
dead, there is accomplished fully for each one the exodus from
Egypt which was begun sacramentally at baptism. This is what
happens in the sacramental liturgy.

But at the same time that humanity enters thus progressively and
partially into the kingdom, it already possesses the pledge of the
kingdom and shares in its life. Together with the mystery of the
sacraments, the paschal mystery calls for the mystery of praise,
the hymn of the redeemed who "sing the canticle of Moses, the
servant of God (the canticle of the Pasch), and the canticle of the
Lamb" (Rev 15:3): hence the *liturgia laudis* which is so characteristic
of the *canonical office.*

Sacrament and praise meet and culminate in the Eucharist, the
characteristic rite of Christian cult which is also *par excellence* the
rite of the new Pasch. All Christian liturgy culminates in the
eucharistic celebration and finds therein its ultimate justification as
mystery of worship. That is why Christian worship tends very

[56]Paschasius Radbertus, *Liber de Corpore et Sanguine Domini,* ch. 3, cited by O.
Casel, *The Mystery of Christian Worship,* p. 58.
[57]CSL 102, 107.

naturally to unite the Eucharist to every other celebration. Whether it is a matter of the great consecrations, of the anniversary celebrations of the "birthdays" (*natalitia*) of the saints on the day on which by their death they sealed the testimony of their faith in Christ and passed with him to the Father to share his eternal Pasch in the kingdom (Lk 22:16), or a question only of calling for the divine blessing on the diverse circumstances of human existence—always it is the eucharistic celebration which seals the particular rites. More than any other it is the sign of the catholicity of the Christian liturgy. In the unique oblation of Christ to his Father, all the actions of men and all the events of history find their ultimate meaning. Through it are truly inaugurated the coming of the kingdom and the consummation of time. The rites can be multiple to signify more fittingly the multiform modes of the active power of grace, but in each of them, it is the fulness of the mystery of salvation which is evoked at least indirectly, and it is the entire order of salvation and the multitude of the redeemed who are concerned. Inasmuch as the Christian liturgy is an action of the Church as the dispenser of the mystery of salvation, the Christian liturgy affects the catholicity of this Church in space and time.

CHAPTER TEN

The Liturgy and the Deposit of Faith

I. H. Dalmais

BIBLIOGRAPHY

L. Beauduin, "Essai de manuel fondamental . . . ," in QLP 3 (1913) 143-8, republished in *Mélanges liturgiques* . . . (Louvain: Mont César, 1954) pp. 38-44.

F. Cabrol, "Liturgie" in *Dictionnaire de théologie catholique* 9 (1926) col. 787-845.

B. Capelle, "Autorité de la liturgie chez les Pères" in RTAM 21 (1954) 5-22.

I. H. Dalmais, "La liturgie comme lieu théologique" in LMD 78 (1964) 97-106.

K. Federer, *Liturgie und Glaube, eine theologie-geschichtliche Untersuchung* (Fribourg: Paulus Verlag, 1950; *Paradosis* 4).

P. Guéranger, "Deuxième lettre à Monseigneur l'évêque d'Orléans, 1846" in *Institutions liturgiques* 4, 2nd ed. (Paris, 1885) pp. 243-583.

J. A. Jungmann, "The Role of the Liturgy in the Transformation of Pagan Society" in *The Early Liturgy* (London: Darton, Longman and Todd; Notre Dame University Press, 1959) pp. 164-74.

J. A. Jungmann, "The Liturgy—A School of Faith" in *Pastoral Liturgy* (London: Challoner, 1962) pp. 334-44.

H. Schmidt, *Introductio in liturgiam occidentalem* (Rome: Herder, 1960) pp. 131-9.

SL 14 (1937): *Le vrai visage de la liturgie.*

C. Vagaggini, *Initiation théologique à la liturgie* 2 (Bruges: Abbaye Saint-André, 1963) pp. 50-141.

The liturgy is indisputably one of the sources (or to use the technical term, one of the *loci*) from which theology can draw the principles which will enable it to elaborate a systematic and scientific exposition of the Christian faith. But the very nature of this *locus* and the conditions for its use derive from the nature of the liturgy, which we have up to now tried to define. The role which should be attributed to this *locus* in the ensemble of the *loci theologici* does in fact depend on the very special situation of the liturgy in the complex organism of "sacred doctrine," which is the communication to humanity, by revelation, of the eternal truth and of its plan of salvation in the world.

The liturgy is an *action*. One cannot then treat it simply as a doctrine and limit oneself to the theological utilization of the texts alone. These texts are properly liturgical only to the extent that they are situated in the liturgical whole of which they constitute only one element. This whole also includes the gestures and melodies which emphasize and specify the theological meaning of the texts. Consequently one cannot draw arguments for theological use from liturgical texts as if they were exactly like the other monuments of tradition. These texts are an integral part of an action, and it is this action therefore, and not solely the texts that it involves, which must be examined by the theologian who intends to draw his arguments from the liturgy.

The liturgy is, however, also a *mystery*, that is, a symbolic and efficacious act which renders present the mystery of salvation. This is a second specific quality which conditions the theological utilization of the liturgy. It is in this respect somewhat comparable to Sacred Scripture, especially the gospels, since there too the doctrinal teaching cannot be separated from the accomplishment of the work of salvation. But whereas in the Bible the message to mankind takes first place, in the liturgy the accomplishment of the mystery comes first, and neither the texts nor the rites aim primarily at teaching. Hence the theologian must not reproach the imprecision of the texts, their utilization of metaphoric forms, or, for example, the use of scriptural passages in an acceptation different from their literal sense. An exegesis which would not take into account the poetic character of the liturgy, the resultant importance of word-associations, and the intentional allusions in the details of a rite or situation, would risk drawing false conclusions. One must put oneself within the categories which are proper to the liturgical and social accomplishment of the mystery of salvation in order to obtain from the liturgy all that it can offer to the theologian.

1 The liturgy, "didascalia of the Church"

The expression "didascalia" was used by Pius XI, who explained it by calling the liturgy "the most important organ of the ordinary magisterium of the Church."[1] It is very difficult to be precise about the teachings of this ordinary magisterium: by definition it requires a study of continual, daily documentation. The common teaching of the Fathers, the bishops, and the theologians is usually investigated; but in fact only the bishops have authority to make the voice of the teaching Church heard. Often this research is disappointing: every author speaks in view of the needs and the culture of a given environment and time. It is extremely difficult therefore to discern to what extent the author expresses the common thinking of the Church

---

[1]Audience granted to Dom B. Capelle, abbot of Mont César, Louvain, and reported by him in *Le Saint-Siège et le mouvement liturgique* (Louvain 1936) p. 22. This affirmation is more fully developed in CSL 33.

or only his personal opinion or a particular tradition. The comparative method, when used to solve this difficulty, can lead only to the least common denominator, sufficient to reveal the main lines of the Church's thought, but not to determine the details of it.

The liturgy—and this is its first advantage—is a *collective* work. In it we hear at the very least the voice of a local church, which speaks not so much to determine its belief as to repeat the word of life to itself and to savor it before God. The liturgy derives from a common foundation going back to apostolic times, according to the most profound currents in the heart of a Christian community. The formulas and the rites which express them can be the work of an individual person; but in order to penetrate into the liturgy, they must be accepted by the whole community and sanctioned at least tacitly by the authority which watches over the apostolic tradition. As a result, the influence of individual factors and of particular teachings is diminished in favor of the properly ecclesial expression of the common faith.

But above all the liturgy is an eminently hierarchic work. If the authority of those who exercise the pastoral ministry and who have therefore the mission to preach with authority the word of truth takes on a particular importance in the eyes of theologians, liturgical traditions offer the same kind of guarantee. They have moreover the direct support of the Christian community which has made them its own, and in addition to this they possess an authority arising from their continuity and from their intimate relation to the fulfilment of the mystery of salvation. In the liturgy it is not only the hierarchy of the Church (the "teaching" Church) whose voice is heard, but also the people of God, the whole Body, according to the diversity of its ministries; in the liturgy each member collaborates according to his role in an action which engages them all. Such a situation is unique among the various organs by which the faith of the Church is expressed and transmitted, and this suggests another likeness between Sacred Scripture and the liturgy, which is its living interpretation. The holy books are—in a completely different way, of course, and under the direct impulse of the Holy Spirit who inspired their authors—the collective work of the people of God; the liturgy is the Church's witness that this sacred history continues to be realized in the midst of the Church.[2]

I THE LITURGY, PERMANENT CATECHESIS OF THE CHURCH

The proper function of the liturgy is not to teach but to bring alive

---

[2]J. Daniélou, "The Sacraments and the History of Salvation" in *The Liturgy and the Word of God* (Collegeville, Minnesota: Liturgical Press, 1959) p. 31.

the mystery of salvation. It is therefore the model of all catechesis, which should aim not solely at transmitting an exact doctrine but above all at introducing men to a living faith. The liturgy emphasizes by preference the fundamental lines of this mystery of salvation in relation to the paschal mystery, which is its center and recapitulation. Through the scriptural readings and psalmody, the basic elements of every Christian liturgy, the faithful are maintained in direct contact with the purest sources from which they can nourish their faith. The distribution of these readings throughout the liturgical cycle, the comparison between the holy books, in particular between those of the Old and New Testaments, aid in the comprehension of their profound meaning in the light of Christ. The chants, the prayers, the rites form a perpetual commentary on the sacred texts.

By putting the faithful in the attitude of prayer adapted to each situation of Christian existence, the liturgy lays the foundations of a dialogue between God and man in which each is seen in his proper place. Thus we can find in the liturgy the material for a whole theology and anthropology, more or less explicitly developed according to circumstances and traditions. Finally, the liturgy, by its communitarian character, brings alive the mystery of ecclesial communion and, in this way, the mystery of the kingdom, the definitive accomplishment of which the liturgy announces and anticipates by means of sacramental symbols.

II LITURGY AND ORTHODOXY OF FAITH

Because of the catechetical value and the ecclesial and active character of the liturgy, the Church has in all ages expressed in it the most significant explicitations of the common faith and the themes which she considered the most important for the safeguard of orthodoxy menaced by heretical deviations. Whether it be a question of the development of formularies and rites, or of the creation of new celebrations, the history of both the Eastern and Western liturgies bears witness to this permanent concern of the Church. At Rome the traditional formularies remained very sober, wary of later developments of doctrine or piety; both have nevertheless found place in the creation of new feasts and in the admission of new formularies and rites which have been added in the course of time. In the East, the great developments of theology stimulated by the trinitarian and christological controversies greatly contributed to giving the liturgy of Constantinople, which gloried in being the guardian of orthodoxy, the doctrinal richness that makes it a popular catechesis while at the same time containing the most essential points of Christian belief.

2 The liturgy, witness of tradition

From the first centuries, the authority of the liturgy seemed so incontestable that it was frequently considered a privileged witness of the apostolic tradition.[3] An exaggeratedly rigid conception of tradition, however, would lead, in this field as in others, to untenable positions. But despite awkwardness of expression or imprudent generalizations, it remains true that the liturgy constitutes one of the most reliable modes of expression in the Church of this continuous apostolic tradition, because it is one of the institutions of the Church most intimately bound to her mission and because its proper object is to render present and active in the Church the mystery of salvation. As a transmitter of tradition, the liturgy is comparable to the role of the Mosaic tradition within the institutions of Israel, which developed and were adapted to the various historical circumstances. The adage, *legem credendi lex statuat supplicandi*, had a precise and limited sense in the *Indiculus* of Prosper of Aquitaine.[4] But its author only summed up an argument of which St Augustine, and Tertullian and St Cyprian before him, had made liberal use. Recourse to the authority of the liturgy is universal in the Church: in recent times the popes have often appealed to this authority in the most solemn acts of their supreme magisterium.[5] Precisely because of this importance, however, appeal to this authority must be made with caution.

I THE DIFFERENT LITURGIES ARE OF DIVERSE VALUE

As privileged witness of the belief of a particular church, the liturgy has no authority other than that of the magisterium which has approved it. In the Latin rite after the Council of Trent, this approbation is reserved to the Apostolic See.[6] But it is necessary to distinguish here between the most ancient liturgies which have not been the object of a revision, the liturgies whose books have been revised by the authority of the Apostolic See, and the Roman liturgy for which the Holy See is directly responsible.

The liturgies proper to individual monasteries and dioceses have the least theological value. A thorough investigation is required in each case before a theological argument can be drawn from these liturgies, especially in the case of recent compositions without

---

[3]Cf. B. Capelle, *op. cit.*

[4]*ibid.*, pp. 6-9; K. Federer, *op. cit.*

[5]H. Schmidt, "Lex orandi, lex credendi in recentioribus documentis pontificiis" in *Periodica* 40 (1951) 5-28.

[6]Cf. above, ch. 4.

traditional antecedents, such as certain liturgies of the eighteenth century. The liturgies of the great religious orders offer stronger guarantees: because they result from the consent of communities whose members differ in origin and formation, it can be assumed that these liturgies are an expression of the common mind, which they in turn helped to shape.

The liturgies which can be called general have a completely different value, since in the course of the centuries they have spread by the participation of various churches in an extensive cultural milieu, especially if this milieu was under the spiritual leadership of an important primatial or episcopal see or patriarchate around which regional or general councils have been assembled. Such liturgies are the heirs of traditions which go back to the first ages of the Church, and it can be supposed that they express the common mind in the style best adapted to a certain cultural milieu. It is particularly interesting in this regard to follow the transformations which liturgical usages undergo in passing from one culture to another, especially if there is a great difference in level of culture. Illustrative of this phenomenon is the relation of the Ethiopian to the Coptic liturgy from which it derives, or, from another point of view, the adaptations which the Roman liturgy underwent in the Gallo-Frankish countries and its links with the Milanese and Visigothic liturgies.

Since the Council of Trent, the Roman liturgy, which has progressively supplanted the other Latin liturgies—not without being enriched by numerous outside elements—constitutes the only living liturgy of the West. It offers the special warrant of expressing the belief of the mother and mistress of the churches and of being organized under the immediate responsibility of the sovereign pontiffs, who have personally written many of its texts.[7] This quality then makes it a theological *locus* of special importance for knowledge of the living tradition of the Church.

II THE LITURGY IS A COMPLEX ACT

The theologian must first fix his attention on the total liturgical action and interpret each element, text or rite, with regard to its place in this whole and in the light of its relations with the other parts.[8] In this way he will guard himself from explaining a sacrament

[7]It will be noted that the organization of the liturgy, like everything else which depends on the power of ordinary jurisdiction, does not always involve the pope as supreme and infallible head of the universal Church.

[8]The role of chant, especially Gregorian chant, in interpreting the sense in which the liturgy understands a particular word and the accent which the liturgy wishes to give it cannot be over-emphasized. See E. Cardine, "Psautiers anciens et

only by the words which are usually considered as essential. The texts of the magisterium, of the Fathers or of doctors of the Church receive from their use in the liturgy a new meaning which must be determined in each case.

Since the liturgy belongs to the realm of tradition, it should be interpreted in the double light of history and of the comparative study of diverse liturgies. By reason of their hieratic character, the liturgies are naturally conservative; many elements are, in their present form, difficult to explain, and it is advisable therefore to re-insert them in the cultural milieu in which they arose. Sometimes historical research does not solve the problem; the comparative method then offers a new instrument of investigation. This method will always be useful for extricating the basic meaning of a liturgical datum from the trappings given it in a particular milieu. It must not be forgotten that the liturgy is a living reality and that the theologian must rely above all on its actual state. The historical and comparative methods are only instruments—indispensable certainly, but still mere instruments—which must be used in the general light of theology, if one intends to elaborate something more than a history of doctrines or institutions.

It is evident that liturgical documents, like all the other documents which the theologian uses, must be interpreted according to their literary or ritual genre. This judgment is often delicate; it requires a deep familiarity with the structure of the diverse liturgies and familiarity with the cultural milieu to which they belong. It is relatively easy to distinguish the readings which aim directly at teaching, the prayers in which the elements of faith are explicitly recalled as grounds for the petitions, and the lyrical parts whose principal role is to create an atmosphere favorable to the contemplation of the mystery. But it is much more difficult to determine the relative importance and the limits of these individual elements in a liturgical complex, and still harder to define the relation of the rites and the words or the exact part of the symbolism and of the basic sacramental character of the liturgy.

Very special attention should be devoted to the texts taken from Scripture or the Fathers. The liturgy sometimes understands them in a sense quite different from the literal meaning. This interpretation is obviously of no help for exegesis of the revelation transmitted by the holy books. But the word of God remains alive in the Church, and in the liturgy this life knows its most vivid expression.[9] Con-

chant grégorien" in *Richesse et déficiences des anciens psautiers latins* (Vatican City, 1959; *Collectanea biblica Latina* 13) pp. 249-58.

[9] L. Bouyer, "The Word of God in the Liturgy" in *The Liturgy and the Word of God*, p. 61.

sequently the liturgical interpretation of the scriptural texts has a theological importance of the first rank. As St Bernard says, when the Church "modifies the sense or the place of the words of Scripture, its composition has more force than the primitive word order, and perhaps as much so as truth differs from figure, light from shadow, mistress from servant."[10] He explains this perfection by the eminence of the contemplation of the Church, which the liturgy expresses. The theologian will therefore be able to appeal to the liturgical use of the Scriptures, and especially to the harmony of pericopes from the two Testaments, which are consciously the aim of many liturgical lectionaries. But he will do so not to Scripture as a source of faith, but to the liturgy as the privileged witness of the faith.

The same holds true for all the other texts. The works of the Fathers and doctors, when inserted into the liturgy, become the expression not only of the belief of one man outstanding in doctrine or of one pastor, but that of a whole community or of a whole group of churches from vastly different times and places. One should not forget, however, that the first function of the liturgy is not to teach but to bring alive the mystery of salvation and, to this end, to make use of modes of expression best adapted to all the faithful. The so-called "historical" texts, such as the "legends" of the breviary, the acts of the martyrs or the synaxaries, obey entirely different laws and spring from preoccupations other than those of history. They witness solely to the admiration which is aroused in the Church by the great works which God accomplishes in his saints.

---

[10]*In vigil. Nat., Sermo II,* 1.

CHAPTER ELEVEN

Pastoral-Liturgical Action

A. M. Roguet

BIBLIOGRAPHY

Directoire pour la pastorale des sacrements, adopted by the French Synod of
Bishops for the dioceses of France, April 3, 1951.

National or diocesan *Directories* for the apostolate of the Mass, especially
Directoire pour la pastorale de la messe à l'usage des diocèses de France, 2nd
ed. (Coutances: Editions Notre-Dame, 1960).

J. A. Jungmann, "The Pastoral Idea in the History of the Liturgy" in *The
Assisi Papers* (Collegeville, Minnesota: Liturgical Press, 1957) pp. 18-31;
republished in the author's work, *Pastoral Liturgy* (London: Challoner,
1962) pp. 368-81.

LMD 77 (1964): complete commentary on the conciliar Liturgy Constitution,
principally pp. 32-41, 52-73, 107-13. Commentary on the first three chapters
of the conciliar document: F. R. McManus, *Sacramental Liturgy* (New
York: Herder and Herder, 1967), especially pp. 60-67.

SRC, *Instructio de Ordine hebdomadae sanctae instaurato rite peragendo*,
November 16, 1955, and a commentary by F. Antonelli, "The Liturgical
Reform of Holy Week . . . " in *The Assisi Papers* (Collegeville, Minnesota:
Liturgical Press, 1957) pp. 149-66.

SRC, *Instructio de musica sacra . . .*, September 3, 1958, French tr. and
commentary in Martimort-Picard, *Liturgie et musique* (Paris: Ed. du Cerf,
1959; *Lex orandi* 28); Engl. tr. by C. Howell, *Instruction on Sacred Music
and Liturgy* (London: Herder, 1959); commentary by F. Antonelli in *The
Furrow* 10 (1958) 700-710; cf. also J. B. O'Connell, *Sacred Music and Liturgy*
(London: Burns and Oates, 1959).

1 Basis and definition of pastoral-liturgical action

I BASIS OF PASTORAL-LITURGICAL ACTION

We have already seen that if the liturgy has for its principal end
the worship of God, it includes at the same time the sanctification of
man as an end. We cannot increase God's glory in itself; we can only
give to God what we ourselves possess. Our holiness gives glory to
him, or, as St Irenaeus puts it: "God's glory is man as a dynamic
being." The Father seeks worshippers who pray to him in spirit and
truth.

Liturgy is the exercise of the priesthood of Christ continued by the
Church.[1] The priesthood of Christ has a twofold end: to give glory
to the Father and salvation to men. In other words, its purpose is to

[1]CSL 6.

present man's gratitude and prayers to God and, in turn, to endow men with the gifts of God. This twofold end of the priesthood also characterizes the eucharistic sacrifice which is a thanksgiving given to God, an expiation for sins and the gift of Christ to men in communion. The sacraments, which are at the same time acts of worship and efficacious signs of grace,[2] also possess this twofold aspect, as does the divine office, the prayer of praise, which is a preparation for and a prolongation of the Eucharist. Thus, it is understandable that, if this prayer of praise goes from men towards God, it requires on the part of men a conscious effort and a purified heart.

The observation might be made that the sacraments work *ex opere operato* and that other liturgical actions are efficacious *ex opere operantis Ecclesiae*. This is true, but it does not exclude the fact that sacraments are signs of faith[3] and that although their validity depends only on their correct celebration with a right intention, their fruits will be so much the more abundant as ministers and subjects approach them with the best dispositions.[4]

Here arises the need for a spiritual effort on the part of priests and faithful, the demands of holiness required for a worthy and fruitful celebration of the liturgy. The encyclical *Mediator Dei* of Pius XII insisted in a particular way[5] on this point in order to remedy erroneous concepts which may still be prevalent. Since Dom Guéranger and especially since St Pius X, the liturgical movement has emphasized how much the liturgy is "the primary and indispensable source of a true Christian spirit," thus the source of all authentic spiritual life, a phrase taken up and canonized by Vatican II.[6]

[2] CSL 59.
[3] CSL 59.
[4] CSL 61.
[5] MD 24, 30-37; cf. CSL 11.
[6] CSL 14. The literature on this subject is vast: C. Callewaert, *De sacra liturgia universim* (1st ed., 1919), 4th ed. (Bruges: Beyaert, 1944) pp. 48-52; G. Lefebvre, *Liturgia, ses principes fondamentaux*, 2nd ed. (Lophem-lez-Bruges, 1922) pp. 182-208; M. H. Lavocat, "La liturgie et la spiritualité" in R. Aigrain, *Liturgia* (Bloud et Gay, 1935) pp. 59-65; P. Oppenheim, *Principia theologiae liturgicae* (Turin: Marietti, 1947; *Institutiones systematico-historicae in sacram liturgiam* 7) pp. 139-204; L. Beauduin, *Mélanges liturgiques recueillis parmi ses oeuvres . . .* (Louvain: Mont César, 1954) pp. 17-35; B. Capelle, *Travaux liturgiques de doctrine et d'histoire* 1, *Doctrine* (Louvain: Mont César, 1955); L. Bouyer, *Liturgical Piety* (Notre Dame University Press, 1950; = *Liturgy and Life*, London: Sheed and Ward, 1958) pp. 243-71; G. M. Braso, *Liturgy and Spirituality* (Collegeville, Minnesota: Liturgical Press, 1960) pp. 160-204; C. Vagaggini, *Initiation théologique à la liturgie* 2 (not available in English), adapted from the Italian by R. Gantoy (Bruges: Biblica, 1963) pp. 145-205; H. Schmidt, *Introductio in liturgiam occidentalem* (Rome: Herder, 1960) pp. 88-130.

However, it is not enough to speak of "liturgical spirituality" and this for two reasons:

(1) Conscious and holy participation at the liturgical celebration, although personal, is a work of the community of the faithful as such, i.e. of the assembly, which is something other than the sum of the individuals composing it.[7]

(2) The faithful are not to be sanctified only in view of the liturgical celebration or as a result of it, but *in* and *through* the celebration itself. The celebration is in itself sanctifying and educative in the virtue of religion, for "it contains a great teaching for the faithful."[8]

This is the reason why the need for pastoral-liturgical action has arisen, i.e. an effort on the part of the pastor with regard to his flock within the liturgical celebration or in view of this celebration.[9]

II DEFINITION OF PASTORAL-LITURGICAL ACTION

Pastoral-liturgical action is closely connected to the liturgy: it flows from its sacramental character which is *propter homines* and is exercised only in the celebration of the liturgy or as an immediate preparation for it.

For all that, it is not to be identified with the liturgy nor confused with it. Perfectly dignified and beautiful liturgical celebrations have taken place which were not concerned with offering to the Christian people the means of participating in them. The "liturgical movement" had for a long time been indifferent to pastoral-liturgical action and was aimed above all at clerics, to the exclusion of the faithful who were considered as simple assistants although "by its nature, the liturgy demands the participation of the people."[10] Pastoral-liturgical action refers to the whole process which will permit the active and conscious participation of the Christian people in the celebration of the liturgy.

---

[7]CSL 26.

[8]Council of Trent, sess. 22, ch. 8, Denz. 1749; cf. CSL 33.

[9]The expression "pastoral-liturgical action" (*pastorale liturgique*), consecrated by Vatican II (CSL 43: *actio pastoralis liturgica*), is not exactly equivalent to "pastoral action and liturgy." It does not mean a juxtaposition or a succession which would accidentally join the pastoral ministry in general and the liturgy in general. The expression "pastoral liturgy" does not convey the same meaning, for it seems to designate the liturgy as seen from its pastoral aspect. It is certainly fortunate and something of a novelty that the Congress of Assisi, statements in *Mediator Dei* and in the decree *Maxima religionis mysteria* (November 16, 1955) have put this pastoral aspect into perspective; some writers had judged it incompatible with the theocentric aspect essential to the liturgy. But pastoral-liturgical action has a more precise meaning.

[10]CSL 14;—cf. SRC, instruction of September 3, 1958, n. 22.

Since the pastoral ministry is the art of governing, instructing and sanctifying the faithful, pastoral-liturgical action can be defined as the part of this art which consists in helping the faithful to participate actively and consciously in liturgical celebration, the primary and indispensable source from which the faithful are to derive the true Christian spirit.[11]

The laws and principles of pastoral-liturgical action must be defined by the hierarchy, who alone are responsible for the pastoral work of the Church. In fact the Apostolic See and especially Vatican II have given it its proper status and orientation. However, considerable authority in liturgical matters from now on falls to the episcopal conference which, assisted by a national commission, will direct the pastoral-liturgical action that comes under its jurisdiction.[12] Similarly each bishop ought to promote liturgical action in his diocese remembering that he is "the high priest of his flock" and that "the Christian life of his faithful depends on him in some way". The bishop also should have one or several commissions at his disposal.[13]

2 Characteristics of pastoral-liturgical action

I IT IS NOT DIRECTLY MISSIONARY

The progress of pastoral-liturgical action has coincided, in different countries, with a missionary awareness, whence it could be thought that pastoral-liturgy action was itself missionary. This would be a mistake. Pastoral-liturgical action has for its object the celebration of the mysteries by and for the faithful. It does not as such envisage non-believers.

This action does not correspond to kerygma, which proposes to non-believers the marvels of the faith,[14] but to catechesis, and more precisely to mystagogical catechesis, which introduces believers to a more intimate understanding of the mysteries. They have been initiated into these mysteries through baptism, and it is the Christian life which helps them to live their commitment day to day according to these mysteries.

Pastoral-liturgical action cannot consist in the creation of forms of worship which would be accessible and attractive to non-believers. This would be radically foreign to liturgy and would not really introduce non-believers to it.

[11]CSL 11 and 14.
[12]CSL 44.
[13]CSL 45-6, 41.
[14]CSL 9.

Q

Moreover the history of Christian beginnings shows that normally the pagans were not attracted to the faith by the display of moving and impressive ceremonies. Their conversion began by questions raised by the purity of life and the love (charity) of the Christians, questions answered by an initial evangelization. Only after a long period of catechesis and initiation were the catechumens introduced to the celebration of the mysteries. But their participation in those mysteries was not complete until after baptism.

If pastoral-liturgical action of itself is not and cannot be missionary, nevertheless a missionary value can be attributed to it in three ways:

(1) in a *mediate* way, insofar as pastoral-liturgical action ought to form communities which would be joyful, united, conscious and proud of their faith and whose members would render the gospel attractive to non-believers;

(2) in a *negative* way, insofar as those responsible for pastoral-liturgical action, themselves animated by a missionary concern, will be on the watch to avoid in their way of celebrating or of explaining the liturgy all shabbiness, inconsistencies and shortcomings to the truth of words, and also all the mannerisms and peculiarities which could estrange non-believers or less convinced believers by showing them religion in an obsolete, infantile or even ridiculous light;[15]

(3) but also in a *positive* way, when the hierarchy adapts the liturgy, according to the rules provided by the Council, to the mentalities and cultures of different people so that it will not appear to them as a foreign import.[16]

II IT IS PRIMARILY EDUCATIVE

Pastoral-liturgical action is educative. It is addressed to the children of God to help them to reach the "fulness of Christ," in the same way as a father brings up his children to help them to acquire a fully developed personality and to permit them to respond to their vocation. The different characteristics of all education will

[15]On these questions, see K. Tilmann, *Die Liturgie missionarisch gesehen* (Freiburg: Herder, 1949); P. Hofinger, "Possibilités de la pastorale liturgique en pays de mission" in LMD 37 (1954) 42-58; G. Weskamm, "La participation active au culte et la vie d'une communauté," *ibid.*, 23-41; G. van Bekkum, "Le renouveau liturgique au service des missions" in LMD 47-8 (1956) 155-76; O. Spuelbeck, "The Liturgy and the Word of God in Parish Life in the German Diaspora" in *The Liturgy and the Word of God* (Collegeville, Minnesota: Liturgical Press, 1959) pp. 172-83; J. Hofinger ed., *Liturgy and the Missions— The Nijmegen Papers* (New York: Kenedy; London: Burns and Oates, 1960).

[16]See above, ch. 4.

help us to give a detailed account of the different qualities which pastoral-liturgical action should possess.

(1) It is *fatherly*, i.e. it treats the faithful not with a tyrannical or capricious authority, but with an untiring patience—a work requiring time and labor—and with respect for persons. It does not seek to impose an authority of exterior comportment only, nor does it seek to train mere actors or robots. Since all education consists in forming good habits, pastoral-liturgical action tries to inculcate right attitudes by explaining the reasons and seeking above all to create interior dispositions.

(2) It is *instructive*, i.e. it ought to impart convictions and not simply impose practices. This is why it comprises an important part of catechetics, to obtain a worship in spirit and truth.

(3) It is *formative*, i.e. it does not aim only to instruct; rather than intellectual notions it seeks to inculcate the meaning of the sacred, a sense of God, the spirit of Jesus Christ, a relish for profound prayer and silence, and at the same time, the meaning of the Church and a liking for common prayer, etc.

(4) It is *progressive*. Education means that man must be taken from where he is in order to be led further. To take man from where he is implies a healthy realism and consequently a certain pluralism. As *Mediator Dei* has well remarked, ways that are better in themselves are not always well adapted to a particular community, for which projects inferior in themselves will be more successful. One sins against this down-to-earth realism when one demands of a community efforts of which it is not capable or when one recommends experiments which have proved themselves successful elsewhere but which may not be advisable in this particular case.[17]

If education takes man where he is, it does this in order to lead him further and to lead him to a higher level. It is not good pastoral-liturgical action when one is content to speak to the faithful in a language which they are capable of understanding, without wishing to lead them progressively to a profounder penetration of the most authentic Christian mystery.

III IT LEADS INTO THE TRADITION OF THE CHURCH

Pastoral-liturgical action is not directed to apparent success, nor to adapting itself only to the immediate needs of the Christian people, especially to a segment of this people geographically and socially confined. It ought to bring the faithful into the worship of the Church and teach them to respect and love everything which constitutes her patrimony of thought and prayer. It does not aim so much at

[17]Cf. MD 107-8, 111, etc.; SRC, instruction of September 3, 1958, n. 29.

forming small, sincere and coherent communities as to incorporate them in the community of all countries and times, the Church. Thus, it has to be founded on a vast and precise knowledge of liturgical tradition, without which it risks being reduced to a short-sighted pragmatism, extemporaneous rites and anarchical experiments.[18]

3 The elements of pastoral-liturgical action

I REQUIREMENTS FOR LITURGICAL CELEBRATION AND ITS EXTERIOR CONDITIONS

The best liturgical celebration, as we have seen above, does not suppress the need for pastoral-liturgical action; and the first concern of this action should be to promote a celebration which is exact, worthy, beautiful and true. Liturgy is a sacred action. Pastoral action consists in introducing the people into this action, in making the signs meaningful to them with a view to participation. For this reason it is necessary that this action be authentic, the signs be recognizable and participation possible.

In certain regards it can be said that the liturgical celebration precedes pastoral effort. Some rites, performed in a worthy, comprehensive and fitting manner, are themselves instructive without any formal catechesis.[19] It is not enough to explain these rites if no one is invited to participate in them. The best catechesis will not substitute for the knowledge which only the living participation in the rites affords. In certain churches of antiquity, the rites of initiation were explained only after their celebration.

Pastoral-liturgical action makes on the liturgical celebration some imperious demands which jar with rubrics drawn up in an era when there was little concern for participation on the part of the faithful. Such demands are formulated in the *Ordo hebdomadae sanctae*, in the instruction of September 3, 1958 and, with more insistence, in the Constitution on the Sacred Liturgy of Vatican II; modern techniques facilitate their introduction.

Active and intelligent participation of the faithful in the liturgy demands that they form, insofar as possible, a single group, and that they see and hear. However, the gathering of the faithful does not depend only on their good will and the exhortations of the pastor; it can be hindered by a poor arrangement of entrances, benches, lighting and heating.

For the same reason, the dialogue of the faithful with the celebrant

---

[18]CSL 23.
[19]Cf. *Directoire pour la pastorale de la messe à l'usage des diocèses de France*, n. 40-41.

will be impossible if they cannot hear him easily. Sometimes acoustical defects must be corrected by means of a good loudspeaking system.[20] However, since "the people have the right to be nourished by the proclamations of the word of God, and by the minister's explanation of it . . . priests . . . will ensure that whatever they or the ministers say or sing will be so clear that the faithful will be able to hear it easily and grasp its meaning; and they will in fact be spontaneously drawn to respond and participate."[21]

It is desirable that the faithful see the rites. In order to accomplish this, it will often be necessary to turn the altar towards them, or at least to move in nearer to them. However, in old churches these changes cannot be done without consulting experts and obtaining permission from the competent authority.[22] If that is impossible, the fact remains that many of the functions of the priest are now done at the chair and ambo; these can be so placed as to facilitate participation.[23]

For the construction of places of worship in the future, pastoral-liturgical action will demand from architects not only a beautiful work but a functional building. A new church must allow all participants a worthy and visible celebration of the sacred actions and not impede in any way the assembly of the faithful.[24] The altar must be given a prominent place, and proper illumination should facilitate reading—all this to create a sacred and serene atmosphere.

Pastoral-liturgical action has to begin with these material conditions. Nevertheless it would be a mistake to believe that they constitute the essentials of this activity, for in fact they only help to eliminate obstacles. The primary pastoral-liturgical action consists in the proclamation of the Word of God in catechesis and the explanations of the "commentator," whose function is to lead the people during the celebration.

II PASTORAL DEMANDS ON THE PROCLAMATION OF THE WORD OF GOD

The Word of God plays an essential role in pastoral-liturgical action. The "pastor" is in effect the one who leads the sheep of Christ to the divine pasture of the Word of God and the sacraments. In the same way the *Regula Pastoralis* of St Gregory the Great is a

[20]SRC, instruction of September 3, 1958, n. 72.

[21]The instruction *Eucharisticum Mysterium* of May 25, 1967, n. 20.

[22]*ibid.*, n. 24.

[23]The instruction *Inter Oecumenici* of September 26, 1964, n. 49, 50, 52, 56, and especially 92, 96, 99.

[24]CSL 124; SRC, instruction of September 26, 1964, n. 90-99.

treatise on preaching and not a treatise on the organization of the diocese or parish.

We have seen[25] that the Word of God convokes and gathers the Church together. Participation required by the faithful will at first consist in accepting the Word and afterwards of responding to it.

1 *Readings*

In liturgical celebration a great importance is to be attached to the readings. As stated above,[26] the readings are designed to be heard: *sedentes auscultant.* This hearing is communitarian, and it is not enough that each of the faithful understands individually what is read, for the Word is proclaimed to the whole assembly. For this reason Vatican II provides, especially for the readings, the use of the vernacular.[27]

This supposes, however, the existence of a single, accurate translation. Paraphrased versions which are not faithful to the original or which disfigure or lessen the Word of God can give the impression that the Word of God can be modified to suit its readers. The difficulties of vocabulary or style ought to be resolved by the homily and by biblical catechesis: the Word of God is a mystery and not always immediately understandable in every aspect.[28]

The reading ought to be clear and distinct and done by a lector who is conscious of the importance of his function. He should so stand as to be heard and seen and should read in such a way that all the members of the assembly hear him.

2 *Psalms and hymns of biblical inspiration*

The psalms too are the Word of God, which the faithful not only hear but which they themselves chant, often in response to his Word.[29] A great effort of pastoral-liturgical action should be concentrated on the psalms in order to make them familiar to the faithful and to put them within their reach in their own language according to the modalities provided by the discipline of the Church. Even when they are translated, the psalms should be explained, and different ones selected for use, according to circumstances and according to the spirit of the liturgy.

[25]See above, ch. 5.

[26]See above, ch. 6.

[27]See above, ch. 6.

[28]Translations can be authorized only by the episcopal conference, according to the norms in the instruction of September 26, 1964, n. 30-31, 40-41.

[29]See above, ch. 6.

3 *The homily*

Preaching had been considered for such a long time as an activity independent of worship that it became too intellectual or apologetical, awkwardly imitating patterned speeches or academic conferences (which serve a purpose but not in the liturgy). Ordinary preaching or the homily is a part of worship: it takes place after the reading and before the Eucharist.[30] Normally, the celebrant gives the homily. Its principal aim is to comment on the texts of the celebration or on certain aspects of them not only to explain them but to adapt them to the concrete life of the assembly present in order to help them to enter into the eucharistic mystery. The homily should elucidate and actualize the Word of God which has been read or sung, the mystery which is going to be celebrated, the part of salvation history which is being commemorated and realized in the course of the liturgical year. Thus the homily should lead the faithful to assimilate these teachings and mysteries and to incorporate them in their daily life.

The familiar tone which characterizes the homily should not result in making it an informal talk, bereft of plan. Its place in the liturgical celebration warrants that it not be reduced to a simple liturgical item without any effect on the real life of the faithful. Such a homily would risk confining religion to the domain of worship, and, through yearly repetition in its narrow perspective, would neglect entire sectors of Christian doctrine and morality. This defect is all the more serious insofar as the homily of the Sunday Mass is the only source of religious knowledge for the majority of the faithful.

III CATECHESIS

BIBLIOGRAPHY

Directoire pour la pastorale de la messe à l'usage des diocèses de France, n. 22-41.
LMD 16 (1948): "Prédication biblique et liturgique."
A. G. Martimort, "Catéchèse épiscopale et monitions diaconales" in LMD 17 (1949) 110-20.

1 *Nature and importance of catechesis*

According to the statement of Pius XII, often repeated in the liturgical Constitution,[31] participation should not only be active but also enlightened. The faithful are to know the meaning of the liturgical action because they are to play an active role in it. For the

---

[30]See above, ch. 6, **1**, **II**, and the references to CSL indicated there.

[31]Discourse of September 22, 1956, in *The Assisi Papers* (Collegeville, Minnesota: Liturgical Press, 1957) p. 236.

same reason, they ought to know the meaning of the gestures and words of the celebrant and ministers and the significance of the gestures which they are asked to perform and of the words which they speak.

Worship and participation in it should thus be guided by catechesis. This word does not designate any kind of religious instruction but a "living and dynamic initiation" which springs from the realities of worship and the rites themselves which it elucidates, and aims at making the people enter into the mystery of worship.[32]

The catechesis which pastors of ancient times directed to their faithful has left some great masterpieces: the *Treatise on Baptism* by Tertullian, the sermons to catechumens and neophytes by St Cyril of Jerusalem, St John Chrysostom, Theodore of Mopsuestia, St Ambrose, St Zeno of Verona, St Augustine.[33] These examples will show that catechesis is not a temporary measure for adapting the liturgy to contemporary needs, nor a remedy for the use of a language which the faithful do not understand. Its importance stems from the very nature of the liturgy which is a mystery, accessible only to believers. Its importance is emphasized by the prescriptions of the Council of Trent concerning the Mass[34] and the sacraments,[35] and in recent times, by the encyclicals *Mediator Dei*[36] and *Musicae Sacrae*,[37] together with the instruction of September 3, 1958[38] and the references of episcopal directories. Vatican II[39] and the documents from the postconciliar commission have also stressed this importance.

[32]*Directoire pour la pastorale de la messe* . . . , n. 24.

[33]A. Hamann, *L'initiation chrétienne* (Grasset, 1963);—Tertullian, *De baptismo*, CC 1, pp. 277-95; Engl. tr., ANF 11, pp. 231-56;—St Cyril of Jerusalem, *Mystagogical Catecheses*, PG 33; text and Engl. tr., F. L. Cross, *St Cyril of Jerusalem—Lectures on Christian Sacraments* (London: SPCK 1951);—St John Chrysostom, in A. Wenger, *Huit catéchèses baptismales inédites* (Paris: Ed. du Cerf, 1957; SC 50);—Theodore of Mopsuestia, *Catechetical Homilies*, text and French tr., R. Tonneau, *Homélies catéchétiques* (Vatican City, 1949; *Studi e testi* 145);—St Ambrose, *De Sacramentis, De Mysteriis*, French tr., B. Botte ed. (Paris: Ed. du Cerf, 1961, 2nd ed.; SC 25 bis); Engl. tr., T. Thompson and J. Srawley, *On the Mysteries, On the Sacraments* (London: SPCK, 1950; also NPF 10, 2nd series, pp. 315-27);—Zeno of Verona, *Allocutiones paschales*, PL 11; the catechetical sermons of St Augustine have not yet been collected in one volume; only a few of them have been translated in various collections of his works.

[34]Sess. 22, ch. 8, Denz. 1749.

[35]Sess. 24, *De reformatione*, c. 7.

[36]MD 202.

[37]n. 47-8 in *Musique et liturgie* 50-51, 1956; AAS 48 (1956)

[38]n. 22d.

[39]CSL 35, §3.

2 *Preliminary and general catechesis*

Catechesis on baptism, Easter, Sunday, Mass, ordination—in short, on the liturgy in general—ought to be included in a general initiation into the mystery of Christ, the plan of salvation, the Bible. This can then be followed up by other means, from the catechesis of children to conferences and writings, as also by the Sunday homily and advice given in the confessional.[40]

3 *Liturgical catechesis proper*

This should be done from time to time in a systematic way. The biddings of the next paragraph cannot explain everything in the course of the rites; it must be left to a detailed catechesis, e.g. a liturgical week, a special series of homilies, conferences, study of the missal, etc.[41] This catechesis would be based on a thorough knowledge of the rites and should be biblical (the actuality of Scripture and its dignity as the Word of God forbid an archaic biblical catechesis).[42] It ought also to be symbolical, not that it has to explain one by one all the symbols—which would risk falling into the medieval defect of allegorism—but that it initiates the faithful into a symbolical language which is that of the Bible and the liturgy, and whose understanding is natural to every man before he is prejudiced by a too rational and verbal scholarly attitude. Liturgical catechesis should fit into a general view of the plan of salvation and never present the liturgy as a curiosity cr speciality; it should be ecclesial, i.e. make it understood that a profound and harmonious Christian life is only developed in the life of the Church. Finally this type of catechesis should always have love for its object, since the grace of the Eucharist, climax of the liturgy, is the unity of the mystical Body in love.

IV BIDDINGS (INVITATIONS TO PRAYER)

The importance of the commentator and the need for direction for an active and intelligent participation of the people in the liturgy have been emphasized above.[43] The instruction of September 3, 1958, followed by numerous episcopal directives, has restored this function, whose necessity was strongly felt in the ancient liturgy. The people need to be guided in their participation. Their movements

---

[40]CSL 35, §2; cf. *Directoire pour la pastorale de la messe* . . . , n. 28.

[41]*op. cit.,* n. 29-38. The directory warns against mistakes to be avoided in catechesis: archaicism, fragmentation, allegorism, rationalism.

[42]CSL 24.

[43]See above, ch. 5 and 6. Cf. CSL 35, §3.

have to be indicated to them; they need direction in the hymns and responses; but above all they need to be helped in order to enter deeply into prayer and an understanding of the rites. The biddings (invitations to prayer) contribute very much to creating or maintaining an environment of prayer and recollection. The conditions which they have to fulfil have been indicated above.

From now on, most of the prayers, including the canon of the Mass, can be said aloud and in the vernacular.[44] This will limit the use of pamphlets, missals, and prayerbooks, which were formerly indispensable. The commentator should be very discreet and should not duplicate, repeat or attenuate liturgical forms. His function, as it has been defined, will continue to be useful if not indispensable. The use of missals and pamphlets is still justified, for the faithful can participate better while reading the texts which they hear (sometimes indistinctly). Besides, this literature can help them to prepare at home for the celebration, to review texts which were heard indistinctly and to perfect their biblical and liturgical knowledge.

4   The place of pastoral-liturgical action in the work of the Church

BIBLIOGRAPHY

CSL 9-12.

LMD 40 (1954): "Évangélisation et liturgie," especially the articles by A. Chavasse and L. Terrier.

Pius XII, allocution of September 22, 1956, in *The Assisi Papers* (Collegeville, Minnesota: Liturgical Press, 1957) pp. 223-36.

I   PASTORAL-LITURGICAL ACTION IS ONLY A PART OF PASTORAL WORK

To reduce all the work of the Church to the liturgy[45] or all pastoral work to pastoral-liturgical action would mean to reduce the priesthood of the New Covenant, which is both royal ("according to the order of Melchisedech") and prophetic, to a purely ritualistic priesthood like that of Aaron.

This would also mean forgetting that the liturgy is made up of signs. Signs cannot be dissociated from their meaning. The liturgical celebration has its ecclesial value assured *ex opere operantis Ecclesiae*, but will be so much the more perfect as it is the action of a "well-ordered people," met to express through the liturgy its poverty, thanksgiving, conversion, needs, its imperfect but real love.[46] Moreover a beautiful liturgical celebration should be the point of departure for a

---

[44]Cf. instruction *Tres Abhinc Annos* of May 4, 1967, n. 10, 28.

[45]CSL 9.

[46]CSL 11.

deeper and purer personal religion and for a more charitable and more radiant communal life.[47]

1 *Before pastoral-liturgical action*

Pastoral-liturgical action must be preceded by evangelization, for the liturgy, as we have said, is not missionary but presupposes the mission which makes up the assembly of believers and baptized: "Go, therefore, make disciples of all the nations; baptize them in the name of the Father and of the Son and of the Holy Spirit" (Mt 28:19). "Everyone who calls on the name of the Lord will be saved. But they will not ask his help unless they believe in him, and they will not believe in him unless they have heard of him, and they will not hear of him unless they get a preacher, and they will never have a preacher unless one is sent" (Rm 10:13-15).[48]

At times the work of Catholic Action must also precede pastoral-liturgical action. Such work would be misconstrued if exercised on a practising, but more or less profoundly dechristianized community, if it does not make the community aware of its condition. So too, those participating in the liturgical action, which emphasizes brotherhood and unity, must be made to realize that they have to make an effort to remedy social injustices and material and moral grievances.

Of course what is said here about missionary work and Catholic Action preceding pastoral-liturgical action must be understood in a logical rather than temporal sense. The work of evangelization itself can only be done by baptized persons who already participate in liturgical life.

2 *After pastoral-liturgical action*

After pastoral-liturgical action the work of Catholic Action is still indispensable as is also the effort for social justice and mutual help in love, so that the liturgical reality celebrated "in mystery" may be realized in daily life and that faith, expressed and reanimated by worship, expand into effective love.[49]

3 *Before and after pastoral-liturgical action*

The pastor must supplement his efforts in pastoral-liturgical action by his example, by exhortations in confession and spiritual

[47]CSL 9-10. Cf. MD 32-7; J. Lécuyer, "Blessed are they who hear the Word of God and put it into practice" in *The Liturgy and the Word of God*, pp. 157-71.
[48]CSL 9.
[49]CSL 10; J. Lécuyer, *op. cit.;* L. Terrier, "De l'assemblée chrétienne à la communauté des hommes" in LMD 40 (1954) 108-17;—see also LMD 24 (1950) "La messe engagement de charité."

direction, in order to prepare people for the liturgical celebration which is deeply personal and at the same time communitarian. He must also help them to grow in holiness by the practice of private prayer, renunciation and fraternal love, by the grace given them in liturgical celebration.[50]

II THE PRINCIPAL AND UNIFYING ROLE OF PASTORAL-LITURGICAL ACTION

Though only a part of the total pastoral ministry, pastoral-liturgical action has a central and unifying role in it. The pastor will not dedicate all his attention and time to it. Many other necessary works will occupy him, but the celebration of the mysteries will be the source, center and summit of all his pastoral activities[51] because this is the privileged moment when he acts *in persona Christi* and as a dispenser of the mysteries of God and where his priesthood reaches its highest dignity and effectiveness.

[50]CSL 12.
[51]Cf. CSL 2, 10.

GENERAL INDEX

R